Jewish Thought

Committed to the principle that "There are no principles in Judaism," Oliver Leaman's *Jewish Thought: An Introduction* presents a fascinating overview of Jewish thought and sensibility from the organizing perspective that the commonalities of Jewish tradition consist in recurring "arguments and controversies" that are rearticulated in new historical contexts across the generations. For a late modern audience whose affirmations and doubts are often both equally suspended and situated in such a way as to ironically play off each other, this book serves as a superb introduction to Judaism.

Aryeh Botwinick,
Professor of Political Science, Temple University, USA

This is a **9** and contemporary introduction to the Jewish faith, its philosop... ...d world views. Written by a leading figure in the field, it explores **10** s that have preoccupied Jewish thinkers over the centuries and exam... ...eir continuing influence in contemporary Judaism.

Jewish T... ...*t* surveys the central controversies in Judaism, including the protracted ...ments within the religion itself. Topics range from the relations ... ...n Judaism and other religions, such as Islam and Christianity, to conte... ...ry issues such as sex and gender, and modernity. Central themes s... ...authority and obedience, the relations between Jewish and Greek t... ..., and the position and status of the State of Israel are also conside... ...e debates are further illuminated by reference to the Bible, as a profoui ...listic text in describing the long interaction between the Jews, their a... ...s, and God, as well as discussions about major thinkers, and passage **To be** ...the ancient texts: the Mishnah, Talmud, and Midrash.

Oliver Leaman's lively approach and light touch makes *Jewish Thought* ideal reading for anyone who wants to understand more about the Jewish faith and its outlook, past and present.

Jewish Thought

An introduction

Oliver Leaman

Routledge
Taylor & Francis Group

NEW YORK AND LONDON

First published in the USA and Canada
by Routledge
270 Madison Ave, New York, NY 10016

Simultaneously published
by Routledge
2 Park Square, Milton Park, Abingdon, Oxon OX14 4RN

Routledge is an imprint of the Taylor & Francis Group, an informa business

© 2006 Oliver Leaman

Typeset in Sabon by
Newgen Imaging Systems (P) Ltd, Chennai, India
Printed and bound in Great Britain by
MPG Books Ltd, Bodmin, Cornwall

Library of Congress Cataloging in Publication Data
Leaman, Oliver, 1950–
    Jewish thought: an introduction/Oliver Leaman.
      p. cm.
    Includes bibliographical references and index
     1. Philosophy, Jewish. 2. Judaism – History of doctrines. 3. Judaism –
Essence, genius, nature. 4. Judaism – Relations. I. Title.

B154.L37 2006
296.3–dc22   2006004861

British Library Cataloguing in Publication Data
A catalogue record for this book is available
from the British Library

ISBN10: 0–415–37425–1 (hbk)
ISBN10: 0–415–37426–X (pbk)
ISBN10: 0–203–08718–6 (ebk)

ISBN13: 978–0–415–37425–5 (hbk)
ISBN13: 978–0–415–37426–2 (pbk)
ISBN13: 978–0–203–08718–5 (ebk)

For Uncle Jack and Aunt June

גַּם כִּי אֶזְעַק וַאֲשַׁוֵּעַ שָׂתַם
תְּפִלָּתִי

And when I cry and call for help
He shuts out my prayer
(Lamentations 3:8)

Contents

Foreword

Many people have helped me with this book and none more so than the many students with whom I have over the years discussed these issues. I have written on these topics very much in response to what they have in the past said and asked, and I am reminded as an author how difficult it would be to write without the stimulus and lively reactions of those with whom we are fortunate to work. There is a midrashic story that every day God is so disgusted with the world that he sends out an angel to destroy it but when the angel comes to a community and sees a teacher with students the divine decree is put aside once more. Let us hope that both divine forbearance and human instruction continues for some time into the future.

I should also like to thank my editor at Routledge, Lesley Riddle, for initially suggesting that I write this book and for supporting it through the preparation process.

Oliver Leaman

Introduction

When I arrived at the University of Kentucky in 2000, I discovered that I was down each year to teach a course called Jewish Thought and Culture. In the first semester this was Jewish Thought and Culture I and in the second semester Jewish Thought and Culture II and these were organized so that part I was basically the Bible up to the expulsion from Spain and part II everything after 1492. This is a logical organization of the topic, and I duly taught it in this way but one of the things that really struck me was how difficult it is to place issues in Jewish history exclusively within a historical context. So often an event in the distant past impinges on a current practice and an event that is much more recent reflects a past controversy. The division between the two periods became very artificial, and I kept on referring to issues in one period while discussing the other. This made me aware of the way in which it is difficult to isolate aspects of Jewish culture within particular periods, since they tend to burst out of those confines and occur in perhaps a slightly different form both earlier and later in time. This is very much the presupposition of this book, that Jewish thought is not about past events that are dead and buried, but that it is based on a past that continues to rebound on the present, sometimes in rather unpleasant ways and sometimes quite delightfully. It is the approach of this book to look at these links and to introduce aspects of both history and culture in ways that hopefully enliven both.

It is worth perhaps spending a bit of space telling readers what this book is not about. It is not an introduction to Judaism, although there is plenty of material about Judaism in it. Nor is it a list of the festivals and other celebratory events in Jewish life. It would be nice and tidy to be able to say that the Jewish festivals and sabbaths structure the year for Jews, but it would no longer be accurate to make such a comment, since for most Jews the festivals are at best a distantly remembered word from Hebrew classes, not a part of their living reality. Christmas is really the festival today celebrated by most Jews, and celebrated in exactly the same way as it is by most Christians, as a secular spending orgy at the start of the winter. This book is not a guide to the major Jewish thinkers, since many of them are not mentioned at all, and that is not because they are not worth mentioning. However, given the introductory nature of the discussion and the relative brevity with which I am carrying it out, I felt it would be more effective to concentrate on a limited number of thinkers and show how they keyed into significant themes in Jewish thought.

The principle on which this book is based is that there are no principles in Judaism. Most authors of books like this provide a list of those principles which they say are basic to Judaism, and it has to be said that such an approach produces a neat and tidy organization of the material. I argue that there are some core controversies that lie at the heart of Judaism, but I would not claim that most Jews agree on any principles or ideas that are axiomatic for them as Jews. My thesis seems improbable, but I hope that as the book gets underway some readers at least will come to appreciate its plausibility. The idea that there are basic principles in religion allows for a logical progression from topic to topic and from historical period to historical period as we investigate each topic and each period. The approach here by contrast is that it is not helpful to consider the basic principles of religion, since these do not exist. What do exist are basic arguments or controversies which have appeared and reappeared over the centuries, and it is these rather than anything else that define a religion.

We are very used to thinking of religions as having basic beliefs and also histories that help explain those beliefs and see them develop in particular directions. We can then write about religions in ways which have a beginning and middle and something of an end, and there is a lot to be said for that as a literary device. It is very satisfying if we can define a religion and then outline the key events in its history. The approach that is followed here is different and so less familiar to the reader. In my view religions are not like novels or histories, although they certainly do participate in both culture and history. Nor do they develop in intellectually satisfying ways from a cruder and more primitive base to a more sophisticated and complex superstructure. Certainly a lot is added to the basic texts, if we can talk in those ways, but it does not seem to me that the issues that are raised in the Jewish Bible, for instance, are changed in the subsequent literature, which is enormous, that comments on the Bible. The same themes arise and are discussed, and that is perhaps why the Bible and other religious works continue to be found interesting.

In the book I will be using material found in the Jewish Bible, which consists of the Five Books of Moses, the Prophets (the books named after prophets), and the Writings (books such as Kings, etc.). Then there will be material from the commentary tradition in Judaism, in particular the Mishnah and the Talmud, the various stories that have developed around the Bible and are collected in the Midrash, and various literary works that reflect on Jewish life and experience. No prior knowledge of Judaism or Hebrew is required, and each concept and term is explained when it first arises. This is also the approach taken to the thinkers who are discussed; they are briefly placed within their cultural context, and then their ideas explained. The thinkers who are most discussed are Levinas and Maimonides, clearly two key Jewish thinkers, and no prior knowledge of them is assumed to exist in the reader. Since the ethos of the book is that Jewish thought is a longstanding and continuing debate the emphasis throughout is on the nature of that debate and not on its historical genesis or social presuppositions. There is certainly plenty of material on issues of context and history, but that is not the focus of the study, which is firmly on the arguments of the thinkers themselves and how those arguments connect up with other arguments and the longstanding controversies that illustrate and enrich the world of Jewish thought.

What are taken here to be the crucial arguments and controversies that have defined Jewish thought and culture in the past and continue to resonate today? The obvious starting point is the Bible and the long history of interpretation and adaptation that has taken place in the Jewish world to this text. Portions of the Bible are read out in synagogues every week and play an important role in the prayers, and much of the Bible is addressed to the Jews and is about the Jews. Yet it is not at all obvious how this text ought to be understood, and indeed, it is issues of interpretation that have raged throughout Jewish history in the Jewish world itself. The example that is taken here is obedience to God and the different ways in which that is understood both in the Bible and in subsequent literature. This emerges as a complex symbol of the crucial relationship in the Bible, that between God and his creatures, and yet like all symbols it may be understood in a whole range of ways.

The fact that texts require a key to open them brings us to the commentatorial tradition, and in particular the Mishnah and Talmud, the two main texts that meditate on aspects of Jewish law and practice and so provide us with a concrete set of ideas about how we might act in accordance with the Bible and with what accompanies the Bible, that is, the oral tradition in Judaism. This consists of a variety of interpretive texts, the opinions of many different thinkers, and, most importantly, a variety of ways of reconciling the different opinions they give or selecting the most plausible opinions as the right ones. It is within this context that the attack on Jewish legalism, the emphasis and some would say overemphasis on law, is addressed, and is linked with the thought of Hegel, the German philosopher, who had such an influence on the Jewish intellectual world, and indeed on our whole understanding of religion. Hegel argued that the important role given to law in Judaism is a defect and that the religion as a whole is a system of thought that should have disappeared a long time ago when it was replaced by what he regarded as more satisfactory and modern systems of thought such as Christianity. The debate between those who accuse Judaism of having an obsession with law is clearly a much older one than is represented in the eighteenth/nineteenth-century thought of Hegel, but he encapsulates much of the debate and presents the anti-Jewish arguments in a highly effective form, one which was to achieve considerable resonance in the Jewish community itself.

The Mishnah and Talmud are impossible to understand without a grasp of Greek culture, since those commentaries employ many of the tools and techniques of Greek logic and argumentation. Greek thought represents rationality and universality, and its application to a particular religion and community raises issues of whether it is appropriately applied and what must change as a result of such an application. As a symbol of modernity and science, Greek culture had a lasting effect on the Jewish world and raised the question that was to be raised many times later of how far Jews would accept modernity, a system of thought that did not stem from the Bible and their relationship with God. If Greek thought was at least as a system of argument so superior to everything else, perhaps the logical step would have been for Jews to abandon their religion and adopt Greek ways of doing things, and as we know many did take this logical step. Others managed to combine what they found valuable in Greek culture with what they continued to want to do in their religion and so did not find the importation of Greek thought to be threatening. This leads to a theme in Jewish culture, the effects of the non-Jewish world on the Jews, and how far they should accede to those effects and how far resist them. This debate continues today, with many Jews assimilating without trace into the modern world, while others steadfastly resist the melting pot process, insisting on their separate identity and doing everything they can to dissociate themselves from secular society, whether in Israel or in the diaspora. Some Jews try to avoid these extremes and go for something in the middle, maintaining some of their traditions while adopting what they find positive about the modern world. The argument about how far Jews should assimilate and how far they should remain a distinct group remains very much a live issue, as it always has been when assimilation was an option for the Jews. It might even be suggested that it is the long period of hostility toward the Jews that has preserved them as an entity, whereas had a different and more welcoming strategy been employed they would have quickly disappeared into the wider world available to them, something that seems to be happening today in areas like the United States and Europe.

A potent source of controversy is the relationship between Judaism and the two religions that have emerged from it, Christianity and Islam. Christianity might have been expected to adopt a fond view of the sources out of which it emerged, especially given the ethnic background of its main figure, but this was not to be the case. Perhaps because of a feeling of rejection by those Jews who were unconvinced by the Christian claims, Christianity quickly came to distance itself radically from Judaism, and especially from the Jews who came to be seen as a radically different Other fit only for persecution and exploitation. The idea that the differences between the religions could be resolved in future by asking the Messiah when he comes to earth whether he has been here before, in which case the Christians could be right, or whether this is his first time, in which case the Jews would be right, was not found compelling by the Christian authorities in the past. Yet it cannot be ignored that Christianity offers a serious alternative to Judaism, and apposite criticisms of the older religion, criticisms that need to be met if one is to be in a position to reject them. The idea of a mediator between heaven and earth is a potent one, and it is certainly relevant to claim that the Jews place God at such a distance from the world of generation and corruption that it is difficult to see how contact between him and his creatures is at all possible.

The Karaites flourished in the Islamic world, where Jews for long periods enjoyed relatively peaceful relationships with the rulers, albeit not quite the idyllic relationship that is often made out to have existed. Like the Christians, Muslims sought to attract Jews to their religion, and as with the Christians many Jews no doubt did convert, but not all. When Muhammad recited the message he received from God, according to Islam, he lived in an Arabia where powerful Jewish tribes had considerable political influence and his relationships with this group was not an easy one, especially when they did not on the whole come over to his side. The Qur'an has interesting things to say about the Jews, something quite friendly and sometimes far from friendly, and the claims of the two religions over the same piece of real estate in Jerusalem are today often put at the summit of the differences between the Jews and the Arabs in the Middle East. The Qur'an presents systematic arguments about how the Jews are to be treated by Muslims, about the Jews' role in the apparent death of Jesus, and their rewriting of the Torah, and these arguments continue to resonate in the interactions of Jews and Muslims.

Although the Christians accept the validity of the Jewish Bible, they reject the Oral Law, the basis of much Jewish law and culture. A Jewish group, the Karaites, also argued that the Oral Law was unnecessary and irrelevant, and the basis of their case rested on the sufficiency of the written Torah, the Bible, to provide the necessary information for how Jews are supposed to live and practice their religion. Although this group is today very small, the argument over the Oral Law continues to have a considerable impact in the Jewish world. For many Jews, it is the main focus of study, and traditionally far more effort has been put into the understanding of the Oral than the Written Law. For one thing, the Oral Law is much more complex and difficult than the Bible, consisting as the former does of a mass of contrasting arguments and examples out of which the reader has to make some sort of conclusion that can be justified in view of the alternative conclusions. Surely, the Karaites suggested, God has told us enough in the Bible to enable us to make decisions about what to do. We do not need to investigate the convoluted and often obscure texts that represent the Oral Law with their uncertain meanings and range of views. This position continues to have many adherents today, and doubt about the role of Oral Law is even more prevalent now than it was over a thousand years ago when the Karaites flourished.

Most religions maintain a distinction between philosophical and mystical approaches to the truth, and Judaism is no exception. The kabbalah in its various forms represents Jewish mysticism and attempts to define a notion of our relationship with God that avoids what might be seen as the over-rational approach of the philosophers, who see that notion in mainly intel-lectual terms. Many people are attracted to mysticism since they see that it presents a more emotionally acceptable aspect of religion to its alternatives, and that it is replete with the sorts of experiences and ideas that resonate with our imaginative lives. On the other hand, philosophers often suspect the possibility of acquiring a deeper knowledge of God than that available to us as rational creatures and accuse the kabbalists of claiming a greater access to the divine than is their entitlement. Interestingly, kabbalah has over time become just as difficult an intellectual exercise as philosophy, which perhaps avoids the philosophical jibe of its being an easy fix, but the controversy between those who support mysticism and those who are suspicious of it continues today.

God represents the ideal in Judaism, and our relationship with him is clearly of overwhelming significance in any religion. However, should it dominate our lives or should we seek to balance our relationship with the ideal with the demands of the everyday and real world? This might seem to be too abstract an issue to resolve and it is generally broken up into its parts, so that we need to consider for example whether the sort of physical love with which we are familiar is a satisfactory form of love for us to employ, or whether we should have ambitions to imitate divine love. The Bible presents the ideal of divine love as something to be admired, and yet at the same time the *Song of Songs* describes a very physical notion as though that is what we should be pursuing. To take another example, Judaism is very much in favor of peace, and there are many references to this effect in the Bible and the commentaries. Yet from a realistic point of view Judaism does accept the necessity in specific circumstances for violence to take place, and seeks to establish rules and conditions for such violence. When is war appropriate? What are we allowed to do in war? How desirable would perfect peace in the messianic age really be? What is particularly attractive about peace? These are issues that are thoroughly debated today, and the classical sources continue to be explored to seek to find a satisfactory route through the contrasting issues that arise in a world subject to conflict.

Is Judaism a natural or an artificial construct? The answer to this seems obvious; a religion like other cultural artifacts is artificial. However, in Eastern Europe a movement called Hasidism arose which interpreted

Judaism as more of a natural phenomenon in the sense that its practice could be based more on feeling and enthusiasm than on learning and ritual. As time went on, Hasidism actually became much more like the rather complicated and artificial form of religion that it originally criticized, but the issue it raised has remained and become very current today. How far is religious performance meaningful unless it incorporates the emotions of the individual? Is a ritual capable of reflecting the piety of the believer? What do we mean by piety in any case? Examples are given where the desire of someone to carry out a ritual strictly makes it look as though he is criticizing other types of performance and by contrast demonstrating his own serious attitude to his faith. Judaism is possibly more complex than many other religions due to its broad legal structure, and the issue of whether that structure gets in the way of feeling and what is natural has to be raised and discussed.

Traditional Judaism and the Bible certainly seem to put women in a very different category from men, and both also take a distinctly dim view of homosexuality. Yet many Jews today think that gender and sexual orientation should play no part at all in restricting religious roles and that the Bible needs to be reinterpreted so that it comes out as supporting what is taken to be a progressive view of these issues. A wider issue arises here and that is what we should do with scriptural passages that seem to be clear and yet present views that we may find unwelcome. Should we just refuse to accept them anymore, and replace them with different passages, or would this amount to disrespect for the text? Is the claim that the Bible treats men and women differently but not unequally of any validity? As women and gays fight for equal participation in Judaism these issues arise in a very obvious way. It needs to be added that some women who were initially in congregations that treat them equally with men have been attracted to more traditional forms of Judaism and claim that this does not contradict their feminism. Many religions today are facing new demands for the rights of their members who have previously been ignored or placed in a subservient role, and Judaism is a particularly lively site for such controversial issues.

The Reform movement arose in the nineteenth century to produce a more user-friendly form of Judaism for people who wanted to be modern and join civil society, and who felt that traditional Judaism was too mired in the past and an ethos of separation from the gentile world. Once Jews were allowed into society they enthusiastically plunged in and many disapproved of the shape that Judaism had acquired during all the centuries when the Jews were cut off from other communities in their localities. Services in churches, after all, were largely decorous and orderly, and often in the local language that everyone could understand, and the Reform movement sought to imitate this for Jewish religious meetings. It argued that the essence of the religion had been preserved, while unnecessary ritual abandoned, and the ritual only applied for the Jews who lived in the past, or so the argument went, and so was no longer relevant.

Traditional Judaism replied that one could be modern and remain a traditional Jew and that in fact there are not different kinds of Jewish ritual, Reform and Orthodox, there are only Jews who carry out their religious duties (the traditional Jews) and bad Jews (the Reformed) who do not. Although the radical measures undertaken by the Reform movement did break new ground in Jewish history, it is also true to say that at every stage Jews had argued about what features of tradition required changing and which should remain the same. The idea that Judaism was fossilized and incapable of change is far from true, since even those very much opposed to change do take on board some theory as to why change is unnecessary and what would make it necessary. All religions that have survived for a long time have only done this by allowing changes to take place, but the question of what changes are acceptable, and why and how they should be implemented, has become a very hot topic indeed in the Jewish community in modern times.

The Reform movement argued that the Jews are not a nation, but just part of a national community, the nation in which they happen to live. Most people have regarded them differently, though, and have not always seen them as ordinary citizens. This discriminatory attitude reached its apogee in the Nazi period when the German government set out to exterminate any-one of Jewish ethnicity regardless of their nationality or actual religion. The creation of the State of Israel was supposed by some Zionists to return the Jews to the status of being ordinary people, since they would be living as a majority in their own state, like the Germans, Italians, and Greeks, all nations that until the nineteenth century did not have their own states either. It has not actually worked out like that, though. In just the same way that Jews were often rejected by the countries in which they lived, so Israel has become something of a pariah country whose existence is often only grudgingly accepted or even positively challenged. This makes it look as though there is something very unusual about the Jews, since antisemitism has remained the world's most successful and longlasting political doctrine. Although the Bible refers to the Jews as the chosen people, much of the world seems to have chosen Jews as prime objects of hatred. This is hardly a new phenomenon, of course, and brings out yet again the issue of whether there is anything special, either negative or positive, about Judaism and the Jews.

The last issue to be outlined is very much on the contemporary agenda and that is the likely nature of the future for Judaism. Low birth rates and high degrees of assimilation suggest that within a comparatively short period the Jews will to all intents and purposes disappear. There are areas of the world now which are entirely, or almost entirely, without Jews, and in some of those places Jewish culture continues as a sort of quaint cultural survival of a long-dead community. Given the rapid decline in the Jewish population perhaps this is the future of Judaism itself, to be a stage on the tourist trail but no longer a living tradition. It is sometimes suggested that Jews are being killed by the kindness of those countries in which they feel so at home that they no longer feel the need to acknowledge any sort of separate status. Not literally killed, of course, and such a fate is far preferable to the murder of the Holocaust, but the end result is not dissimilar. How far Jews should allow such assimilation to take place and even welcome it, and how far it should be resisted, and by what means, remains today a hotly debated topic.

These are the main controversies that are raised in this book and linked with earlier events. It would be wrong to claim that these are the only controversies that have emerged in Jewish thought; quite the contrary. Yet these are all interesting areas of debate and important ones also. They all have a role to play in helping define the problematic nature of Judaism and the Jews, and they link the past with the present in ways that bring out the continuing relevance of the discussion. As Wittgenstein put it when talking about philosophy, "In the race...the one who wins is the one who can run slowest. Or: the one who reaches the finishing line last." The fact that we feel compelled to return to these issues almost in every generation is evidence of their significance. Those who are hostile to religion tend to think that this ever-recurring series of issues is a sign of the intellectual bankruptcy of the whole enterprise. They see religions as making claims for our acceptance and if over thousands of years we cannot resolve those claims, then the claims themselves must be unsatisfactory in some way. Interestingly, many of the supporters of religion also think that a faith must be capable of identification with a set of beliefs that have to be accepted by those who call themselves adherents of the religion. The difference between them and the skeptics is that the former argue that the claims are true and often can be shown to be true. Yet neither side of this dispute is able to acknowledge adequately the complexity of the sorts of things that are said about religion and by religions, and the way over time the familiar issues become better defined and linked closely with the cultural contexts in which they continue to arise. Judaism is no exception here, and presents a variety of theological responses to longstanding theoretical problems. Readers of this book will find that they, like the whole chain of commentators and rabbinic authorities in the past, will have to sift through competing claims and interpretations and find a resolution to the issues that refuse to go away but continue to make their presence known and demand a response.

Abbreviations

BCE   Before the Christian Era
CE   Christian Era
GP   Guide of the Perplexed
MT   Mishneh Torah
NE   Nicomachean Ethics

I have not followed a strict transliteration schedule for non-English terms, I have just used the spelling that seems to me to be most familiar to an English-reading audience. Biblical references are given as chapter:verse, Qur'anic references as sura.aya.

Jewish History: A Timeline

The Biblical Period

c.2000–1700 BCE Middle Bronze Age	The Patriarchs: Abraham, Isaac, and Jacob
c.1700–1300 BCE Late Bronze Age	Israelite Slaves in Egypt
c.1250 BCE	Exodus from Egypt and the Conquest of Canaan
c. 1025–928 BCE Iron Age	Rule of the Great Monarchs (Saul, David, and Solomon)
c.1000 BCE	Solomon Builds Temple in Jerusalem
928–726 BCE Iron Age	Divided Kingdoms (Israel and Judah)
726 BCE Iron Age	Northern Kingdom (Israel) Falls
586 BCE	The Destruction of the First Temple, Judah Falls
586–538 BCE	Babylonian Exile and the Freeing of the Jews by Cyrus

The Second Temple Period

515 BCE	Second Temple Completed Under Persians
332 BCE	Alexander the Great Conquers Israel
167 BCE	Hasmonean Uprising
80 BCE	Roman Victory over Maccabees
37–4 BCE	Herod the Great
CE 66–72	The Great Revolt
CE 70	The Destruction of the 2nd Temple

The Talmudic Period

135	Bar Kokhba Revolt
200	Mishnah Compiled
c.425	Palestinian Talmud Completed
c.550	Babylonian Talmud Completed

The Medieval Period

638	Muslim Conquest of Palestine
762	The Karaite Schism
1096	Crusaders Massacre Jews in Rhineland
1135–1204	Maimonides
1240	Paris Disputation and Burning of Talmud
1290	Jews Expelled from England
1492	Expulsion of the Jews from Spain
1516	First Ghetto in Venice
1567	Joseph Caro's *Shulkhan Arukh*
1665	Apostasy of Shabbetai Zevi

The Modern Period

1730	First Synagogue in New York
1760	Death of Baal Shem Tov
1770–1880	Haskalah Movement
1791	Jews Granted French citizenship
1820s	Reform Judaism begins in Germany
1878	Petah Tikvah established in Palestine
1881–1924	East European Migration to North America
1882–1903	First Aliyah (going up to Israel)
1886	Conservative Judaism created
1894–95	Alfred Dreyfus accused of espionage in France
1897	First Zionist Congress
1917	Balfour Declaration
1933–45	The Holocaust
1948	Creation of the State of Israel

Chapter 1

Jews and the Bible

The obvious place to start a discussion of Jewish thought is the Jewish Bible, a book in which Jews take the leading role. But it is not a book in which they necessarily come off well. There are many instances in the Bible where the Jews, both as individuals and as a group, behave badly. They certainly do not obey God always and often seem to have a rather problematic relationship with him. It is the purpose of this chapter to explore some of the issues that arise through these varying degrees of obedience. Other themes could have been highlighted, and are also very important, but obedience is particularly useful in that it brings out the relationship between an authority and those subject to that authority. This issue, of how far God's commands ought to be obeyed and how they should be understood, is a constant in Jewish life and thought.

Jews have a complex relationship with the Bible. They are in it, and it constantly addresses them, and others also, but the text often leads to problems of interpretation. For one thing, what is the relationship of Jews today, the apparent descendants of those who stood at the foot of Mount Sinai waiting for Moses to return, to those who witnessed such events? The whole notion of covenant is implausible, in the sense that an agreement made between God and Abraham many millennia ago can hardly bind the descendants of Abraham today. Or can it? When God promised not to send a flood again to destroy the world we are supposed to see in the rainbow a sign of his promise (Gen 9:13–16), but the promise is made to all humanity, and God is quite clear that he does not make it because we have got any better. We are still capable of evil, yet God has committed himself not to punish us in this way ever again, however beastly we might become. One might think this is a case of God tying one hand behind his back, and diminishing his deterrent capacity, but of course there are other ways in which the world could be destroyed apart from flooding. (It may though be that the promise not to send a huge flood again is meant to cover all the natural disasters that could occur.) This sort of covenant is at the heart of much Judaism, in that relationships are established between what happens today and what happened in the past. One might think that this is not true of all Jews, since many do not believe in the historical truth of the account given in the Bible, nor do they think it comes from heaven. Some Jews reject the supernatural as a category and adopt an entirely humanist and secular approach to both themselves and the history of their people. Other Jews not only reject the supernatural but act positively to break the rules of the Torah whenever they can and speak critically of it and Judaism in general. Even in the case of these Jews the notion of the past forms part of their self-identity, since in order to reject a role one has to at least acknowledge it as significant enough to be rejected.

Who is a Jew?

A good deal has been written on the Jewish sense of identity, on who is a Jew, and on the ways in which Jewishness is constructed often in tandem with antisemitism. This issue revolves throughout the Bible also in prescient ways. The distinctive feature of the Bible, to my mind, is that many of the characters in it are taken to be heroes and yet are also deeply flawed. Many religious works present their main characters in an entirely positive or negative light, so this feature of the Jewish Bible is rather unusual. Even the great hero, Moses, the person who can be said to have established the Israelites as a political community for the first time, the person who took them out of Egypt, the house of bondage, and the person who is said to have had contact with God "face to face," the only person in the Bible to enjoy such a relationship with God, even he had faults. He was not allowed to enter the Land of Israel, yet everything in his career was building up to precisely that moment. It is not like the case of Abraham who was told to sacrifice his son to God, as God reminds him several times "his only son," the son whom he never expected to have and for whom he had to wait so long, the son that he loves. In this case, God changes his mind, or at least he changes what he wants to happen, so Abraham does not suffer the pain of actually sacrificing his son. Yet poor Moses does not manage to enter the Land, and this seems cruel, just like asking Abraham to sacrifice Isaac. It is worth noting how ambivalent the Bible is about its heroes and indeed how ambivalent its heroes often are about their heroic roles.

Bargaining with God

When Abraham is told by God that the latter is going to destroy the evil cities of Sodom and Gomorrah Abraham starts to haggle with him about the number of good people in those cities that would prevent him from destroying them. This is hardly a very respectful attitude, rather like Moses pointing out to God that he is not much of a speaker and so probably would not do well trying to persuade the Pharaoh to let the Israelites go.

The Bible does not take a dim view of their apparent criticism of God's plan; on the contrary, it presents their disagreements with him as entirely reasonable. And they are entirely reasonable, even Moses' impatience at the tardiness of the divine response in the desert to the thirst of the community is reasonable. Moses strikes the rock and water appears, but God did not tell him to do this and in fact told him not to do it. This is the immense crime for which entry into the Land is apparently denied him. One might think that God is particularly cruel here to deny Moses the culmination that his entire life had up to that point led up to, something worth bearing in mind when we look at the *akeda*, the binding of Isaac by his father Abraham, and the apparent willingness of Abraham to sacrifice his son (his only son, whom he loves, as God, twisting the knife, reminds him). It is sometimes said that Abraham knew that God would intervene eventually, but we know from Jewish history that God often does not intervene in this way eventually or otherwise. Waiting for God is not something that the Jews got much out of during their history.

Other Jewish stories do not treat challenging God as a crime at all. There is the story of a rabbi who on the Day of Atonement had led his congregation through the long and fervent prayers for forgiveness. It was coming to the conclusion of the service, the Neila session, which brings the long fast to an end. The rabbi was transported to heaven to discuss issues of importance with the Almighty, and during the discussion, the rabbi looks down and sees a member of his congregation looking faint. He apologizes to God and asks to be sent back so he can complete the service and the man can eat. God agrees but says that had the rabbi only argued a bit longer for the Messiah to be sent, God would have done it. This is similar to the Moses situation. The rabbi wanted to respond to the simple needs of a member of the community and rejected abandoning those needs under the broad label of doing what God wants or would expect. Yet the story seems to approve of the rabbi. Instead of ignoring the petty concerns of his congregation, he might have concentrated on bringing about the Messiah by continuing to argue with God. These stories tend to disapprove of such a strategy, they imply that it is the little things of life that are important, maybe more important than the big things like the coming of the Messiah. Can we really believe that God would have sent the Messiah had the rabbi argued a bit longer? After all he has had plenty of opportunities to send him in the last few thousand years and has steadfastly withheld him. It might then be better for us to concentrate on doing good in so far as we can and avoid speculation about what God is going to do.

Yet when Moses did this, albeit on just a few occasions, he was punished for it and severely punished at that. Is this because the Bible takes a much harder line on disobedience than later Jewish texts? Toward the end of the Five Books of Moses when Moses gives his final address to the Israelites, he threatens them with the consequences of disobedience, and these are severe. One of the entertaining aspects of this long passage is that a phrase from it, "it is not in heaven" (Deut 30:12), referring to justice, was later used in the Talmud to suggest that in later times it is not God who establishes the Law but the rabbis (*Bava Metzia* 59a–b). God points out that it is not difficult to behave well; justice is not in heaven nor is it over the sea but its performance is all about us and knowing how to perform it is readily available. It is also worth remembering a line of Jeremiah, referring to King Josiah, one of the few people in authority of whom Jeremiah approved, that "He judged the cause of the poor and needy; so it was well. Is this not to know me? says the Lord" (Jer. 22:16). Before we conclude that the Bible takes a stricter line than later writings we should acknowledge the existence of all those parts of the Bible where disobedience is readily excused or brushed over.

Running away from God

Jonah provides an excellent example, he is told to go east to Nineveh to warn them of their imminent destruction and instead goes west in the opposite direction to avoid the task. The sinking of the boat on which he is traveling does no more than inconvenience him, he is saved, unlike presumably his unfortunate companions, and then he becomes the most successful prophet in human history. All he has to do is say "In forty days Nineveh will be destroyed" and everyone repents. So his disobedience is rewarded by complete success, something for which he continues to be bad-tempered, since toward the end of the book he regrets that Nineveh accepted his message and saved themselves. One might have expected God to have been disgusted with Jonah, yet this book is the haftorah reading on the Day of Atonement afternoon service. The haftorah is the reading from the Prophets that comes after the reading of the Five Books of Moses in the synagogue, a different reading being selected to accompany each portion from the Pentateuch. It is often taken to show that God will forgive anyone and that no one can escape him. Yet it might be taken to show also that even extreme disobedience will be excused by God and indeed used by him.

It can hardly be argued that Jonah carried out his task adequately despite his total success. We do not think of him as having the stature of some of the great prophets like Isaiah or Jeremiah, but actually Jonah was much more successful than they were, which perhaps reflects the fact that gentiles are much easier targets for prophecy than Jews. His stock phrase "Nineveh will be destroyed in forty days" looks like the sort of thing that a child would say if it was coerced to recite some formula. It almost sounds as though Jonah put no effort or thought into his task, hardly surprising since he did his best to avoid it. Yet the message was very successful, perhaps illustrating the principle that less is more in the Bible as elsewhere. There is a tradition that Moses' prayer for his sister Miriam when she was ill

(O God, heal her please) in Hebrew, just the words *El na refa na la*, was instantly answered since God was so delighted by its brevity. Yet a prayer that something that presumably God brought about should be reversed might be questionable, smacking of disobedience itself. On the other hand, one might see divine action as a process of testing and inviting prayer as an appropriate response.

Suffering and slander

Why was Miriam punished? There is a rabbinic discussion which says her sin was slander or *lashon ha-ra*. To a degree this is because of the similarity between the terms *metzora* (leper) and *motze sham ra* (defamation) in Lev Rabbah 16:1 and the report in Num 12:10 of Miriam's leprosy. Jewish law takes a very dim view of slander or speaking ill of someone, although we need to remind ourselves that slander is not only speaking ill of someone, it includes the idea that this attribution of evil is misapplied. In some religious circles the avoidance of speaking ill of someone is interpreted as never criticizing those in authority, which is surely off target. On the other hand, a general intention to criticize is designed to undermine the authority of the authority and perhaps it is for this that Miriam was punished. Our close relatives are prime agents of evil reports, they have seen us at our worst and enjoy a familiarity with us that can make them frank.

This still does not help us explain why Jonah seems to be constantly helped and supported by God, while Moses who very occasionally lapsed from the very highest standards of behavior was punished. Even right at the end of the book when Jonah is annoyed at the inhabitants of Nineveh and regrets their having been saved, God chides him with his attitude, but there is no sense that he is going to be punished. We shall see later on in the book how important slander is in Judaism and how seriously it is treated as an offence. It certainly takes us a long way from the ideal of truth telling and frankness. On the other hand, it is something for which we may be forgiven by God, should he choose to do so. God realizes why Jonah feels aggrieved, it is after all God who has made him hot through killing what was sheltering him, a plant that had until then kept him out of the heat of the day. Yet when Jonah reacts angrily to his circumstances and is intemperate, as we often do and are, God is quite mild in his response, and throughout the book he is very forbearing in his dealings with an obviously recalcitrant prophet. We shall come to see later, when we look at the details of the book, how the account brings out the complexity of God's interaction with us, but at this stage it is worth highlighting that there is not just one attitude that God has to our failures to act as he would wish. It is these differences in what we do and in what God then does that lead to a whole tradition of commentary, since we need to work out some reasons for these differences and an account of the text that makes it more than a random collection of perplexing stories.

Complaining to God

Perhaps the most puzzling case of all is that of Job. He spends most of the book complaining about the lack of justice in the world and moaning about God's role in all this. He calls for God to answer his charges, often intemperate charges, and in the end God does. While this is going on, Job's friends present a variety of explanations for what is happening to Job, and these all vindicate God to some extent or another. His friends present the normal range of religious responses to suffering; that is, he must have done something wrong, God organizes everything justly whether we understand it or not, we cannot question God, and so on. Yet at the end of the book it is Job who is rewarded, getting everything back and doubled at that, while his friends are only forgiven by God because Job intercedes on their behalf. Yet it is they who one might well expect should be rewarded and Job punished for his boldness and lack of respect toward God. Although he certainly does not ever deny God, which his wife raises as an option, he hardly speaks of God with what might be considered as the necessary respect.

Contrast Job with Aaron's sons Nadav and Avihu, who use strange fire in their ritual and are rewarded by being destroyed by God (Lev 10:1–2). All they did, as far as we know, is use fire that they should not have used, yet everything else was as it ought to have been. There is a suggestion that they were drunk, which certainly would explain a good deal of what happened, but that is not actually what the text says, it refers to strange fire. It is a case apparently in which a ritual is carried out not entirely as it ought to be, and swift retribution follows. Yet as Job points out time after time, our experience suggests that God does not punish the wicked and reward the virtuous in this world. The virtuous like Job suffer horribly on occasion, and the wicked die old and respected in their beds, surrounded by their children and possessions. God does not seem to interfere then, so why is he so excited by a ritual incorrectness, as in the case of Nadav and Avihu, or by a degree of impatience in the case of Moses?

God's treatment of people

It might be thought that God has particularly high standards for certain people. Moses of course was very close to God, he saw him face to face, and Nadav and Avihu were the sons of Aaron, the high priest. Indeed, this could be used as an explanation for the dire warnings that God makes to the people of Israel at the end of the Pentateuch, which refer to future events that in fact did take place. It might seem unfair for God to punish a particular group of people, but if he makes an agreement with them and they break it, then why should he not exact the penalty? Perhaps because the individuals who are actually punished are a long way away in time from those who made the agreement, and how can they be held responsible for breaking an agreement which they themselves did not make? This brings up other and unrelated issues like whether we should be held responsible for the actions of our predecessors. To a degree we should, since any attempt to insulate successors from the failures and achievements of predecessors is impossible to achieve. After all, one of the things we should fear when we act is the consequences that those actions have for others, in particular those close to us. The children of criminals are likely to suffer as a result of their parents' sins. It is not the children's fault but the likely consequence of what the parents should have taken into account, in just the same way that parents should consider the desirability of smoking or drinking while pregnant or doing anything that harm someone else. If I disobey a traffic light and hit a car moving in accordance with the law, it is not fair that the innocent party should be hurt, since everything she did was right. Yet if some people are disobedient this affects other people, and that is something we should take into account when we consider how to act.

Perhaps this brings out why disobedience is such a serious offence. It is not that God makes arbitrary demands and reacts aggressively when the demands are not met, although that is often how the Bible reads. It is because the orders that God gives are given for a reason, they express how God wants people to live. He established a good many more rules for Jews than he does for gentiles. It is often argued that there are 613 laws in the Torah which specifically relate to the Jews. By contrast, there are only seven rules for gentiles, the basic rules of social life sometimes called the Noachide laws. They all express ways of doing things that are in our interests. So when God warns us of the consequences of misbehavior he is pointing to the fact that doing the wrong thing does have consequences for us, and this is not something he can really change. When he talks about justice and says, "it is not in heaven" (Deut 30:12) he is referring to the easy nature of doing the right thing. There is, as we have already mentioned, a much-quoted talmudic passage which uses this phrase to argue that it is the rabbis and not God himself who has the right to decide legal issues. Whatever the plausibility of such a reading, it is certainly plausible that God would establish a law that is not difficult to follow. Whether the direction that halakhah has taken is true to the spirit of this principle is perhaps doubtful. On the other hand, the principle that is embodied in the Talmud, that there is often no obvious resolution to legal issues, does raise the issue of what it would be like to know that one has got it right.

Prophecy

A very relevant issue when considering disobedience is the nature of prophecy. The prophet, as traditionally understood, is the intermediary between God and the world, and he transmits the divine message in ways that resonate with the public at large. When prophets perform miracles, as the Torah sometimes says they do, how are we to understand this? The normal interpretation is that God permits them to act in violation of nature in order to emphasize their credentials as people in tune with the divine.

This line was rejected by Moses Maimonides. He is the outstanding personality in Jewish thought. Born in Cordoba in 1135, he was forced to leave Islamic Spain, al-Andalus, owing to the expulsion of the Jews by the Muslim rulers, and spent some time with his family in what is today Morocco. He finally found refuge in Fatimid Egypt, where his medical skills found him employment at the court, and his intellectual power led him to the leadership of the Jews in the Islamic empire. There is a Hebrew saying that from Moses to Moses there was no one like Moses, and this is not an inaccurate summary of the period from the Moses of the Bible to the medieval thinker, since Judaism has, ever since the work of both the bearers of this name, been tackling the consequences of their work. Maimonides wrote many works, and among the most important of them are his commentary on the Mishnah, the *Mishneh Torah*, which has become a classic in Jewish law ever since, and the controversial *Guide of the Perplexed* (GP). In this latter work, he deals with some of the issues that arise in reconciling, or trying to reconcile, traditional Judaism with the philosophical understanding of religious topics. A huge corpus of commentary has built up over both works, not to mention over the rest of Maimonides' many works, and they have become ubiquitous in Jewish thought even before his death in 1204.

According to Maimonides, we should not understand miracles as events that are counter to nature and designed to force us to acknowledge God's power and will. The trouble with miracles like that is that they would force us to side with God for reasons of prudence, and that can hardly be what God wants us to do. In any case, if the course of nature were to be thoroughly upset by God whenever this might be effective, we would soon lose faith in natural necessity and regularity. So Maimonides thinks that the miracles in the Torah cannot prove anything at all; what they do is confirm what we can work out anyway (GP 3.24). In fact, the first two of the so-called Ten Commandments do not need to be acquired by prophecy at all, since we can work them out entirely rationally. Moses is labeled by Maimonides the prophet par excellence, almost the Prophet, since his prophecy is so different from the other prophets. But what is the difference? It is not in more and better miracles, nor is it in better-expressed argument with his community, but rather in the fact that he played a crucial role in establishing the Jewish people as a political community. They only saw themselves as such during his leadership, so his prophecy was marked by enormous success in that department. He was able to achieve this because he had much closer contact with God than the other prophets, all of whom without exception were obliged to distance themselves from God due to their allegiance to material issues. The veil of matter, which proved to be so helpful when explaining divine matters to ordinary people, got in the way of their relationship with God, and so also in the way of their production of the divine message. They were themselves confused by matter and so could not reach very high in their understanding of the nature of the divine.

Although Moses did have a healthy suspicion of matter, according to Maimonides, he accused Moses of falling foul to matter nonetheless. His passion and impatience at God's apparent tardiness resulted in his jumping the gun and striking the rock with his staff in order to provide water for the people, and for this he was banned from entering the Land of Israel. The main problem with his action was not his disobedience of God, however, but the effect that this passionate action would have on the community, who modeled themselves on him as someone trying to live in accordance with the divine attributes. God does not behave emotionally, hence Moses gave a misleading picture of divine action and nature through his emotional action. This is not just a personal error, but one capable, and indeed likely, to lead the community as a whole awry. It is hardly surprising that God felt that this failure on Moses' part to obey him completely deserved a considerable punishment, a refusal to allow Moses to enter the Land of Israel.

The intellectual versus the social

Moses was both an intellectual and a political leader, according to Maimonides. Here we have a reflection on a theme that must have been felt very deeply by Maimonides, the duty of the intellectual involved in public affairs. Left to himself, the implication goes, he would just spend his time thinking and thinking about abstract topics, but once he has obligations to those around him, he has to involve himself in their affairs and this can be rather troubling. For one thing, it means that he has to spend time thinking about things, that are not abstract and are not issues that really interest him as a theoretical operator, and so these sorts of thoughts take him away from his personal opportunity to attain salvation through intellectual perfection. Maimonides is firmly of the view that it is the duty of the individual to think about the needs of the community, as the Mishnaic saying goes, "do not abstract yourself from the community" (Sayings of the Fathers II.5). He himself often complained of the affairs he had to take care of and which had nothing if anything to do with his more theoretical interests, at one point even telling his translator Samuel ibn Tibbon that he did not even have an hour to spend talking to him as he was so busy. Presumably he was exaggerating here, but the notion that he was busier with public affairs than he would have liked makes sense, especially when one considers his many roles as head of the Jewish community in the Islamic world, physician to the vizier, business partner of his brother, and so on.

Maimonides is at something of the ascetic end of getting the balance right between satisfying the demands of the body and our higher ends. On the other hand, he certainly gets it right in thinking that there is some sort of problem here, a problem that Samuel alludes to when he is asked by the Jews to create a king for them. He points out that any king will take their money and their men and aggrandize himself at their expense in much the same way that a parent will warn his children about the consequences of strong drink. And Samuel received just about the same response; they wanted to do it anyway. If there is one topic that the Bible is very perceptive on, it is the desire by human beings to act in what is probably not going to be their best interest. Adam and Eve disobey God and eat the only thing he has told them not to eat; Moses is told not to hit the stone with his staff and yet he does. People are warned and they promptly submit to temptation, and it has to be said that God sets up the situation in such a way that it is difficult for them to resist. After all, Moses is told not to hit the rock with his staff, but he is told to take the staff with him. For this disobedience he is condemned never to enter the promised land, something that represents the meaning of his whole career up to that stage, and indeed even beyond it.

Hegel versus Judaism

This is a point that Hegel (1770–1831) makes very well about Judaism, and it is one of the reasons which he uses to condemn it as a primitive and early stage in human social development. Hegel was a philosopher who had a great impact on Jewish thought, largely because his criticisms struck a nerve. On his account of the Bible, the Jews are given orders, they are told to obey, and yet the reasons for those commands are often obscure or even impossible to divine. Hegel suggests that there is not here a system of thought that is capable of being universal or rational, and these go together since something that has a reason will be universally acceptable by all who can acknowledge that reason. Judaism is then always going to be a fossilized faith, it makes extreme demands of a limited and restricted group of individuals. It may affect other religions, and indeed did, but this is only to emphasize its difference from the progressive growth of human consciousness over the evolution of societies in time. This charge was deeply felt by contemporary Jews, and they tried to respond to it, as we shall see. Hegel challenged Judaism with an overemphasis on obedience to the divine, a challenge that in many ways was taken up by the varieties of Judaism that emerged in the later nineteenth century and beyond.

Another claim that Hegel made was that Judaism emphasizes the distinction between God and humanity to such a degree that it drives God out of the world. God becomes perfectly transcendent and Other, and the question of how we are to relate to him is as a result mysterious. This difficulty is eventually resolved by Christianity, which in the person of Jesus manages to bring God back into the world and establish for his creatures an appropriate channel for interaction with him. One of the awkward consequences for Hegel's theory of religion is that Judaism should really have been subsumed under more modern and developed religions such as the Greek religion and Christianity. Hegel sees religions as existing in a progressively expanding cycle of human consciousness, and so as problems arise in older religions they are solved in newer ones, and rational believers should move from the old to the new, rather in the way that people often move from older cars to newer models. Yet this did not on the whole happen. It did happen to a part of the Jewish community who moved with alacrity to what they saw as perhaps more modern faiths, but not to the whole or even a major part of the community.

Hegel's challenge remains highly apposite, though, and deeply felt by many Jews. Here are these newer religions which may have emerged from Judaism, like Islam and Christianity, and also entirely different and similarly ancient faiths such as Buddhism (if it is a religion) and Hinduism, and a Jew might consider which religion would best suit his or her requirements. There is no inevitability about sticking with Judaism since that only represents a starting position, the religion into which someone is actually born. The existence of such alternatives has produced over time a debate about the respective merits of the different religions, and why Judaism might be worth upholding despite them. At the same time Hegel did manage to identify aspects of Judaism that were often felt by Jews to be difficult features of their religion, and his Jewish followers felt obliged to show that an account could be provided of Judaism that would survive his critique.

God versus ordinary life

One of the reasons why the Jews are so intimidated by God is because they put him at such a high level with respect to humanity. God is so far above the world that the world is to a degree bereft of the divine. This brings out nicely something of the role of obedience in the Bible, in particular its absolute nature. There certainly is such a strain in the Bible where God says what the Jews are to do without providing any sort of argument or explanation. It is worth noting a phrase that occurs throughout the Bible when God gives the Jews orders, and the phrase is "I am he who brought you out of Egypt" or "I am the God of Abraham, Isaac and Jacob," as though this was enough. And of course in the rhetoric of the text it is enough, since this level of authority explains why the laws that are to follow are obligatory on the Jews. That is what authority is, the ability to issue orders and the right to expect those orders to be obeyed. Whatever one thinks of this level of explanation, there is no attempt in the Bible except in a very few places to give reasons for such orders, since this would be irrelevant.

Does this mean that the Bible just gives orders and expects people to obey them, and punishes them if they do not? This would be too simple. One of the familiar activities in any religion is working out why particular rules have been given to us. We are rational beings and we like to know why we have been ordered to act in particular ways, and yet, as Maimonides often points out, many of the rules we have been given are really mysterious as regards their rationale. He is probably reacting to the sort of account of the rules provided by earlier thinkers like Sa'adya who blithely argues that all the rules rest on an entirely obvious rational foundation, if we only look hard enough at them. Sa'adya Gaon (882–942) was the head of the opposition to the Karaite movement, the latter being those in the Jewish community who rejected the Oral Law and sought to establish a form of Judaism based entirely on the written Torah. He also seems to have been impressed with the thought of the Mu'tazilites, an Islamic theological school who sought a rational basis to religious law. The project of discovering the rationale of law is an interesting one and could be regarded as part of the process of justifying it. It has to be said that some law is easy to explain and justify. It is difficult to think of any viable society that allowed theft for example and we can find good arguments as to why stealing from each other is not a good idea. On the other hand, why we are told to sacrifice a bull rather than a sheep or a white cow rather than a black cow, these are mysteries which are not available to us to understand in detail. We just have to go along with what we are told, in rather the same way that when we are in school we accept much that we are told because we trust those who tell us. Any child learning her arithmetic tables may learn them by rote without really understanding why they are true but needing to come to the correct result quickly. In just the same way, a person working around her house may carry out a plumbing task that has for a long time eluded her, as in connecting a faucet for example, and not know why it works finally when it does, and yet on previous occasions when she did exactly the same thing, or so it seems to her, it did not work. We accept that there is a reason for something going right, at last, but we also accept that we do not really understand why it has gone right and what we did right on this occasion.

How to be charitable

This brings us to an important point about Judaism, and that is that it often leaves many blanks in what we are to do and believe. Let us take the example of charity, something that is constantly praised in Jewish literature. But what does it actually mean to be charitable? Maimonides produces a famous series of distinctions here, with eight levels of *tzedakah* or charity (MT *Hilkhot Matanot l'Ani'im* 10.1.7–14):

> The highest degree... is that of one who assists a poor person by providing him with a gift or a loan or by helping him find employment—in a word, by putting him in a situation where he can dispense with

other people's aid. With reference to such aid it is said: "You shall strengthen him, be he a stranger or a settler, he shall live with you" (Lev 25:35) which means: strengthen him in the sense that his falling into want is prevented.

A step below this stands the person who gives alms to the needy in such a way that the giver does not know to whom he gives, and the recipient does not know from whom he takes. This is doing a good deed for its own sake...

One step lower is where the giver knows to whom he gives but the poor person does not know from whom he receives. Thus the great sages would go and secretly put money in the doorways of poor people...

A step lower is where the poor person knows from whom he is taking but the giver does not know to whom he is giving...

Lower than this is where someone gives a person a gift before he asks.

Lower still is one who gives only after the poor person asks.

Lower than this is one who gives less than is fitting, but does so with a friendly face.

The lowest level is one who gives ungraciously.

Now, this is a psychologically acute description of a variety of forms of charity, and one can also see how one could try to rise through the hierarchy in just the way that Maimonides recommends. For instance, one starts off perhaps not really wanting to give charity, but because we know we ought to we force ourselves to give grudgingly, until we do not mind it so much, and even feel quite cheerful doing it. We may then start to give without being asked, but still for motives that are not entirely pure, perhaps just because we think this is something we ought to do but do not really want to do ourselves. Practice makes perfect, according to Maimonides, and the more we do it the more we find it a natural action and one that we feel called upon to extend and build on until we are in a position to help people quite impersonally to leave poverty entirely behind them.

It is interesting to speculate on why this is so significant and at the same time note that a good deal of Jewish charity has a very practical bent. The Society for Trades and Agricultural Labor (ORT) system was very effective in training Jews to learn an occupation from which they could support themselves, and this form of charity puts the giver and the poor person on the same level, since they both end up being able to support themselves. This is so important since it preserves the dignity of both parties and especially the poor person, and once she can earn a living then she is an entirely different position vis a vis society. It is worth noting here that Maimonides does not prioritize anonymity here, and this is probably because the benefactor can be more effective if he knows the individual he is trying to set up in employment.

This brings out nicely how religious law works. We start with a general principle, and that is that God wants us to be charitable and help others.

The question then is, if we are to fall in with his desires, what we are to do. The answer is not simple. Many people today are in favor of just giving people who are in want money or things, as though this would solve their problems. Sometimes it will, of course, but sometimes it will not, since the reason they are suffering is not because of what they lack, but because of a political or economic structure in which they are systematically denied property and sustenance. Being charitable can disintegrate into stimulating dependence and passivity, and Maimonides' principles here are designed to prevent that. What is important about them is not that they are accurate or not, but that they replicate the complexity of what it is to help others who require our assistance. What is important about that is that it brings out how obeying God is far from simple. The whole of Jewish law might be seen as a reflection of this complexity, and this is worth bearing in mind when we are confronted with criticisms of that law or claims that it is empty and legalistic.

Causing harm

There is a famous story discussed by Rabbi Akiva about a conversation between Rabbi Shimon ben Gamliel and Rabbi Yishmael as the former was being led off by the Romans to his execution. Shimon wondered why he was about to be killed and in a typically painful manner so characteristic of the Romans. One suggestion is that on one occasion he had unwittingly upset a widow, here taken as a representative of the most downtrodden class in society (Ex 22:21). A widow came to him for some advice on a legal matter, and he might have been sleeping in the afternoon, having just come in after a difficult morning providing spiritual support for his fellow Jews in Israel during the time of the Romans and their persecution of the Jewish community. His attendant suggested she wait for him to wake up, which she did but while she was waiting it occurred to her that had she been a more important person the man would have woken the rabbi up to speak to her immediately. Or it might have been that he had been asked for advice by a widow and he had paused to finish a drink, thus again making her wait. So, in the words of the text, this thought caused her heart to miss a beat, and she felt demeaned, something for which the rabbi was to pay dearly later on at his death (*Yevamot* 62b, 121b). And yet, we might say, he was not even aware of what was going on, he was exhausted and sleeping, having carried out difficult and dangerous work for the Jewish community, and so how could he be blamed for the feelings of the widow? To a degree one can see how he might have trained his servant to allow anyone however humble to disturb him lest she or he feel demeaned by having to wait, or compare their treatment to those with a higher position in society.

This is why Maimonides stresses dignity, as it is such an important part of our lives and of our sense of well being, and not wealth. It is possible for a person in a humble occupation to feel entirely proud of himself and what he does, even though to others it seems far from desirable, and the source of the feeling of pride may be that the individual can, through that occupation, support himself by doing something useful for society. We are reminded here of the 36 virtuous people on whom the world rests, all people who may be in very menial occupations and far below the radar of social attention. We are also reminded of the stress in the Mishnah on the importance of combining study of Torah with work, with making a living and not making a living out of studying or teaching the Torah. The occupations of the great rabbis of the Mishnah and Talmud were often very humble, they were shepherds, carpenters, builders, and so on, and yet it is their thoughts that we study today when we read these books, not the much wealthier Jews of the time who no doubt hardly noticed their poor compatriots. Charity, in the sense of providing employment, is a wonderful thing, though, since it enables the wealthy to provide not only work for the poor but also dignity, and to create a community in which people are dependent on God for help, not each other.

The significance of dignity

This is very much a theme of the postbiblical literature, and it clearly has its source in the Bible, in a sense, but only quite indirectly. What the Bible has to suggest is that charity is an excellent human virtue, but how we carry it out is up to us to devise. It is Maimonides who works out the eight levels of charity, not the bible or the Talmud, and it is for us to work out what charity means and how to become more charitable as part of our ordinary lives. Similarly with dignity, we need to establish for ourselves what it actually means. In the Talmud, we have this interesting comment:

> Great is human dignity, which overrides a negative commandment in the Torah. Which one? Rav b. R. Sheva explained in the presence of Rav Kahana: the negative commandment "You shall not turn aside from the thing that they [in this passage the Levites but the implication is the rabbis] tell you" (Deut 17:11)—i.e. where following a rabbinic injunction would undermine human dignity, the injunction is overridden.
> (*Berakhot* 19b)

Is not this what we would expect a religion to tell us? Not really, since we would expect a religion to say which sorts of actions it approved of. But apart from that it is up to us to interpret how to embody those principles in our lives. Most people follow a particular religious school of interpretation and so they think that they are doing the right thing by doing what Rabbi Shneerson, the late leader of the Lubavitch movement, said they ought to do, or what some other authority suggested. In our diverse society what counts as an authority is itself diverse, it could be a line from "Fiddler on the Roof" or something one saw on a billboard somewhere.

It is difficult to define disobedience in a religion which seems to prize individual responses to what Jews are told to do. Of course, we should not make too much of this, since many Jews just follow a particular line in theology, and so give up their independent judgment on these issues to a type of synagogue or rabbi or organization. Yet the individual still has to decide which group to join or whether he or she should stay in the group in which they were raised and so it is clear that the rules of obedience and disobedience have to be interpreted in accordance with the rules and traditions of a particular approach to Judaism.

Chapter 2

The commentatorial tradition
Mishnah and Talmud

Judaism is often characterized as a very legalistic religion, and the main legal texts do seem to confirm this view. The Mishnah, written around CE 200, is a systematic exploration of the rules and regulations surrounding Jewish life in Palestine, with an emphasis on agricultural laws and procedural issues. The Talmud in both its forms, that produced in Jerusalem and the longer Babylonian version, is a discussion of the law as expounded in the Mishnah but with the emphasis on producing a range of views of that law. Given the democratic character of the text, it is perhaps surprising that so much emphasis should be placed on the legalism of Judaism, since any system of law that is based on different legal authorities presenting different views is difficult to define as straightforwardly legalistic. That is, law is clearly important but what the law is remains a live issue in such a system of norms. It is not as though the letter of the law is invariably applied since there is a good deal of discussion what the letter of the law actually is. As we have seen in the Chapter 1, the issue of how the law is interpreted remains at the heart of much Jewish thought, and will continue to be described and discussed in this chapter.

There is little doubt about the intellectual headquarters of the Jewish world in the Islamic Empire during the first part of the Geonic period (the whole period extending from mid-seventh to the mid-eleventh century), and it was Iraq. The Geonim were heads of the various colleges or *yeshivot*, and came to be based in the capital of the Abbasid Empire, Baghdad. From here they communicated with the rest of their part of the world, sending out their decisions on leading legal issues and publishing their reasoning, thus making available to everyone who could read the methodology they were employing. The Palestinian Talmud from the Land of Israel is a much slimmer document entirely and is evidence of the reduced size of the community out of which it emerged. Actually, Israel tended to concentrate on producing other sorts of literature, in particular the midrashim or rabbinical stories that have proved so important in the development of the Jewish tradition, as well as some of the early kabbalistic works such as the *Sefer ha-Yetzirah* (Book of Creation) and *Hekhalot* (Temples) that provided an imaginative backdrop to the rather dry legal material that was being produced at the same time. We tend to think of the centers of Talmud in Babylon and Palestine as transmitting the text to other parts of the Jewish world, but in fact it tended to be just summaries that were sent out to more distant communities. The original 50 volumes were soon slimmed down to summaries of relevant legislation (so abandoning mention of temple rituals, for example), and a long list of geonim produced what they took to be decisive summaries of precisely what the law was. The fact that there were so many summaries, and that they were all different from each other, is revealing in the fluidity of how the law could be interpreted. Yehuda ben Nahmanin in the eighth century produced the *Halakhot Pesukot* (Decided Laws), an Aramaic text from which all the debate in the Talmud has disappeared but a highly usable series of decisions are explicated and shown to relate to each other. This text was itself the source of many variations and commentaries over the centuries, being variously translated into Hebrew and interspersed with Arabic commentary. As commentaries developed, they interestingly became a bit more similar to the Talmud itself, foregoing the very spare style of earlier works that merely present concise decisions. It is not clear why this is the case, but perhaps communities had used the additions to these commentaries to reconstruct something of the structure of the Talmud itself and so were prepared and even eager for additional texts which were rather similar to the original work itself. Yitzhak Alfasi in the eleventh century produced an outstanding text, the *Halakhot Hilkhot Rabbati* or Great Lawbook which not only includes decisions from the past and something of the discussion and debate that led up to those decisions, but also links the material with modern and more recent legal rulings. Another strand of condensed readings was provided by Sa'adya Gaon in the tenth century, and concentrated in particular on Jews in the Arabic speaking world, the text being in Arabic and the structure of the argument owing a good deal to the sorts of debates that predominated then in the Islamic world. Jewish thinkers were adept at using the local culture to discuss Judaism and its law and even the structure of Hebrew using the theoretical tools which were developed to analyze the foundations and structure of Arabic! This may seem surprising, especially as some of the accounts of Arabic at that time were designed to prove the superiority of the language and the culture of the Arabs over other communities and people. On the other hand, it was not that difficult to use the same techniques employed by Arabic literary theory to reverse the argument and suggest that Hebrew was the superior language. In fact, where the debate tended to go was to prove that Hebrew was at the very least no worse than Arabic and so was just as useful a language to work in as is any other.

Hegel's challenge

According to Hegel, the trouble with Judaism is that it separates God too radically from the world. Judaism is an advance on some idolatrous religions because they bring God too close to the everyday world. Indeed, he is part and parcel of that world as far as idolater religions are considered. So Judaism is an advance because it appreciates that God has to be distinct from the world. On the other hand, it drives God out of the world by basing the religion on law and denying humanity any direct connection with God. Whether this really describes Judaism is doubtful, and perhaps the real issue is whether Hegel has his finger on an important aspect of the religion here, which he surely does. Judaism in most of its versions does insist on the problematic nature of divine/human interaction except in the case of a few special individuals, and their interaction is often reinterpreted also. Law is also important in Judaism, but then law is important in several religions. It is certainly true that Jews spend a lot of time discussing legal issues, or some Jews anyway, but there could be a good reason for this. The assumption of Hegel and his supporters, especially his Jewish supporters, is that the emphasis on law is because Judaism makes impossible an emphasis on God since it puts God so far away from his creatures.

Judaism and principles

Given the significance of law in traditional Judaism, one might think that there would be a series of basic legal principles or axioms from which the rest of the law, and indeed the religion itself, would stem. There was a huge controversy in Judaism about whether the religion has principles or not. This controversy has something to do certainly with the long experience that Jews had of living in an Islamic environment. Muslims have from the start of Islam been enthusiastic producers of creeds and as one might imagine they differ from each to a degree, since different thinkers adhere to different sets of principles as more basic than others. These differences often serve as the dividing lines between different schools of legal and theological thought in Islam, and so they are far from being minor aspects of debate. A similar process emerged in Judaism, where there was a controversy not so much as between different principles but whether there are principles at all. Of course, there was also a debate about the principles, and this proves interesting, in that some emphasized abstract principles while others selected more practical or procedural principles.

Levinas (1906–95) was a philosopher whose output can be neatly divided in half. He stressed the significance of practice and ritual in Judaism, arguing that this in fact represents the essence of the religion. His early work was in phenomenology and dealt with metaphysical issues in general, and he was very much influenced by Heidegger, an outstanding thinker who enthusiastically sided with the Nazi party when it came to power in Germany. Levinas' later work was on Jewish philosophy, where he produces a moral theory that he claims is based on the Bible and reveals a universal message despite its limited transmission to the Jews. Through his writings on how the self and the other are irretrievably connected he has become very influential in a wide range of disciplinary areas.

Levinas was strongly of the view that there is no point in adhering to a creed unless there is a way of translating that creed into practice, and this is not just a point worth making about Judaism. Perhaps as Levinas suggests, the halakhic route is the path that Jews undertake when they embody their beliefs in practical action. This is very much how he takes it, and his long discussions of talmudic passages are built on the idea that traditional Jewish practice is the physical expression of the ideas in Judaism as a system of thought. It is worth pointing out that he might be right in thinking that ideas, in particular moral ideas, need some practical application, but not right in identifying that practice with the traditional. As we shall come to see, the issue of how to embody Jewish ideas in practice has remained very much a live issue throughout history.

Judaism and rituals

But what is this practical action? We would tend to look for things like charity or the pursuit of justice, or even prayer, but carrying out a sacrificial ritual in itself does not appear to be very important. One would tend to think that it is what is behind the ritual that is significant and that the ritual itself is merely the exemplification of something deeper and could easily be different. This is something that Maimonides, the great champion of both rituals and what underpins them, the principles on which they rest, argues. He suggests that the principles are unchanging since they embody the will of God, but the actions which we carry out to make them material could take another form. It would be difficult to argue that the precise kind and color of animals to be sacrificed was important, so long as one accepts the need for sacrifices. But Maimonides presciently points out that once we start to question the ritual, its hold on us has disappeared and we are likely to adopt a skeptical attitude to all rituals.

If he thought that rituals could be different, and indeed do change over time, how could he argue that they must be followed exactly and without variation? We know what happened to Nadav and Avihu for apparently not being precise enough in their completion of ritual, but this is not his point. He suggests that at any particular time the ritual we are supposed to follow has been set for us and should not be questioned. At another time and in another place perhaps we would be called on to do something else. This has no consequences for whether we should perform the ritual or not. To give an example, right now I am typing in English because I am writing a book for an English-speaking audience, but I could be writing in a different language if I were writing for a different audience. My contract is to write a book in English and I shall honor that, but the contract could have asked me to write it in a different language and had I signed such a contract

I should honor that. There is no contract of contracts that embodies everything that one ought to do regardless of the time and place. On the other hand, what a contract is in itself does not change, and this is what Maimonides meant when he said that we need to examine the underlying principles on which our actions rest. After all, it is only if we grasp the principles that we shall be able to resolve difficulties as they arise, such difficulties often being based on a poor grasp of what the point of the ritual actually is.

Yet there is a common belief that Judaism is riddled with obscure and irrelevant legislation, rather like countries that do not periodically revise the laws on their statute books. The reason for not changing the law is that it is eternal and comes from God and so cannot be changed. But of course this is an evasion of the issue, because whatever we may think, law is always being revised as our practices adapt and change.

Let us take as an example the mezuzah and the tefilin. A mezuzah is a small box that is placed on the door of every room in a traditional Jewish home in response to the Biblical injunction repeated in the *Shema* prayer "and you shall write them upon the door posts of your house and upon your gates." It contains a small scroll inscribed by a scribe and Jews may kiss it on entering and exiting, thus acknowledging their acceptance of the command by the Almighty. The tefilin are small boxes that are worn on the head and the arm and they also contain biblical passages. They are worn during morning prayer on weekdays that are not festivals. The tefilin reflect the passage "and you shall bind them as a sign on your hand and in front of your eyes." Over the centuries, a good deal of legislation has developed over these items of Jewish ceremonial life, such as the exact positioning of the mezuzah on the doorpost and the tefilin on the head and arm.

Now, it is undoubtedly true that a majority of Jews do not observe the rules of tefilin and do not even own them. If they were given a set they would not know what to do with them. Does this mean they are not following the Bible? Not necessarily, since they might interpret the Bible differently. They might say that remembering God when entering and exiting the house does not require a box on the door, nor does holding God in your mind and heart require having close to your heart and on your head a little box with a relevant text.

This is very much the argument of the Reform movement and its branches which as the name suggests are interested in reforming Judaism to make it both more relevant to contemporary times and events and also to bring out the real meaning of the biblical text. The reformers argue that the real meaning has become occluded over time and obscured by the complexity of the laws that have grown up around it. We discuss later the details of the arguments of the Reformers and examine the logic that they say underlies Judaism, which is independent of the legalism that in their view bedevils the religion.

The reply to this is that an eternal law cannot be changed, and there seems a lot to be said for such a view. God presumably had a plan in mind when he created the world, and this plan may not be available to us, given our relative ignorance. So who are we to suggest alternatives to what God commands? Human laws are different, of course, in that legislators have to explain and justify them to us, and we may decide with some right on our side to reject a civil law if it offends some wider concept of justice, in our view. Divine law is not subject to such variation, though, as it is perfect and eternal, so the response to the criticisms of it is that they do not cohere with the special nature of the law.

This objection only works if it can be argued that the Oral Law, whose formulation is represented by the Mishnah, Talmud, and other legal texts, is also divinely inspired. Such a claim is indeed made that Moses received both an oral and a written Torah, and he passed both on to others, the oral Torah to a limited group for transmission to the community at large. The Written Law as we know was broadcast openly to the community present at the foot of Mount Sinai and subsequently to their successors. Indeed, the *Ethics of the Fathers*, which is a chapter of the Mishnah and is found in many prayer books, starts by describing a long line of transmission of the Oral Law, thus seeking to establish its own authenticity as an important source of information in the Jewish canon.

Of course, if one does not see the Oral Law as divinely inspired in some way, then one might be free to interfere with it. However, this is a step that one does not need to take since the Oral Law itself is hardly specific and uni-vocal. There is a whole range of problems in coming to an agreed position on the basis of the Oral Law. Maimonides, in his book the *Mishneh Torah*, tried to sort out this problem by specifying a list of solutions and answers to a range of legal questions, in fact to every legal issue that could arise both at his time and in the future. This brave attempt was not surprisingly heartily resisted by many in the rabbinate, since it went against the principle of not privileging any particular rabbinic authority. It may be for this reason that Rabbi Akiva, one of the greatest Jewish personalities who died *kiddush ha-shem*, in sanctifying the divine name, at the hands of the Romans for refusing to stop teaching Torah, is often ridiculed in the Talmud. Perhaps this is to establish that even Rabbi Akiva is not so great that we have to accept his rulings. He did after all accept Bar Kochba as the Messiah and supported his disastrous revolt against the Romans, so why trust any of his other judgments? Bar Kochba led a revolt in CE 132 against the Romans, and despite initial successes, the eventual result was a complete disaster a few years later, with Bar Kochba being killed in battle and Akiva skinned alive.

As Maimonides puts it so trenchantly:

> Do not think that King Messiah will have to perform signs and wonders, bring anything new into being, revive the dead, or do things like that. It is not so. Rabbi Akiva was a great sage, a teacher of the Mishnah, yet

he was also the armour-bearer of Ben Kochba. He affirmed that the latter
was King Messiah; he and all the wise men of his generation shared this
belief until Ben Kochba was slain in [his] wickedness, when it became
known that he was not [the Messiah]. The rabbis had not asked him for
a sign or evidence. The general principle is that our law with its statutes
and ordinances is forever and eternal; nothing is to be added nor taken
away from it.

(*Hilkhot Melakhim* 11:3)

Judaism and law

Why did Maimonides try to resolve the legal problems arising from the
various Jewish legal texts? One answer might well be, as he says, that in difficult times when there are not established legal centers that can adjudicate
on legal issues, it is important for Jews to have a way of working out how
they are to act. Maimonides was a great supporter of terseness and clarity,
and critical of what might be thought of as the rather confused and confusing nature of Jewish law as found in the various competing texts and
authorities.

The arrival of Maimonides' work was to become only one more legal text
in an already well-supplied market, albeit one of extraordinary influence. In
the printed versions it is invariably put together with the disapproving commentary on it by Rabbi Abraham of Posquières which immediately signifies
that this is just another text in a long debate, albeit one of outstanding quality. And so we return to what is surely the crucial issue here—even if the
Oral Law is divinely inspired, how can we tell which version of it is the
right one? Or, how do we know that one authority ought to be followed on
a particular issue as opposed to another authority? The way in which these
issues are sorted out is by discussion and argument, so that one can explain
why a particular approach is acceptable.

Does that mean, as some suggest, that these Jewish texts are representative
of a relaxed and rather postmodern attitude to getting the decision actually
right? If that is the case then what would be important would be the
arrangement of texts and decisions in a way that one found aesthetically
pleasing or appropriate on some other criteria. That would make the
Talmud and Mishnah rather like a complicated game that could end in any
sort of way at all. It is true that heaven is supposed to prefer the School of
Hillel over the School of Shammai because the former always gave due consideration to the views of the latter, and even priority, when coming to a
decision. Hillel and Shammai were leaders of competing legal schools, often
identified with the Pharisees, in the first century CE. Yet this might be seen
as being fair-minded, not as validating the idea that the final decision does
not matter, and all that matters is the process. There is indeed a sort of
pleasure to be found in producing a well-argued case for an implausible or
obviously inappropriate conclusion, but this does not make that conclusion

any more viable. What we need to remember is that religious law is about trying to get to grips with how God wants us to live, and although there is undoubtedly merit in trying to get it right, shrugging our shoulders if we get it wrong is not the attitude with which one is supposed to operate.

But why not? If we do our best to get it right, is that not enough? It is obviously better to try to get it right than not to care at all, but it is not enough just to try. If one believes that ritual embodies divine legislation then it has a meaning and impact of great importance in the lives of Jews, and cannot be set aside if we are to live as God wishes. It is here that the distinction between principles and practices becomes disassembled, since it is plainly not much use if someone understands the principles of mathematics but is unable to get any calculation actually right because of errors in the practice of mathematics. A linguist need not speak many languages, nor may an engineer be much good at actually putting up something like a bridge. They all have a grasp of the theory, but not of the practice, and when it comes to religion this is more than a minor practical embarrassment. Failing to act as God has commanded is to place our lives outside the range of practices that are divinely ordained and so we might assume that our lives would then be far less satisfactory in a whole range of ways.

We are used to seeing theory as something that tells us how to follow practice, and that is surely correct, since unless we understand the theory we will not be able to understand why we do what we do. It was the ideal that Maimonides set himself and indeed the whole of Judaism to understand the principles on which the religion rests, so that its practitioners are aware of why they do what they do. An important question here is whether there is enough depth in Jewish legal material to constitute an appropriate theory upon which to base practice.

Hegel for one certainly thinks Judaism is not up to this task. It is not what he calls a "world historical" religion. He follows here Herder who in his discussion describes the Jews as

> the people of God whose country was once given to them by heaven itself, have been for thousands of years...a parasitical plant upon the trunks of other nations; a tribe of cunning brokers throughout almost the whole world who, in spite of all oppression, nowhere long for their own honor and habitation, for a country of their own.
>
> (On World History, 1997, 263)

The point here is that the Jews are so limited in their outlook that whatever their ethos it cannot extend over territories and civilizations but is limited to where they themselves exist. The Jews are stuck in the local and eschew the universal. On the other hand, he describes Abraham as someone who totally cut himself off from his family and background. He rejected rootedness for perpetual wandering, and in just the same way modern Jews are not really part of the state—they see themselves as separate from it. The result is that they do not think in line with the Christian ethos of love and universal ethics. Of course, it might be argued using Hegel's categories that the Jews are precisely world historical in the sense that some of their ideas have become part and parcel of global civilization, and they have demonstrated the power of Jewish thought to transcend the restrictions of location so that their thought could become part of the world's thinking.

It was not only Hegel who professed such a view, but the peculiar status of the Jews in nineteenth century Europe had led to a number of thinkers, including Jews, to disparage the role of Jews in history. Eduard Gans (1798–1839) was one of the leading participants in the *Verein für Cultur und Wissenschaft der Juden*, an organization dedicated to the study of Jewish culture and an enthusiastic Hegelian. He accepted entirely Hegel's analysis and sought as his role the integration of Jews in civil society. Hegel, with great perspicacity, understood the role of Abraham as of someone who was to leave his own community and set up a new and separate community. Hegel contrasted this with what he took to be the impulse to unity in Christianity. After all, there is a good deal in the Bible about the movements of the Israelites, and God's command to Abraham to go and leave his home very much sets the process going, and the history of the Jews in the Bible and beyond is very much one of transience. We receive constant information in the Bible about travel, the routes that the Jews followed, and the problems and successes they met on the way. They also are encouraged to take a hostile attitude toward many of their neighbors or the original inhabitants of the areas they are to enter and occupy. Once they get a system of law it distinguishes them radically from everyone else, and the acceptance of that law means that they are unable to join in with everyone else and do the same things. Jews would find it difficult even to eat with gentiles if they obey the laws of kashrut, the rules defining the food that Jews are allowed to eat.

Gans argued that if the Jews are to join in with everyone else they have to change their practices from their previous adherence to their distinctive customs and practices and behave like everyone else. It is not a matter of chance that the Reform movement started in Germany, since so many German thinkers were critical of the attempt by Jews to isolate themselves from civil society. This is really an attempt at evading the legislation that is part and parcel of the Mishnah and Talmud. Maimonides had argued that Mishnah and Talmud need to be put on a rational basis, so we understand why we are expected to interpret the law in a particular way. Then we can maintain a traditional religious practice, while not rejecting a commitment to reason. Gans and the Hegelians argued that these commentaries cannot be rescued, since they are part of a premodern way of living that cuts the Jews off from normality. It is only normality that allows the Jews to enter history and produce ideas, and people who participate fully in world events.

Jews and history

This seems to be wrong since surely the Jews have always been participants in history, and indeed the Bible is an indication of the significance of their history. Hegelians would say that that was in the past, but in early nineteenth century Europe Jews did not have the cultural impetus to affect anyone outside of their own sphere. Yet they do now and Jewish culture and ideas have become widespread all over the world. Perhaps they did in the past also. Ludwig Börne said that the Jews have always embodied the modern principle (p. 79). That might be true, but it is clear that what has become powerfully transmitted has nothing to do with the Mishnah and Talmud, and everything to do with what rapidly became the secular trend in Judaism. There is no surprise in this, since the commentaries have nothing really to say to gentiles, as they are specifically there for Jews, not as universal ideas. On the other hand, what might be said to have been very helpful to Jews entering the modern world is the methodology of the commentaries, since that methodology in many ways represents the main principles of modernity. It involves questioning what one is told, working with ideas and texts, and seeking to construct a rational solution to intellectual problems.

We can see from modern history how the Jews have taken Hegel to heart. Most Jews are secular and are firmly part and parcel of the societies in which they live. Even very Orthodox Jews earn their living as part of society, albeit sometimes in rather specialized areas which allow them to carry on their religious practices. This might be seen as a Faustian pact, the choice being to participate fully in society at the cost of abandoning one's distinct faith, as compared to remaining in separation from civil society and consequently failing to affect it. Where Hegel was wrong was in seeing religions as having an essential core which leads them to shape political life distinctly. Christianity, with its ethos of "love," is supposed to bind people together and help them project their power over others. Hence the success of European countries in their former relationship with their colonies or less powerful countries. We might wonder though how far colonialism and imperialism was experienced as love by their victims or even by the victimizers. Hegel of course was the essentialist par excellence, the thinker who thought one could encapsulate a whole culture and time period within a few descriptive terms that define it once and for all. We do not have to agree with his methodology to accept that occasionally he hit the target, but what is important here is not whether he was right. What is important is whether many Jews thought he was right, and they undoubtedly did, abandoning ritual in so far as they felt it interfered with their full participation in civil society. The question at this stage of the twenty-first century is whether this throwing off of ritual will lead to a complete throwing off of Judaism itself, a question which will probably be resolved one way or another in this century.

Judaism and nature

The idea that ritual is important, the idea that runs throughout the Bible but especially the commentaries on it, is nicely encapsulated by this passage from the Mishnah.

> Rabbi Yakov says, Someone who while walking along and thinking about his studies interrupts his review and says "How beautiful is that tree! How pleasant is that ploughed field!" He is regarded by Scripture as someone who has forfeited his soul.

This passage is to be found in many prayer books in the *Ethics of the Fathers* 3.7, and to the modern reader it is quite shocking. Why should Jews not enjoy the beauty of the natural world and indeed the beauty of cultivation? There are in fact in the same prayer books prayers which are to be said on specific occasions when we are captivated by beauty in nature. There is a particularly delightful prayer to be said when seeing the first tree in bloom in Nissan: "Blessed are you, O Lord our God, king of the universe, for nothing is missing from his universe, and he created in it good creatures and good trees, in order to bring humanity pleasure."

Now, it will be said that what this passage from the Mishnah refers to is not the overwhelming importance of study and the crime of letting one's attention stray, but the need to acknowledge that the world is beautiful because of its Creator and the plan behind it. There is certainly the implication that learning, and here is meant religious learning, is so significant a part of our role in life that any time spent away from it is a dangerous distraction. Yet it is always dubious to take one of these passages by itself and weave a complete thesis around it, however entertaining that might be, since there are plenty of other passages even in the same tractate of the Mishnah that go against that serious view entirely. What about all the passages criticizing making a crown of the Torah (*Ethics of the Fathers* 4.7), in other words, making one's living through one's religious learning? The commentaries praise the idea of a balanced life, as indeed does the Bible, and so prayer, study, and commercial activities all have an important role to play in what is a fulfilling activity for human beings. The professional rabbis who exist today are very distant from their peers of 2,000 years ago, who all earned their living through fairly menial occupations like cobbling, shepherding, building, and so on. On the other hand, someone who is easily distracted from his studies is clearly not going about things in the right sort of way, and it is not surprising given its authorship that the commentaries tend to have a rather middle aged and male ethos. They are on the whole written by teachers who no doubt were often fed up with the antics of their students, and so fulminated against their capacity to miss the point, avoid their studies, be frivolous in their approach to what they ought to be doing, like students everywhere. So it would not be correct to see 3.7 as an indication that Judaism advocates a total lack of interest in nature and the natural world in favor of a complete commitment to religious learning and commentary. We should in any case know by now that taking a passage from any religious text in isolation from the religion as a whole and placing great weight on it is a very dubious way to proceed. Nonetheless, it is very popular to do this, and few religious thinkers can resist identifying what they regard as key texts or ideas around which the whole of their faith revolves. Theology might be seen to result from the fact that different thinkers select different texts and ideas.

Commenting on commentary

So the passage does not say it is wrong to abandon study for love of nature, it says that even a minor interruption in study in order to appreciate nature is wrong. Yet this is something we often do when studying, we have a break, a cigarette and a cup of coffee, we look outside the window, we go for a swim, and then we return refreshed to our studies. Here we come to an interesting and quite characteristic theme of Judaism, the idea that study is difficult and has to be continued to the end. This is an important idea about ritual and involves the spider's web model of the community, where what holds everything together is a complex set of interweaving relationships and practices, and any break in one may threaten the whole structure. It is represented in the idea that the Messiah will come if the whole Jewish community observe the Sabbath for two consecutive weeks or that the correct sequences of Hebrew letters will trigger the creation of life or the Messiah again. It is the rather tragic notion that everyone has to do what he or she can to increase their own learning and improve the world, and we can never really know if we have done enough. Although we are told that it is not our task to complete the job, it is also not good enough for us to say that we have done what we can do and so can relax (Rabbi Tarfon at *Ethics of the Fathers* 2.21). This is a good example of how different passages have to be taken together with each other in order to provide an overall view of one's obligations, but it is worth pointing out the problems with this in that it is very much up to the individual and the community of which he is a part to resolve precisely what the implication of these passages is. In some ways, it is like a mysterious piece of writing being interpreted differently in different places, with some people thinking it means one thing, some thinking it means something else, but there is often an acceptance that it is up to each community to work out what it means. This is why the whole emphasis on commentary might be called tragic, since it places the commentator in the position of trying to get something right where he or she has no criterion of success. Saying in the postmodern way that what is important is the effort not the outcome just does not work for religious texts, for here the outcome is crucially important since it relates to how God wants us to live and what sorts of activities on our part can fit in with the ways in which he has constructed us. If I place my bicycle on the wall and regard it as just a beautiful artifact I am missing something very important about it, namely, that it is (primarily?) a means of transport. If I investigate the bicycle, suppose one just appears to a community who do not know what it is, then if I do not regard it as a means of transport I have missed the point. Not that it could not also be seen as an art object, or many other things as well, but we really need to acknowledge that religion sees itself as having a close link with the truth and has to be seen thus if we are to preserve an accurate view of how it sees itself.

This is where ritual and the commentaries really come in, they are trying to preserve and comprehend this link by discussing practices that will represent how things should be regarded, given our relationship with the divine. That relationship, it has to be emphasized, is always a rather distant one in Judaism, or at least has been up to now. It might be that if a form of Judaism emerges as a result of women rewriting and reexamining some of the classical texts then we might end up with a God who is far more immanent or present in the world than the transcendent God we have at the moment in most of the literature. Until we reach that stage, however, and we may never reach it since the whole project may turn out to be ill-conceived (see the chapter on gender and sexuality), we are constrained to using some sort of commentatorial tradition in order to interpret the text, legal or otherwise. The Bible may speak in the language of human beings, as the Talmud tells us, but in many places it is far from clear what the point is that it is trying to get over and why. Hence the need for some system of explanation and interpretation.

Chapter 3

Jews versus Greeks

One of the first prayers in the traditional *siddur* or prayer book is a *baraita* of Rabbi Ishmael, and it deals with the rules of inference that we ought to employ when studying the Torah. A *baraita* is a rabbinic teaching that is not included in the Mishnah and yet is regarded as relevant when working out the appropriate legal ruling on an issue. There can be little doubt about the Greek origins of this observation, since Greek philosophy and logic swiftly had an impact on the Jewish cultural world in Israel, just as much as it did on other cultures in the area. Greek argumentation was very economical and perspicuous by comparison with other approaches, that is, it expressed concisely and clearly what the rules of argument and debate are in a way that made them very difficult to reject. The transmission of Greek culture to the Jewish world is a symbol of what then represented modernity, and on the whole, it was grasped with both hands by most Jews, as it continues to be today. Yet, modernity leads to a host of problems when it is received by a community that adheres to traditional ideas. It may well be that the modern and the traditional point in different directions or even contradict each other. In this chapter, we will be looking at the impact of rational ideas on religion and in particular of how the universal rules of rationality came to feel at home within Judaism.

This emphasis on Greek views of argument, for that is what it is, shows explicitly what the Jews took from the Greeks. Greek culture attained great heights of intellectual awareness, and in particular, philosophy and logic flourished. To some Jews this appeared to be a threat to Jewish culture, and indeed, the imposition of Greek culture in the land of Israel often was just that, the imposition of an alien way of living. The festival of Chanukah commemorates the overthrowing of Greek culture in Israel and the victory of Judas Maccabeus over the idolatrous foe. The Maccabees fought a protracted guerilla struggle against the force of Hellenism represented by the Seleucid rulers of Israel. When the Temple was captured in 164 BCE, a lamp was lit that should have only lasted one day but lasted eight, and ever since the Jews have burned up to eight candles to recall the miracle. What is worth saying about this period is that the enemies of the Maccabees were probably largely their fellow Jews who were perfectly happy to take Greek culture on board. Like other groups, Jews have usually leapt at the opportunity to integrate with wider cultural forces when they were allowed to and the broadening horizons brought on by Greek culture would no doubt have attracted many. If it involved worshipping gods in temples that might well have been seen as a sign of modernity, as adhering to the beliefs of an advanced culture and people.

Levinas puts his finger on the issue when he distinguishes between the Greek and the Hebrew. The former represents the universal, the latter the particular. Levinas quite rightly sees Jews as stuck in between the universal and the particular. They may be attracted to ways of living that are followed by everyone and anyone, while at the same time they are aware that as Jews they might be expected to follow a more specific path. It is here that one of the real paradoxes of Judaism arises as a religion that is also connected to an ethnicity. People can be members of other religions and yet still regard themselves as Jews and be regarded by others as Jews. For example, there exist Messianic Jews who think that Jesus is the Messiah and who follow vaguely traditional Jewish rituals while holding this belief that is anathema to all other Jews. Perhaps we could say that they are just wrong. On the other hand, some people who were undoubtedly Christians, and even priests, were murdered by the Nazis because ethnically they were Jewish. This was just about the only group of victims that the Vatican could raise the energy to take up with the Germans at the time. It is certainly also the case that many of those killed by the Nazis had no religious beliefs at all but were killed because of their ethnicity. In some cases, they only realized they were in this ethnic group when they were arrested and taken away. This really does bring out nicely the distinction between being a member of a specific ethnic group and sharing religious beliefs with members of that group. Anyone can become a Jew by going through an appropriate ritual and preparation, depending on the particular kind of Judaism that is involved, and yet they will be linked then with a large number of other Jews who have no interest in "their" religion. Of course, it is a well-known phenomenon that converts are much more enthusiastic than those brought up in the religion; after all the converts have made a conscious decision to accept a faith not originally their own. They must have a strong motivation and will also have to acquire training in the principles of the religion that those within it originally may never have undergone.

Religion as rational

One of the problems with Greek influence is often taken to be its overrationalization of religion. When we look at many Jewish texts, they appear to be highly rational, logically structured and articulated, and only really accessible by those who are capable of quite advanced theoretical work.

Maimonides tends to suggest that only really intelligent people can understand what goes on in the Bible and how they should act, whereas the less intelligent are obliged to do what they are told by those better able to understand the scope and nature of our duties. It is against this sort of intellectualism that movements such as kabbalah arose, together with thinkers who defended a traditional attitude to religion in marked contrast with the rather artificial constructions of those like Maimonides and Gersonides where the emphasis is very much on reason and on the overwhelming significance of reason in religion. Gersonides or Levi ben Gershom lived from 1288–1344 in Provence and frequently disagreed with Maimonides, but was in total agreement with him about the significance of philosophical, that is, rational, thought itself. To take a small but useful example, Maimonides is always critical of anything that suggested belief in magic such as the use of amulets or the insertion of additional material in mezuzahs, the little boxes that are placed on the doors in Jewish homes and places of work with particular texts in them. Some think that when a family has ill fortune it may be linked with an imperfection in the mezuzah, and it might be advisable to change the mezuzot. Maimonides was totally out of sympathy with these aspects of popular religion and argued with some justification that it smacked of idolatry. In fact, he argued that Judaism is a religion on a progressive growth to an ever-purer form of faith, starting with sacrifices and ending with quiet contemplation of the deity alone on one's bed! But of course it is worth saying that this last form of religion, replacing both sacrifices and public prayer, would be regarded by many as a very thin form of faith, one that does not pay nearly enough attention to the emotional side of the religious life. It is that Greek emphasis again on reason, an emphasis that leaves out a whole range of motives and connections that are important for many members of the religious community.

Yet the Greek response will be that it is important to put religion on a secure intellectual foundation. People may associate all sorts of weird ideas with their religion, but they are better off without these ideas, comforting though they may be at early stages of the development of the religion. It is worth adding that mystical approaches to Judaism such as kabbalah end up being just as intellectual and theoretically complex as anything else. Shabbetai Zvi lived in the Ottoman Empire in the seventeenth century and after training in kabbalah managed to persuade a lot of Jews that he was the long-awaited Messiah. But when the Sultan threatened him with death he promptly converted to Islam and as a result many of his supporters also converted. What is interesting about this event is some of the language that accompanied it. The conversion was justified in kabbalistic terms of plunging into the depths of evil in order to oblige the forces of good and light to shine on the world and hasten the messianic event.

For those with what might be called a Greek temperament, the sort of enthusiasm that was exhibited during the Shabbetai Zvi period is an excellent example of what is wrong with enthusiasm. Instead of calmly considering the evidence for the messianic status of the imposter many in the community allowed their wish for a messianic deliverance to overcome their better judgment, including the distinguished scholar Nathan of Gaza. In fact, it is a familiar feature of false messiahs that they have no difficulty in attracting to themselves important thinkers who promote their cause, and the "messiahs" garnish a lot of support from other members of the community as a result.

Pharisees and Sadducees

One of the intriguing aspects of discussing that other effect of Greek culture, the debate between the Pharisees and the Sadducees, is that we know very little about either group, especially the latter. The main sources of information are the New Testament, early rabbinic texts and Josephus, but by the time they were written these groups had already disappeared. Josephus was a first century CE Jewish historian who provided a fairly dispassionate account of the wars against the Romans and a lot more about the culture of the time. From what we are told, the Pharisees were strict in their adherence to what they took to be the law, emphasized divine power, and had a strong belief in the afterlife. The Sadducees by contrast did not believe in an afterlife, emphasized human freedom of action, and were not so popular as the Pharisees. Of course, the latter held onto two beliefs that might be thought to contradict each other, namely, an afterlife in which there will be reward and punishment together with divine determinism that makes it difficult to understand how human beings can make significant moral choices or act of their own accord. Although the Sadducees may not have made a reference to this point, they did question the idea of a reward and punishment in the next life on the grounds that it was likely to motivate us improperly when we decide how to act, since such action might well be in search of a reward rather than just obeying God. The deniers of resurrection are often labeled "Epicureans" and there is some truth in the idea that repeated disasters in Palestine lead to a change of direction from concern for this world to emphasis on the next world. Yet the whole notion of the afterlife only really gets much purchase in either a positive or negative way once Jewish thought meets Greek culture. Greeks had many views on this topic, whereas in earlier Jewish thought it hardly seems to have been an issue at all. We then find in the commentary tradition, and certainly in the Midrash, the stories that grew up around Jewish texts, a firm belief in an afterlife. This doctrine is targeted by some Jewish thinkers who were impressed with Aristotelian doubts about the idea of a corporeal afterlife and by other Jewish thinkers who debated as to what form of an afterlife might be feasible, employing a range of Platonic, Neoplatonic, or Aristotelian ideas. What is worth noticing about all these ideas is their origin in Greek thought and their very rapid naturalization in Jewish culture. This was to become something of a theme throughout Jewish culture, its omnivorous attitude to what it found in other cultures and its ability to make them part of its own.

The nature of the afterlife

Why should the afterlife be such a hot issue? This might seem a strange question, since is it not natural for people to welcome the possibility that this life is not all that there is? For many it is the prospect of an extended afterlife that makes religion and a relationship with God have significance. This leads to the question much debated in Jewish thought as to how literally the language of the afterlife ought to be taken. Maimonides suggests in much of his work that the afterlife is not literally going to be a place where something like this life continues and where we are rewarded and punished in terms of what would please us or displease us in this world. Indeed, such an image would seriously interfere with our pure attitude to God, since we would forever be looking to rewards and seeking to avoid punishment in our service to God, hardly appropriate for such a relationship. It makes God look like he is supposed to be a person like us, someone who will be pleased if we do what we should and annoyed if we do not. Yet for Maimonides this is the effect of imagination on our thinking about God, where we use material images to make sense of an abstract notion. For many of us, the idea of an afterlife in which we do not do many of the same things as we do in this life is vacuous, and so religion gives those who need such images scope to use them, since for them this is how they could make sense of a much more difficult idea, that of an afterlife in which the individuality of the person disappears and the physicality of his life and its activities are entirely dissolved.

This is not only an issue for understanding the afterlife, but for a whole range of religious ideas in Judaism, such as the Messiah or miracles. According to Maimonides, it is a mistake to think that miracles constitute an interruption in nature, since nature is a system that is based on regularity and order. How could it be suddenly diverted from its path without making a nonsense of the pattern of nature that is so characteristic of it and of our experience of it? So miracles are then natural processes which we do not understand as connected with the rest of nature and which are designed to make us marvel at the power of God, but they are nonetheless part of nature in a way that we do not understand. Similarly with the Messiah; when he comes the laws of nature will not be suspended, people will still get hungry, die, and need to work to live. It is not a miraculous period in which everything becomes entirely different, although there will of course be a new set of conditions operating throughout the world, a set of conditions that improves what already exists but does not change its nature.

Understanding the Bible

We can understand how the debate between the Pharisees and Sadducees might have reflected this sort of debate which came to dominate much Jewish thought, the controversy on how literally the Bible is to be taken. We do not really know if we should take the Pharisees to have been skeptical of the literal understanding of the Bible and other similar texts, but it seems to follow from their opponents' insistence on divine power that the Sadducees thought that God could do absolutely anything, and certainly anything that he was said to have done in the Bible. If we see the world as the product of God's actions, then what difficulty is there in thinking of God doing anything that he wants to do? If he wants the Messiah to change entirely the basis of the world, then he can do this, and if he wants us to sit in heaven with crowns on our head in the next life (*Berakhot* 17a), what difficulty exists for an omnipotent being in carrying this out? The Pharisees seem out of line with the Bible if they deny that God can do any of these things, can in fact do anything at all that he wishes to do and for reasons best known to himself.

But of course those who challenge the literal interpretation of the Bible do not seek to deny God's ability to do what he wants. They rather seek to establish a role for divine action which makes it fit in with what they see as the nature of the world that he has created and the purposes for which he has created. The aim is not to restrict God from doing what he wants but rather to try to understand how he would act and what he would do. This makes their opponents worry about whether they are really giving enough scope to God to do absolutely anything he wishes to do. For example, at the start of the Bible in Genesis when God establishes a covenant with Abraham we get no explanation as to why this is done. Noah is saved and linked to God with a covenant because Noah was good, at least good for someone living at his time, and so it was appropriate for God to establish such a relationship. On the other hand, when God says that he will never destroy the world again with a flood despite our evil nature this appears to be an entirely gratuitous act of kindness. God does not tell us why he did it, he just does it, and this is similar to his subsequent favoring of Abram, later to become Abraham, where we are not told why he was picked out and preferred to others. Establishing some principle of divine action that would insist that he explains what he does, or only does things that appear rational, would undermine the absolute freedom of God to do whatever he wishes to do, or so the Sadducees might have put it.

This issue of what God can and cannot do is raised by God himself in the Bible where he asks Abram, as he then was, whether it is too difficult for God to enable him to have a child with Sarai, as she then was. As God says in his response to Job, the person who creates all the wonderful things in the world can surely bring about all sorts of unusual events that exceed our normal expectations. But this does not really address the issue of whether God can construct for us an afterlife that is rather like this life, or issue strange events that serve as miracles, or even respond to our prayers and bend the pattern of nature to do so. What is at issue here is not so much what God can do but how much like us he would have to be to do these sorts of things.

This raises an issue that no doubt separated the Pharisees and the Sadducees, and it separated many of the major thinkers in the Jewish rabbinic and philosophical traditions. When God says that he made humanity in his image does he mean that he looks like us? Some kabbalists did think that this was the case and that it was possible to measure God, but this is not the normal view among Jewish thinkers. God is beyond human description and the sorts of things that are said about him, and that he says about himself in the Bible, are to be taken figuratively. How we reconcile the unity of God with his many qualities and the fact that he acts and so presumably changes from time to time are all traditional problems in religions that have a deity who is supposed to be just one being who is unchanging and perfect. We are not going to address this persistent problem here, but we are going to look at the ways in which the apparent humanity of God can be reconciled with the definitions of him as very far from human and indeed entirely beyond us and our abilities to describe him.

The kaddish

The first thing to notice here is that the Bible consistently describes God as very much like us but more so. The same has to be said of many of the commentaries such as the Talmud and the prayer book. The latter seems quite relaxed about the idea of addressing God; many of the prayers in the liturgy of all the varieties of Judaism address God and presumably this implies his ability to hear and pay attention to us. If he cannot do this, one wants to ask, what is the point of talking to him? Many prayers in the liturgy take the path of praising God, and perhaps the perfect example of this is the prayer that is traditionally said to commemorate a death, the kaddish or literally sanctification. This is normally recited in its Aramaic version and the translation goes thus:

> May his great name be exalted and sanctified in the world which he has created, according to is will. May he establish his kingdom during your lifetime and during your days, and during the lifetime of all the House of Israel, speedily and very soon and let us say Amen.
>
> [The response is:] May his great name be blessed for ever and for all eternity
>
> [The mourner continues:] May the name of the Holy One, blessed be he, be blessed and praised, glorified and exalted, extolled and

honored, adored and lauded above and beyond all the blessings, hymns, praises and consolations that are uttered in the world. And say Amen

May there be abundant peace from heaven, and life for us and for all Israel and say Amen

May he who makes peace in his high places grant peace for us and for all Israel, and say Amen.

Some synagogue services have replaced the phrase "for all Israel" with "for all humanity," but the form of the prayer is fairly clear, and it might be regarded as a defiant declaration of faith in God even in the face of grim circumstances such as death. Strangely perhaps it does not ever mention death or sadness, but appears to be a celebration of God and his power over all things. Presumably the reasoning is that God has a plan for the death that is being commemorated, and so praising him is to express one's faith that it did not happen for nothing, since we live in a world fashioned and controlled by God.

One feature that all this religious language clearly exhibits is the idea of a relationship with God. Yet how can we have a relationship with a being who is so unlike us? We even find it difficult, although not impossible, to have a relationship with another human being who is very unlike us, yet the difference between us and such a person is tiny compared to the difference between us and God. The chasm is so great that Hegel criticized Judaism for driving God out of the world, a move that was only to be finally countered by Christianity and its sending of Jesus Christ as a mediator between this world and the divine. We do not have to be Hegelians to agree that many of the accounts we find in Judaism of God do insist on his considerable distance from the world, a distance that is often referred to in the Bible.

The significance of study

A very considerable rabbinic thinker, the Maharal Rabbi of Prague, is supposed to have said that when we pray we talk to God but when we study God talks to us. This is an interesting idea and brings out something of the remoteness of the divine/human relationship. When we study we try to make sense of the various things that have been reported to us of God and that involves working with what he has made available to us and what we can work out ourselves (with our divinely given powers). Here it looks as though both God and we are active, as opposed to when we pray since then only we are active. The idea of God listening to our prayers, an idea often referred to in the prayers themselves, is difficult for many Jewish thinkers to accept literally. Maimonides in particular has huge problems with it, since for God to listen he would need some listening equipment, and for him to see some visual equipment and so on. In any case, the idea of a God who is always in charge of what we do, since he is good and always aware of what we do, is an idea of a world in which there is no human freedom and there is complete divine domination. It might be a more comfortable world than the one that we inhabit, but it certainly does not seem to be our world. So a good deal of the language we find in the Jewish Bible and prayer book has to be taken in a nonliteral sense if it is to make sense.

For example, "when it is written 'When I whet my flashing sword (Deut 32:41)'. Has God a sword and does He kill with a sword? It is a metaphor and all such phrases are metaphors" (MT *Hilkhot Yesode ha-Torah* 1.9). Of course, it will not have escaped Maimonides' attention that this phrase of the flashing sword is typical of biblical language about God, and so we are presumably to think of all that language as metaphorical. He goes on to deny that we can say anything positive about God at all and so underlines the significance of where a rational approach to the text can take us.

Translating the Bible into Greek

An interesting way of dealing with this issue is explored by Levinas. Levinas makes a sharp distinction between what he calls Greek and by this he means the universal role of philosophy and he contrasts this with what he calls Hebrew, the language representing the culture of a particular people. He starts by replacing the usual starting point in metaphysics of ontology with ethics. The obvious place to start philosophically is to ask the question: what is a human being? Once we know the answer to that question, which includes other questions like what can we know, we can then start to work out our duties and responsibilities for others. Yet Levinas turns this starting point entirely the other way around. The first question we need to ask, he suggests, is not who we are, but what our responsibilities to others are. Only once we can answer the question who is the other are we in a position to know who we are. Again, the normal way to start constructing a metaphysics is to build up a model from the self to the other, and then suggest that I have certain responsibilities for others, as they have for me. But these responsibilities for others are limited, since it is unreasonable for them to be otherwise. Levinas reverses this commonsense idea to argue that our responsibilities for others are not limited but are infinite. This is because if one starts with the self and then moves to the concept of the other one is always in the position of trying to demarcate between the roles of different selves in ways which limit, perhaps too severely, the links between these selves. In saying that we have infinite responsibility for the other, Levinas means that we must, if we are to remain who we are, always be able to respond to the other, since unless we do, we lose our identity as a subject. As he says: "The word I means here I am, having to answer for everything and everyone" (*Autrement que d'être* 145). This is a reference to the Hebrew expression *hineni* which is so often used in the Bible by those who wish to announce that they are present, ready and able to take on their roles in response to God's communication.

This radical turn in philosophy has radical implications for all the familiar philosophical problems, but one implication which one might assume it would have is to direct attention away from the individual and toward groups of individuals, or indeed the whole of humanity, since it is to the whole of humanity for which the self is answerable. This implication is drawn by him, and Levinas seems to have a horror of the solitary life, in marked contrast to Heidegger who appears to value above all retreating from the world into oneself and being alone with nature. Heidegger was a vast source of how to philosophize for Levinas, and for many others, and yet he became an enthusiastic Nazi during the regime of the Third Reich. For Levinas, the attempt to withdraw from the community is a dangerous process, since the more one tries to retreat into oneself, the less self there is to retreat to. This raises the question of how far one can ally oneself with a restricted group in society, as compared with the whole of society. Hence Levinas' criticisms of love between people, which he sometimes sees as limiting the links of responsibility that we establish between each other. Yet loving particular people may help us accept our responsibilities for the wider community, since we could extrapolate from our relationship with one person to many more. For Levinas the relationship we have with other people is not reciprocal. It does not depend on their behavior or even their personal level of merit and deservedness. Our responsibility even extends further than our lives into the infinite.

This is so distant from our normal understanding of who we are responsible to, since in our everyday life we strictly demarcate and limit responsibility. Social life is the formalization of ethics within a rational system, which serves to replace ethics, according to Levinas. Civil responsibility is precisely a form of responsibility which denies responsibility, since it makes it abstract and so no one's responsibility. Given his criticism of the state, one might expect that Levinas would be similarly scathing of the institution of the family, since it is the case, after all, that for most people their primary responsibility would be seen to be for their family as compared with those outside of their family. But Levinas holds up the family as a sort of ideal. The production of children within the family brings home to the individual how infinite and eternal her responsibility is, since the products of the family will continue into the future in ways that are entirely beyond our consciousness. Within the context of the family, individuals do not limit their responsibility, and even an unpleasant and unresponsive child is often cared for by his parent. There is nothing surprising about this, on Levinas' account, since within the family it is this attitude of affection that serves to construct the self in the first place, and if I fail to feel affection or concern for my child, I fail to be me. The disinclination to enter into relationships like this is a disinclination to develop and take risks, the sort of risks that involve becoming a person in the fullest sense.

Universal ethics and Judaism

What is Jewish about this theory that seems on the contrary to apply to everyone? According to Levinas, Judaism has a number of features which enables it to fit into the account of ethics and morality that he defends. Judaism is profoundly ethical, in his view, and so it emphasizes the practical as against the theoretical, the group as compared to the individual. It compares speech with prophecy, has a messianic future in prospect for humanity, and is generally suspicious of the capacity of the state to embody ethical life appropriately. In his Jewish writings he illustrates these points evocatively, examining a wide variety of biblical and other literature which he interprets as bringing out some of the key aspects of his philosophy. So the Bible is not just a history of God's relationship with the Jews but with the world at large, which fits in nicely with how the Bible sees itself, of course. But is he right in thinking that Judaism is an especially ethical religion? What Levinas is doing in his writings on Jewish thought is using his philosophy to bring out what he thinks are the meanings of Jewish texts, and in this he is of course following in a long and distinguished tradition of Jewish philosophy. What we need to examine is the claim that there is something specifically Jewish about his central philosophical claims.

Levinas is naturally interested in those parts of the Bible which refer to the individual as responsible for others. When God asks Cain "Where is Abel your brother?" (Genesis 4:8) the response that Cain is not his brother's keeper is entirely inappropriate, although technically it is correct. Nor is the question only directed at Cain, but at everyone. Everyone is responsible for those who are murdered even if they are not directly involved in the crime, he argues. Levinas picks out those parts of the Torah in which individuals respond to God by saying "hineni" or "I am here." What is meant by that is that the individual recognizes the claim of God to be heard, he accepts that he is the person to whom the divine question is to be put and acknowledges responsibility for the task which God may have in mind. But is this not just the individual responding to God? What is specifically ethical about it? For Levinas references to God are not references only to a being. After all, "The direct encounter with God, this is a Christian concept. As Jews, we are always a threesome: I and you and the Third who is in our midst. And only as a Third does He reveal himself" (*The Levinas Reader* 247). The point of religion is to bring out to the individual the significance of her links with others, so that when she is involved with others God is close to her, but when she is thinking only of how to come close to God, he is distant.

There are plenty of passages in the Torah and other Jewish writings which emphasize the presence of God as contingent on a certain way of human acting. Buber, for example, was impressed with Hasidic stories of quite ordinary actions being imbued with spirituality when those actions were carried out for the sake of others. Martin Buber (1878–1965) is often regarded as a Jewish existentialist, and was committed to defending a form of Judaism that he thought captured rightly the freshness of our relationship with God. Levinas is quite right to criticize the smug attitude of believers who seek "the artificial peace of synagogues" as though there they could find "the peace of private worship" (*Nine Talmudic Readings* 193). The idea that religion is about a personal relationship with God which could exclude others is a fallacy, he argues, but if it is a fallacy then in spite of what he says it is surely wrong to accuse Christianity of it. Most Christians would also insist that their followers accept widespread social commitments, and their worship would be expected to result in action. Many Christians would be critical of coreligionists who concentrate on contact with God at the expense of what might be seen as their social responsibilities. It is worth adding that there have also been Jews who have tried to make contact with a personal God and who have devoted their lives to preparing themselves for such contact. As a result they may have abstracted themselves from the matters of the ordinary world and refused to acknowledge the responsibilities to others which in fact are incumbent on them. Would we wish to say that someone such as the Jewish mystic who acts in this apparently selfish way is not really following the principles of Judaism? Certainly some would want to say that, but others would urge the view that a religious community, like any other community, will include within it a wide variety of different forms of belief and practice, and tolerance of variety is a religious as well as a political virtue. In any case, the solitary worshipper may well see himself or herself as working on behalf of the wider community, albeit not directly.

What of those Jews, probably today the majority, for whom the language of the Torah is "empty wrappings of musty perfumes" (*Beyond the Verse* 8)? According to Levinas, in times of emergency such as the Holocaust and danger to the State of Israel they feel again that they are a chosen people, that their realm of responsibility is widened, and what had previously been empty of meaning suddenly fills up with significance. But it is not clear what the point is here. Do all Jews have to have this feeling, or is it a feeling which they should have? Again, some Jews may feel, mistakenly in Levinas' view, that their primary aim is communion with God. Is Levinas claiming that they cannot have this aim and remain Jews, or that they should not have it? He presumably cannot claim that it is not possible for Jews to seek communion with God, since many Jews have claimed that this is their objective. Of course, we could reinterpret that language into something different, something in terms of action and work with others, but surely this would be very forced in many cases. One could be prescriptive here and insist that Jews who see such communion as their objective are not really Jews, or not proper Jews, yet Levinas seems to accept that even nonhalakhic Jews are Jews, so it would be difficult to argue that some of their more orthodox coreligionists do not pass muster. There are Jewish communities who do all they can to isolate themselves from the secular and especially the gentile world. Presumably the argument is that Jews should have the attitude which Levinas recommends, since in so thinking they will fit into the notion of Judaism which accords with his general philosophy. There is nothing wrong with such an approach, which has been followed by many Jewish philosophers in some form or another. The only problem arises if we cannot translate the ordinary language of religiosity into the new philosophical interpretation of that language.

Judaism and practice

Is Judaism then specifically directed toward practice, toward the ethical? It certainly looks like it, and its legal structure, the integration of the life of the Jew within a ritualistic system, is evidence of the significance of behavior, in particular behavior which is linked with the behavior of others. The idea is that the sorts of rituals that arise in Judaism point toward wider interactions between Judaism and the rest of humanity.

> The way that leads to God therefore leads ipso facto – and not in addition – to man; and the way that leads to man draws us back to ritual discipline and self-education. Its greatness lies in its daily regularity. Here is a passage in which three opinions are given: the second indicates the way in which the first is true, and the third indicates the practical conditions of the second. Ben Zoma said: "I have found a verse that contains the whole of the Torah: 'Hear O Israel, the Lord is our God, the Lord is one'." Ben Nanus said: "I have found a verse that contains the whole of the Torah: 'you will love your neighbour as yourself'." Ben Pazi said: "I have found a verse that contains the whole of the Torah: 'you will sacrifice a lamb in the morning and another at dusk'." And Rabbi their master stood up and decided: "the Law is according to ben Pazi."
>
> (*Difficult Freedom* 18–19)

The point of this discussion is that the verse which is finally selected as embodying the whole of the Torah is the one which one would least expect to accomplish the task, yet as Levinas points out, it emphasizes the importance, the overwhelming importance, of practice. The Torah is not (just) about beliefs, it is primarily about deeds, and it is only through appropriate actions that it can be realized. This passage comes in an essay titled "A Religion for Adults," and brings out Levinas' view of the maturity of Judaism as a faith. The implication is that there is no point in the Jew retreating into himself in order to pray to God, he is not at home by himself in his house but first of all only in society, with others (ibid. 22).

The important question we need to answer here is whether this is really true of Judaism. Does the emphasis on practice dominate the religion in the ways in which Levinas suggests? It is certainly important, but whether it is so overwhelmingly important for everything which can be accepted as Judaism is difficult to accept. Could one be a Jew and yet not regard oneself as indelibly linked with other human beings or even other Jews? Could one be a Jew and not respect the laws in the Torah? Again we come to the conflict between working out precisely what Levinas is arguing. Is he advocating a particular definition of Judaism which accords with his account of how it should be or is he reporting on how it actually is?

There is no doubt that this methodological question bothers him a lot, because he is continually raising it in one form or another. It comes out in his accounts of universality, in the contrast between the particularity of Judaism, or indeed any religion, and the universality of philosophy. Judaism, he suggests, is particular but aspires to be universal. It does this because it links the divine to the moral (ibid. 21). The very election of the Jewish people is itself a symbol of the election of everyone to undertake and accept "responsibilities on which the fate of humanity hangs" (ibid. 22). But is not being Jewish primarily a matter of origin, not a matter of faith? According to Rabbi Meir, Levinas tells us, a pagan who knows the Torah is of equivalent status to the High Priest. He also refers in a very interesting way to the move from the particularity of Judaism to the universalism of philosophy as part of a process of liberation which needs to be continued. This means that "we have not yet finished translating the Bible" (*Beyond the Verse* 75), in the sense that we have only just started bringing out its universalist message. We tend to get it the wrong way around, he suggests, in that we often try to invest a biblical idea with a universalist notion already specified in Western or Greek thought, whereas what we should do is bring out the universalist idea which is already there in the Hebrew, and explain it in Greek (ibid. 199). So the apparent clash between Athens and Jerusalem, between reason and revelation, comes out as a pseudo-conflict after all, since revelation contains everything which reason does, albeit in a different form.

This is also a familiar solution to the apparent conflict between the Torah and philosophical thought within the tradition of Jewish philosophy. Levinas is thus moving through familiar territory here, although the ways in which he characterizes his theoretical environment differs from his predecessors. One difference lies in the sort of philosophy which Levinas argues runs through the Bible and the Talmud, which is of course his philosophy. The other difference is in the ways in which he approaches Judaism, which he defines thus: "Judaism is definitely the Old Testament, but through the Talmud" (*Beyond the Verse* 136). This in itself is not unusual as a definition, although it does appear to exclude the lived experience of the Jewish people which might seem not to be entirely encapsulated by this definition, but it is worth acknowledging that he often identifies Judaism in a much wider sense than one would expect given the above definition.

What is unusual about his approach to Jewish texts, which he calls Hebrew, is the freedom with which he operates. He appears to trawl the Torah and the Talmud for interesting quotations in the way that is so common among the nontraditionalist Jewish community. The idea is to find interesting and perceptive sayings that work out of their context and which can be used to give a "Jewish" gloss to an issue that looks impressive.

It is particularly marked when he comes to investigate the Hebrew words themselves, often reorganizing them and reinterpreting them to extract further meanings from them, meanings which match the arguments about their meanings which he produces at the same time. This again is a perfectly acceptable technique and much used within Jewish tradition, which even compares words in terms of their numerical value (since every Hebrew letter represents a number, so that apparently distinct words may have the same numerical value and lead to speculation about comparisons between them on the basis of that numerical value). But the ways in which Levinas carries out such operations goes against the general approach by talmudists in that he limits himself to a few such alternative readings often as few as one, the readings which fit in with his philosophical thesis. The appropriate method in the tradition would be to explore a range of alternative readings and then establish a case for a particular reading being the most plausible. What Levinas' methodology entirely misses is the tentative nature of the talmudic approach. The talmudist builds up an argument by slowly assembling evidence and then presents what he takes to be the most plausible conclusion. Levinas selects just a few pieces of evidence, and weaves around them a philosophical story which presents them as having a determinate reading, a reading in line with the philosophical meaning. There is nothing wrong with such an approach, of course, and Levinas is entitled to approach the text in whatever way he wishes. It is interesting that he describes his approach as one of *sollicitation* of the text, or rubbing the text, and one of his collections is entitled Beyond the Verse (*L'au-delà du verset*), both of which hint at the rather free way in which he is going to deal with the text. The important point to make here is that he comes to the text from outside the tradition of examining such texts, as it were, and so he finds the text ready to receive whatever interpretation he wishes to impose on it. He transforms what is already a knowing and sophisticated text into an ingénue waiting to be transformed by the creative power of the visiting philosopher.

As Levinas himself acknowledges in his essay "Revelation in the Jewish tradition" (*Beyond the Verse* 129–50), the Talmud does not consist of a body of finished and final doctrine. It consists of arguments, often pointing in a wide variety of directions. The Bible, of course, is in exactly the same position, so that one finds within it a whole range of different stories and forms of writing, some of which seem to have one meaning and others which appear to contradict that meaning. As an exposition of the Bible the

Talmud appears not to be a great help, since it is replete with the same sorts of contradictions and different points of view as the Bible itself on which it concentrates. But it is a help, since there are ways of working with these texts to arrive at a satisfactory intellectual and practical answer to a particular problem. What is this way? It involves assessing the strength of some of the competing arguments of the Talmud, and using those arguments in tandem with the Bible to build up a solid case for a particular interpretation. Since both the Bible and the Talmud consist of such varying ideas and arguments, it is not surprising that it is relatively easy to find anything in either or both texts to support virtually any view. Does that mean that these texts should not be given any respect, since they are so replete with contradictions that they can be used to imply anything at all? Certainly not, what makes these texts problematic is precisely the ways in which they reflect the complexity and depth of the lives of human beings in this sort of world.

Making sense of commentary

If we are to make sense of the apparent contradictions in the Bible and the Talmud, we have to go about it in the right sort of way, the sort of way which has been developed over many years within the traditions of the religion which is concerned with these texts. What this tradition does is balance carefully different readings, both in the Bible and in the Talmud, and then come to some conclusion about where the balance should lie. That conclusion may well be countered by alternative conclusions, which are constructed out of different readings and an alternative marshaling of evidence in the form of quotations and commentaries. Now, this is not to criticize Levinas for not being a talmudist, which is not something he is pretending to be, nor a role which he thinks he could undertake. But it is worth pointing out that if one goes to religious texts in order to select bits which are going to help one defend a particular interpretation of the religion, it is really not acceptable to select a few texts which fit in with one's existing view. That misrepresents how those texts are meant to be used within the religion. Again, it is perfectly acceptable to try to show how a general philosophical position may resonate through a particular religious text, but not if it is taken to show that the philosophical point is already there in the religion itself. It is certainly there in some of the texts of the religion, but before we can say finally that those texts represent the fixed view of the religion, we need to introduce the gamut of competing and contrary texts which in fact represent the context within which any of the texts of the religion take place.

Does that mean that the only way in which one can understand religious texts is by exploring them in detail, and certainly in combination with many other similar and related texts? This would be unduly restrictive, and one can only admire the flair which Levinas brings to his partial representations of Judaism in his work. One of the wonders of his enthusiastic style is that he takes the reader with him, in much the same way as when he was alive he would almost seduce the listener to accept his reading. Some of his talmudic readings are remarkable literary constructions, with a subtle blend of reason and emotion, sometimes leaving the reader to ponder what seems like a blank assertion with no argument, while at the same time introducing the argument in such a slow and surreptitious manner that the reader's feeling of confusion throughout the reading is suddenly resolved right at the end. It is worth pointing out that Levinas' interest in the Talmud is far from just being an academic interest. Although in his early years he appears to have been content to pursue philosophy purely as a technical enterprise, after the Shoah (Holocaust) he felt the need to link his theoretical interests with the practical aim of serving the Jewish community. So the talmudic commentaries are apparently calm works which float on a sea of passion, and they are a very effective way of bringing out his general philosophical principles. They represent the practical application of the theory, and they introduce into everyday human life the complexity of the theory. Hence their capacity to seduce, since they persuade us how interesting and complex we are, how significant every apparently minor ritualistic activity is, how close our links must be with others for us to be ourselves. We want to hear this, and if we are Jewish we want to hear how Judaism embodies this more deeply and surely than alternative faiths.

But does it? An immediate problem here is how we define a religion. Judaism is defined by Levinas as the Bible mediated by the Talmud. What he has in mind here, of course, is his Old Testament and his Talmud, that is, those passages from these texts which he is going to use. What about the Judaism of those Jews who give no particular authority to the Talmud but like the Reform movement which started in Germany emphasize the Prophets? Are they not really Jews, and is what they are doing not really Judaism? Certainly there are many who would say that. There are some Christians who would say that being a Christian means that one cannot kill another human being, and they would doubt the credentials of Christians in the military services as Christians. Some Jains are so concerned about killing anything that they sweep the ground in front of them to warn insects that they are in danger and to brush them out of the way. Is a Jain who swats a fly no longer a Jain? Is a Jain who murders a human being no longer a Jain? Is a Jew who ignores the laws of kashrut no longer a Jew? What these questions are supposed to suggest is that the character of a religion is far more complex than can be encapsulated by some formula which seeks to define it. This is a point which is obvious to Jews in particular given the extraordinarily complex ramifications of defining who a Jew is for halakhic reasons and in accordance with the laws of the State of Israel. Yet many of the people who Levinas talks about as Jews would not have accepted the definition of Judaism which he puts forward. Perhaps they are wrong, but

Levinas does not tell us that they are or why they are, and it is worth asking where they come in his account of Judaism.

Jews and Christians

We have problems in working out who Jews are, who are the "real" Christians, who is a genuine Jain, and we have similar problems in working out what their religions are. Levinas claims that religions other than Judaism interpret the religious being as transcending the ethical, while Judaism identifies the religious with the ethical. Tamra Wright refers to Kierkegaard here as "of course, the paradigm" of religions other than Judaism in placing God above the world of ethics ("Translating the Bible into Greek" 41). For Judaism, one can only live a religious life if one responds to God by trying to bring about justice, if one responds to God by helping other human beings, which will result in his response to us being *hineni* (here I am) as in Isaiah 58:8–9). Let us ask a few questions about these claims, questions which I admit are rather naive. Can Kierkegaard be taken to be the representative of religions other than Judaism or even of Christianity as such? He is certainly representative of some forms of Christianity, but many Christians would be surprised to discover that Kierkegaard has become their paradigm. Or, to take a different tack, is it the case that Christianity by contrast with Judaism does not identify the religious with justice and the ending of servitude? Many Christians would argue that their religion is entirely about the ending of inequality and poverty, and they would point to those passages in the New Testament in which Jesus through his actions and words seems more of a social reformer than a potential messiah. Indeed, many Christians would claim that Jesus was a critic of the transcendental notion of God, which is generally taken to be a feature of some forms of Judaism during his time, and his mediation in the world as linking this world with God as a solution to many of the problems that the Old Testament cannot resolve.

This is not the place to debate these enormous issues but their significance is that they are issues. One cannot just brush aside all other religions as less concerned with ethics and justice when compared with Judaism. One could go further and suggest that the whole attempt at characterizing religions within a particular formula is itself suspect. It is just the sort of thing which Levinas quite rightly accuses Hegel of doing to no great purpose. Hegel's aim is to construct a sort of league table of religions, but Levinas seems to have a simpler process in mind. He has a dichotomy between Judaism and the Rest, as though one could distinguish religions in the simple ways in which one can distinguish other organizations. There are distinguishing aspects between different religions, to be sure, but they are not along the lines which Levinas suggests. We can discover no predominantly ethical flavor to Judaism which does not also exist in many other religions.

There certainly is a powerful ethical strain in Judaism, but then there is exactly the same orientation in some forms of Christianity, and also Islam, which is hardly surprising given their origins in Judaism. Indeed, the enthusiasm for ritual that we find in many versions of Judaism could be seen as profoundly unethical and particularist, since it invites us to think a lot about whether we have got the ritual right, and this may have nothing to do with our relationships with other people. The fact that Jews see themselves as members of a specific group could militate against relating to everyone else outside the group. One would expect a religion that develops into other religions to stress particular aspects which are then taken in different directions by its successors, and for those successors to emphasize rather differently what had previously been important. Christianity, for example, often represents itself as following Jesus in no longer giving any prominence to halakhah, which it sees as unduly restrictive of our relationship with God and each other. It is not clear that this was Jesus' view, but this is in itself a highly controversial issue. Islam also sees itself as mediating between the extremes of Judaism and Christianity and as the final revelation getting the balance exactly right. All these three religions make social justice and ethics extremely important. One could go further, of course, and look at a far wider range of religions, and again one would find that ethics is usually, although perhaps not always, a feature which is taken to be crucial to living a religious life, a life in accordance with the faith. There are some religions like Buddhism, if Buddhism is a religion, that stress our responsibility for everything else in an even more radical way than Levinas suggests. Other faiths like Jainism practice extreme care lest one destroy the lives of even tiny insects, something that does not seem to occur to Levinas as being a significant step at all.

Levinas makes an even stronger claim then that Judaism is the unique paradigm of ethics. He also claims that halakhah is, for Jews, the route to ethics. In "A Religion for Adults" he suggests that "The ritual law of Judaism constitutes the austere discipline that strives to achieve…justice. Only this law can recognize the face of the Other, which has managed to impose an austere role on its true nature" (*Difficult Freedom* 18). One wonders what this means for the followers of other religions, who of course have no such law, or for the followers of no religion at all. Are they denied access to ethics in its fullest sense, can they not recognize the face of the Other whatever they do or think? One wonders what this means for Jews, surely the majority today, who are not committed to halakhah. Are they also excluded from ethical life? It might be that the thesis is that for a fully ethical life to be achieved it has to be embodied in some set of rituals, and halakhah does this perfectly, so that other forms of life may come close to this level of perfection, but never reach it nor replace it. Yet the rituals often have nothing to do with linking us with others, and it is not clear to many Jews why those rituals should still be followed.

We should remember the audience which Levinas is addressing in his Jewish works. He is speaking to assimilated Jews, to Jews who see themselves as part of the Greek world of the West, for whom Judaism is a faith in which they are born and which plays little part in their intellectual and personal lives. He wants to show that the Greek ideas which dominate their lives have their origin in Hebrew and are greatly enriched by going back to the Hebrew and exploring the profound web of meaning which surrounds the Hebrew. Hence halakhah, which otherwise might seem to be a remnant of an unenlightened and burdensome past, can emerge as a path to ethical life and the sort of freedom which is acceptable—the freedom to acknowledge and carry out human responsibilities. Halakhah is part of the warp and woof of ethical life, and it is not open to the Jew to wonder whether she should practice that life within or without halakhah. The argument then concludes with the proposition that halakhah is ethics for Jews.

Levinas and the defense of law

When we examine the detailed defense of halakhah that Levinas produces a number of questions arise. He tends not to defend the practices of halakhah as a whole but the principle of there being a halakhah. We are supposed to accept that once the principle of there being a halakhah is understood, the details of what to do will be in accordance with the legal texts. Perhaps it does not matter so much exactly which understanding of the precise nature of the law one follows, so long as one adheres to an appropriate legal rule that determines the nature of the law. The general point which Levinas makes is certainly appropriate, that Jews seeking to find a way of embodying their ethical behavior in a practice need look no further than halakhah, which is a form of practice specifically designed to replicate the truths of faith. Yet since Levinas often says that when he talks about Jews he means humanity at large, we are still left not knowing how most people ought to behave. He relishes the prospect of Jews being obliged to follow 613 commandments, while the rest of humanity only needs follow the seven Noachide laws, since this exemplifies the idea of owing more to the other than one asks in return ("Assimilation and the New Culture," *Beyond the Verse* 200)! But is the only route to such an ethical life for the Jew the halakhic route? It is one thing to defend the acceptability of such a route but quite another to demonstrate its inevitability. Since Levinas is firmly part of the demythological tendency in modern theology, he cannot argue that one should follow halakhah because God had commanded us to act thus in the Torah. Such appeals to what Levinas rather scathingly calls the numinous are ruled out from the start.

Then we have the problem of knowing how gentiles are to live. Are they to follow the laws of their faith? Are they to consider conversion to Judaism? Are they limited to the seven Noachide laws? These are the rules established at the time of Noah, according to the rabbis, and incumbent on all humanity, regardless of religion or nationality. They too may wish to be in a position to say *me voici* even if they cannot say *hineni*. Their route to reaching that position is presumably through Greek, since they cannot go through Hebrew, but if they can attain their end along the Greek route, there seems no reason to deny such a route to assimilated Jews. It would be invidious to suggest that a particular ethnic group is especially advantaged in knowing how to live as compared with others, unless one can appeal to some supernatural rationale, which Levinas rejects. Even if my ancestors opened themselves to God in a way different from other ethnic groups, it is difficult to see how that elevates my consciousness above those of members of other ethnic groups. In a celebrated discussion Levinas argues that what made the Jews unique was that they undertook to obey God's law even before they heard what that law was and in this way acknowledged the priority of the ethical over the ontological (see his "Temptation of the Temptation," *Nine Talmudic Readings* 30–50). That is, they accepted that the first question to be answered is where our responsibilities lie, and the second question follows from that, and concerns who we are. But what is the link between that event and the nature of halakhah, as it has come down to us today? There is obviously some sort of link in terms of tradition, yet it is the case that for many Jews the ties of tradition no longer have any emotional resonance. The only way for them to find that resonance again is through the Greek, and that is why Levinas seeks to reinvigorate tradition by exploring its universal values in language which is accessible to those who have lost the ability to understand the Hebrew. When he talks of them no longer understanding Hebrew he does not refer to technical mastery of the language, but the ability to link the Hebrew to present-day ethical and political issues. What needs to be brought out is the universalist message of the Hebrew, so that it is not seen as the repository of a small and remote community, but as implicit within the rules of behavior everywhere and at all times.

Does he succeed? He succeeds in the sense that he shows that the detail of the law, of some of the law anyway, is far more than merely a technical exercise in legal reasoning. It is appropriate as the embodiment of an ethical lifestyle which is capable of guiding us today through the realm of responsibility. He may be taken to have presented useful arguments to establish halakhah as a sufficient condition of such a lifestyle, but does he establish it as a necessary condition? That is, does he show that the Jew can only participate in that lifestyle if she is a halakhic Jew? He does not establish that, and perhaps he does not intend to. It might be enough for his purposes to show that halakhah is validated as a practice through its suitability for ethical life. But is this really enough? What the modern Jew may ask is why she should obey a system of law which she does not feel is appropriate to her participation in ethical life. She knows that halakhah is available to her, but she does not feel that this is the right way for her; she cannot react to it as though it is a way of life which she is called upon to follow. Levinas' arguments may establish that halakhah represents the universal aims which she has in mind, but those arguments do not establish the uniqueness of halakhah in representing those aims. If we cannot appeal to the divine origin of halakhah, as we cannot for Levinas, as justifying halakhah, then why choose halakhah over some other comprehensive lifestyle? The identification of halakhah with ethics gets us away from the problem of justifying a practice in terms of its supernatural origin, but it lands us with the problem of knowing how to assess varying interpretations of lifestyle which seem to be ethical and yet not halakhic.

What in the end can we say of Levinas' project of translating the Bible into Greek? The relevant question is what the project illuminates. Does it illuminate the Hebrew or the Greek, the works of Judaism or the works of philosophy? The answer has to be that Levinas is not really translating Hebrew into Greek but one form of Greek into another form of Greek. The talmudic readings do not shape the philosophy, rather, they are shaped by it, which is hardly surprising given his argument that Judaism is a universal system of thought. So denying that he is really translating the Hebrew into the Greek is not to criticize what he sets out to do, although it is to criticize one way of portraying his approach. Many commentators tend to copy his approach, jumping from Jewish texts to philosophical texts as though one were in that way establishing links of meaning between them. What Levinas does is show how Jewish texts may be interpreted philosophically, and in this he is following in a long tradition of Jewish philosophers examining Jewish texts. The danger lies in our thinking that he is doing more than this, that he is really showing how the philosophical texts are reflections of the Jewish texts or that the Jewish texts in some way validate the philosophical texts. Another danger lies in our thinking that he has produced good arguments for prioritizing Judaism over other religions as the paradigmatic ethical faith or that he has shown that halakhah is the exclusive route to ethical life. Once we acknowledge the limited nature of what can be derived from translating Greek religion into Greek philosophy, we shall be in a better position to understand the real significance of Levinas' writings on Judaism.

Chapter 4

Jews versus Christians

One of the assumptions one has to make about the difficult relationships that have existed for many centuries between Jews and Christians is that most Jews found Christianity to be a profoundly unsatisfactory alternative to Judaism. After all, for much of that time it was very advantageous for Jews to convert, and indeed converts as a whole often find they have engaged on an entirely new career, a career on which they are immediately placed on the fast track. Sometimes converts were treated with some suspicion, and the Spanish Inquisition was initiated in order to weed out those who had not really converted but were just pretending to be Christians in order to stay in Iberia and hold onto their property. One of the interesting phenomena of the Inquisition is that it put Jewish ethnicity to the fore, the assumption being that Jews who converted were never really the same as other Christians, but that there was something still "in the blood" that made them a dangerous and dubious group in society.

Jews had on the whole an unhappy experience of living in societies dominated by Christians. In this chapter, we shall examine some aspects of that experience and see what it is in Christianity that Jews did not appreciate. The original message of Christianity could be seen as quite friendly to Judaism, indeed a mere development of it. Jesus does not seem to have set himself up as offering a different religion and his first followers were of course, like himself, all Jews. What often happens though when an ethnic or religious group rejects the message of one of their own is that he and his supporters turn away from that group and feel hostility toward them. The attempt of Christianity to proselytize the Jews was not a brilliant success and had as its residue the notion of the Jews as a stubborn and ungrateful bunch of people who had rejected and even killed their own coreligionist who was trying to help them reach salvation. This is not a very promising way for religions to relate to each other, especially as the Jews were profoundly unsympathetic to a leading Christian claim, namely, that Jesus was the Messiah.

Jesus the Jew: Messianic issues

As anyone who has followed the recent literature will know, the notion of Jesus the Jew is hardly revolutionary any more. It is widely accepted that in order to understand the role of Jesus and Christianity one must pay due attention to Jesus' origins and not treat these as something to be glossed over as standing in the way of the universal message of Christianity. What is the main difficulty in Jews accepting Jesus as the Messiah? The standard answer is that Jesus did not satisfy the criteria for this role according to Jewish law. For one thing, he was extraordinarily unsuccessful as the Messiah, since he did not lead the Jews back to Israel, he did not bring universal peace, and nor did he conquer death, despite what priests and ministers often say. Let us examine these claims and counterclaims one by one.

There is in Judaism a lot of controversy over the nature of the messianic age, not surprisingly since there is a lot of controversy about everything. Some like Maimonides argue that the messianic age will not be very different from our age. People will still die and have disputes with each other and the normal range of Jewish law would still apply to the behavior of the Jewish people. In fact, for him it is a sure mark of a false messiah if the individual wishes to change even a tiny aspect of Jewish law. Halakhah will stay the same because the laws of nature will stay the same, and if they were expected to change radically, would this not imply that there was something wrong with them in the first place? That would in turn imply that there was something wrong with what God had produced.

The Messiah in Judaism will revive everyone at the end of time and not just one. Although Christians often argue that Jesus prefigures the eventual revival of everyone, or at least those who deserve to be revived, this is not the story of the Jewish Messiah. On the other hand, we cannot rule out the extension of the Jewish idea as valid in its Christian form, since it would be wrong to see Judaism, or indeed any religion, as being narrowly defined in terms of a few narrow principles.

Perhaps the telling objection is that Jesus did not lead the Jews back to Israel; it was quite different individuals who set that in motion and those Jews who returned only came in most cases to get away from a worse alternative elsewhere. Nor did Torah go out from Zion, which is generally taken to mean that the world will accept some basic aspects of monotheism, perhaps the Noachide laws, the seven basic laws given to Noah and his descendants, and so join the Jews in the project in establishing a new and close relationship with God. Again, it might be argued that this is going to happen in the future, but that is rather like saying that the Messiah has not yet come and will come in the future.

Christian persecution of the Jews

As we know, when Christianity became more established in the state it turned on the Jews, not surprisingly, with a ferocity that limited their scope for action. The idea that the Jews were the murderers of Jesus is still hotly debated today, and the film *The Passion of Christ* was attacked by some as depicting the Jews' guilt in the death of Jesus. What seemed to annoy the Christians particularly was the refusal of the Jews to acknowledge Jesus and his role, although they were the group to whom he first preached and from which he emerged. Individuals who feel that they have been slighted often bear a grudge for a long time, and Christianity certainly has. The idea of the Jews as the Other, the opposite and opponent of Christianity, validated the discrimination that Jews suffered in the Christian world and their restricted living and occupational framework. Occasional massacres and forced conversions were also a feature of Jewish life in the Christian world, and it was only when religion started to relax its hold on Europe that the Jews became members of the society. Once this became a possibility, rapid assimilation took place; it was as though the most effective form of conversion was not after all force but acceptance. In modern Europe, when Jews could join civil society as Jews they often became Christians to become even more ordinary and normal members of society, and the "Why not become a Christian?" debate became much discussed in Jewish intellectual circles in nineteenth and early twentieth-century Europe. Today, the debate has become more general, and a large number of Jews do convert to other religions and practices, Buddhism being particularly popular as a Jewish destination in the United States (leading to the nomenclature of "Jew-boos").

Christian Jews or Jewish Christians?

It is an interesting question whether a Jew can be a Christian and remain a Jew. There is a group of people who call themselves Messianic Jews and who claim to regard themselves as Jews and who argue that Jesus established a form of faith which is particularly appropriate to Jews, one which does not call for the abandonment of normal Jewish practices and rituals. They argue that Jews who join their group do not convert to Christianity, they merely continue to follow Judaism, with the slight difference that now they acknowledge Jesus as the Messiah. One might well feel that this claim is disingenuous and that this is yet another ploy to convert Jews to Christianity, but in fact, this raises an interesting point. From a legal point of view, there is no doubt that a Jew who acknowledges Jesus as the Messiah is no longer to be counted as a Jew in anything but an ethnic sense. During the Second World War, many ethnic Jews who happened to be Christians were murdered along with those who remained within the Jewish religion, so the idea of a Jew being a Christian at the same time as remaining a Jew is not exactly new. Christianity from early on in its history regarded itself as a potential faith exclusively for Jews until the decision was taken to open up the religion to everyone regardless of background. This must surely be regarded as one of the best marketing decisions in human history, given the rapid success of Christianity as a world religion.

There is no doubt that a Jew who acknowledges Jesus as his savior is no longer a Jew according to Orthodox Judaism. This is because that brand of the religion adheres to a set of fairly clear criteria of what is involved in being a Jew, and a criterion to be accepted is that the Messiah is still awaited. Presumably, when he comes he will tell us whether he has been here before, and if he has then the Christians are right; if he has not then the Jews are vindicated in their obstinate rejection of Jesus. (I suppose we should keep open the possibility that the Messiah has already come but no one recognized him at the time.) For other kinds of Jews though the position is different, since there are often no clear criteria of being Jewish either in the ethnic sense or in what has to be believed. If there are Jews who admit that they do not believe in God, who adhere to no rules of behavior based on religion, and who perhaps have no views whatsoever which distinguish them from anyone else, then why should there not be Jews who believe that Jesus is the Messiah?

Should Christians continue to try to convert Jews to Christianity? This practice raises a lot of hackles in the Jewish world, and this is hardly surprising when one recalls the long history of persecution and compulsion that conversion represents. In the past it was often not a voluntary issue, Jews were compulsorily converted or killed, and their refusal to convert was often given as a good reason for treating them poorly. The disputations in the middle ages were good examples of this. Jews were obliged to listen to a preacher, often himself a former Jew, and then sometimes to one of their own representatives, a rabbi. The debate was on the merits of Christianity and the demerits of Judaism, and the appropriate result in the view of the organizers was a mass conversion when confronted by the obvious truth. The fact that many Jews did not convert is remarkable given the onus on them to do so and the material advantages in so doing also. From what we know of such debates, they were usually highly slanted in favor of the Christian advocate and the rabbi was under many difficulties in making his case, but there was despite this, often an interesting exchange of views, albeit what was expected was that the Jews would be converted to Christianity, not the other way around, so the very notion of a debate was rather stretched.

On the other hand, the rabbis were sometimes very animated in their defense of Judaism, despite the difficult circumstances, and even seem to have won the argument. For example, in Paris in the thirteenth century Rabbi Samuel ben Abraham was confronted by Paul Christian, a converted Jew, in the Dominican residence and obliged to debate over a considerable period on Judaism versus Christianity, and the only topic which seemed to embarrass him was that of the death of Jesus and the involvement of the Jews in that event. Over time, the Jews responded to the charge of killing Jesus in a variety of ways. For example, the Talmud refers to Jesus the Nazarene being killed (by stoning!) for witchcraft and deceiving the people (*Sanhedrin* 43a). It was also argued that if God sent Jesus on earth to die then the Jews were only fulfilling divine wishes. Also, the link between the few Jews at the time and the Jewish world today seems rather a distant one. Interestingly, today some of the most vocal support for the State of Israel comes from evangelical Christians who are enthusiastic about converting Jews, and others, but who also think that Jews in the past played an essential role in sacred history and will again. They believe that the Middle East will see extreme violent conflict, which will bring on the end of the world and the second coming of Jesus. They see the reestablishment of the State as part of the divine plan for the eventual coming of final salvation and the judgment of everyone in existence. One would not expect Jews to do well in such a judgment, not if they stay Jews that is. This was a line that was used during some of the debates, and it seems a reasonable one. After all, God had a plan for Jesus, and the Jews fulfilled their role in that plan. In any case, what is the link between Jews many centuries after the incident or even at the same time, unless they were directly involved? On the other hand, exactly the same point could be made about the covenant between God and the Jews, an arrangement made a long time ago between entirely different people (on the human side, that is), and yet many believe that agreement is still binding today.

Christian accusations against the Jews

There were various charges made against the Jews apart from just not getting it, and they were supposed to be involved in a variety of anti-Christian activities. A religion that believed in the literal truth of the Mass representing the blood and body of Christ suspected Jews of profaning the host in order to persecute Jesus as he became physical on a regular basis. It was a small step from this to suspecting them of actually killing Christians, in particular children, in order to incorporate their blood in some ritual. Missing children were often credited with having fallen into some Jewish trap, and this resulted in expulsions and murders of the minority, when it was not under the protection of some greater power such as the king or local aristocrat. Since Jews were progressively denied employment except in very specialized professions such as money lending, they became a mysterious and threatening presence in many towns, with apparent power over those to whom they lent money, but also without the opportunity to participate in civil society. Jews were often obliged to wear distinctive and humiliating clothes when out in public, and it is hardly surprising that this small group of people came under a good deal of suspicion for their behavior given their virtual exclusion from ordinary society and exotic customs. The status quo was often interrupted as in the Crusades when popular fury at the Jews led to their massacre in many towns en route, and in Palestine itself. The Black Death renewed the hostility to the Jews, since they were accused of causing it. Indeed, any disaster improperly understood could be laid at the door of the Jews or so it seemed. This was important since the link between the Jews at the time of Jesus and contemporary Jews must have seemed distant even in the Middle Ages, and any putative crimes that the Jewish community continued to commit against Christianity was valuable in preserving the sense of outrage at the existence of any sort of Jewish community at all.

Jews in Spain and Portugal

One of the most traumatic events that occurred to Jews in the Christian world occurred in the Iberian Peninsula, once a territory that had spasmodically been a favorable location for Jews. The constant fighting between the Christians and the Muslims left Jews with a degree of breathing room, since they could be useful to both sides. It was when one side became successful that the real danger started. So when the Almohads conquered most of Spain they expelled much of the Jewish population and when toward the end of the fifteenth century the Christians completed their reconquest of Spain they celebrated by expelling the entire Jewish population in 1492 (Portugal was to follow in 1494). But in fact this was merely the culmination of many anti-Jewish measures in the rapidly growing Christian part of Spain; previously, there had been mass conversions and also a suspicion of the genuineness of the conversions, leading to the institution of the Spanish Inquisition to investigate whether former Jews had really become Christians for the right sort of reasons, and whether they were performing in secret any of their previous Jewish rituals.

This was an interesting phenomenon. One might have expected that the Spanish Christians would have been pleased that so many Jews had embraced Christianity and had now seen the error of their ways. Why this emphasis on the genuineness of the conversion? After all, it was not as though the Jews were not under pressure to convert. They were. The frequent debates by former Jews against their coreligionists, which were far from pacific, and academic exchanges of view succeeded in obliging many to give up their religion. The material and social advantages of conversion also took a toll, and finally the choice between emigration and conversion was a very bleak one indeed. It is hardly surprising that there was some suspicion of the genuineness of the conversion. It is rather like a man boasting of his wealth to a prospective partner and then wondering whether she loves him for his money or for himself. No doubt some of the converts were enthusiastic about their new religion, in just the way that converts are often far more serious about religion than are those brought up in it. On the other hand, the circumstances of the conversions must also have led to a lot of pragmatic decisions to take the easier path and become a Christian, and the result of that would have been that most of one's friends and business partners would have remained Jews, or people who were originally Jews. It is difficult to believe that people who converted were especially religious in their Jewish lives since presumably they would not have taken the decision to convert but would have left, suffered disadvantages, or even died. During the Crusades, some Jewish communities actually killed themselves and each other rather than be forced to convert. What seems to have happened in Spain is that many of the conversos continued to practice a sort of social Judaism in which they gathered in secret and persisted in some Jewish practices, albeit as time went on the practices became more and more eccentric and disconnected from tradition. Had Messianic Judaism then existed they would no doubt have felt very at home in that sort of movement since they could have continued with some Jewish prayers and customs while acknowledging Jesus as the Messiah referred to in the Jewish literature.

But in Spain the conversos were not given the opportunity to take this approach; they were sometimes labeled Marranos, a derogatory term, and widely believed to persist in their Judaism, while pretending to be Christians. Presumably, the source of this criticism were people who felt shut out of the various commercial and political groups that former Jews constituted, and this was how Christians or old Christians as we should call them sought to raise their status against the newcomers who may have been after a free ride. It is difficult to avoid believing also that what we can see here is an aspect of a persistent feature of racism, namely, that there is nothing that the despised group can do to escape being disliked. If they maintain their original religion and practices they are disliked because of their religion and practices. If they give up their religion and practices they are disliked because they are suspected of having given up their religion and practices for pragmatic reasons or for not having given them up at all. This approach to the Jews came out clearly in recent years in the opposition of many Europeans to the notion of a viable Jewish state in the Middle East. To some Jews this looked very much like the Europeans not wanting the Jews to live in Europe, as evidenced by the Holocaust and the lukewarm reception that the survivors received in many parts of Europe, and also not wanting them to live in the Middle East, since their situation there was causing so much apparent aggravation. This represents a classic form of antisemitism whereby the despised group can do nothing to avoid being despised since it is held to be despicable in its very nature or essence. It is worth remembering that the point of hating a group is often to have the concept of an Other against which one can define precisely who you are. Once the Other becomes, or tries to become, the same as you, it is difficult to define who you are anymore. That can easily lead to even greater hatred.

Chapter 5

Jews versus Muslims

The relationship between Judaism and Islam has not usually been easy. For one thing, Islam as a later religion was always subject to the criticism or anxiety that it is only a derivation of earlier religions, something that certainly is not seen as a viable option for Muslims. An effective way to downplay the significance of Islam is to stress its putative origins in other religions and the non-Islamic factors that influenced it. Orientalist commentators have spent much energy stressing this sort of dependence, and Muslims have often countered this approach by stressing the originality of the event of the message presented to Muhammad. This spat between the two religions has often been replicated in far worse and violent behavior and as with that other new religion—Christianity—it is always awkward to know how the new should relate to the old. Too much respect of the new for the old raises the issue of why a change needed to be made at all. Too little respect suggests that there is something wrong with the source of the new, challenging its credentials as the genuine path to God.

When the Prophet Muhammad received the revelation over a period of a couple of decades, he had different expectations of how it would be received by the Jews and Christians. There were significant Jewish tribes in Arabia and it was important to gain their support or at least acquiescence in the message of Islam and the growth of the new political and religious movement. The Qur'an after all represents itself as confirming the earlier messages from God to the Jews and the Christians, and many of the figures that occur in the Qur'an are also to be found in the other holy books, at least in the sense of sharing the names of biblical prophets and characters. On the other hand, the charge was leveled against the predecessors of Islam in monotheistic religions that they were not really monotheistic (the Christians) or that they had changed their scriptures (especially the Jews). Yet, it is not clear how we are to know which parts of the Bible have been superseded and which have not. One charge often made by Islam is that those parts of the Bible must have been changed by the Jews if they involve negative accounts of the prophets. It is a powerful charge, since there is no doubt that many of the accounts of the main participants in the Bible present them as highly dubious moral characters. They lie, they steal, they mislead and cheat others on occasion, and it has been argued that this must represent a deviation from the real message of God, since how could God hold up these individuals to be messengers and exemplars if their behavior was often so disgraceful?

Jews as stubborn

There are friendly references to both religions in the Qur'an, and also some much more hostile references, especially to the Jews, perhaps a reflection on the opposition by the Jews to the Prophet's mission and their lack of enthusiasm for the religion of Islam. A similar process seems to have occurred in Protestant Christianity. Luther's earliest references to the Jews in the mid-1520s are quite gentle, and apparently he had hopes of converting them through his proposed reforms. Yet once they proved obdurate he turned on them, in the 1530s and 1540s, labeling them parasites, kidnappers of children, thieves, and well poisoners. He suggested that the civil authorities expel them or use them as forced labor. It may well be that the change from the positive or at least neutral to the more negative image of the Jews that arises in the Qur'an is a response to their early and protracted opposition to what they regarded as a new religion, after an initial period of optimism at the potential as converts.

One of the claims in the Qur'an is that God punished the Jews by imposing very strict dietary laws on them, and this certainly seems a plausible claim given some of the extremities of that legislation. On the other hand, this punishment for disobedience could easily have been disobeyed in turn and so have turned out to be no punishment at all. There is a range of rather unpleasant comments on the Jews and their apparent failure to stick to high standards of ethics in business, particularly the practice of usury. One of the causes for complaint with the Jews may well have been their disinclination to convert to Islam, although there can be no doubt that large numbers did convert. But as with the Christian reaction to the Jews, the fact that some held out must have annoyed the Muslims, and they held out despite the many practical advantages of embracing Islam. This led to a developing relationship, which was often mutually unsatisfactory. On the one hand, the Jews were enthusiastic participants in the general culture of the Islamic world and became some of the most proficient Arabic and Persian poets, scientists, physicians, and philosophers and were of course involved in commercial life in its broadest sense. On the other hand, they often had to cope with discriminatory treatment, forced expulsions or conversion, and indeed murder, all of which emphasized their difference from other inhabitants of the Islamic world. The so-called Golden Age in al-Andalus (Islamic Iberia) was often far from golden as far as the Jews were concerned. The idea that

Jews, Muslims, and Christians were living in some sort of harmonious and tolerant state is far from the truth. There were periods of relative tranquility between the different communities and periods when the relationships were far more difficult. Yet, when the great Jewish thinker Moses Maimonides, most of whose work was written in Arabic, was expelled with the rest of the Jewish population from Islamic Cordoba and had to leave the whole of the Iberian Peninsula, he found uncertain sanctuary first in Islamic North Africa, finally ending up in the Fatimid city of Cairo. Muslims both obliged him to leave his own land and also established him in a new domicile.

Jews seeking refuge in the Islamic world

When the Jews were finally driven out of Spain and Portugal by the Christian rulers they often found sanctuary in other parts of the Islamic world, in particular the Ottoman Empire, where they were seen as useful allies for the Sultan as commercial entities throughout the empire. The fact that they were not Muslims was not a huge issue in an empire which had many non-Muslim subjects and the formal disabilities under which they worked as non-Muslims were often rather minor compared to what they had had to put up with in the past.

Even when antisemitism got going in Europe and the Germans in the twentieth century tried to instill some of the standard European stereotypes of Jews in the Arab world they found it quite difficult to inspire much hostility for the Jewish minority in their midst. It is only in more recent times, since the establishment of the State of Israel, that the standard antisemitic images and slogans have gained much purchase in the Middle East and the recent popularity of the *Protocols of the Elders of Zion* in Arabic suggests a protracted future for this well-known forgery. Sometimes, one has the impression that these slogans are used to annoy the Israelis rather than resonate with the Arab public, but the latter has taken to a European style of antisemitism with alacrity. It is rather like Holocaust denial, a popular pastime in the Arab world, but not really having any connection with anything of relevance to the experience of the Arabs themselves. In so far as Israel owes the moral claim for its existence on the Holocaust, the enemies of Israel can set out to challenge that claim by challenging the existence of and significance of the Holocaust. Another effective strategy has been to compare the actions of the Israelis to those of the Nazis, and this serves also to undermine the basis of the state, since if the Israelis are as bad as the Nazis, why don't they deserve the same kind of delegitimation and destruction that the Third Reich received at the hands of its enemies? Finally, the claim that the Israelis are racists and the State of Israel is based on genocide works effectively to put the country rhetorically in the same category as apartheid South Africa and to suggest that it be treated in the same sort of way. What often works with a local audience are those passages from the Qur'an, and the *hadith* (traditional sayings of the Prophet and his Companions) that are derogatory of the Jews and which suggest that there will be constant conflict between the Jews and the Muslims.

The Jewish Antichrist

It is useful for this rhetoric that the Dajjal, the Antichrist, is often represented as a Jew. He will appear shortly before the arrival of Jesus and the Mahdi, and he will dominate the world with his power and strength, but will ultimately be defeated by the forces of good. The Islamic community is often warned to be careful of those who would like to lead it astray. Among those who were to come after the Prophet the most notorious was the Dajjal, the false Messiah, whose wickedness is so effective and compelling. Therefore, the Prophet related many details of his character, how he will operate and his distinguishing marks, so that there remains no room for the community to doubt his dangerous nature whenever he appears. Similarly, among the positive figures in religion, Jesus is the most distinguished whom God blessed with the role of prophecy, he kept him alive in the heavens to come to the rescue of the Muslim community during the wicked period of the Dajjal and appointed him to kill the Dajjal close to the Day of Judgment. This is why it was deemed necessary that the community should be given the most clear indications of his person and qualities as well so that no human being remains in doubt identifying Jesus when he comes on the second occasion. The information is given in the literature of the Traditions (*hadith*) and not in the Qur'an, yet it is certainly true to say that there is plenty of it, and there is enough there to guide the believer.

This image of the savior and his determined enemy has worked well with traditional antisemitic messages and toward the beginning of the twenty-first century standard antisemitic literature such as the *Protocols of the Elders of Zion* and more recent and popular anti-Jewish texts are widespread in the Islamic world. Having driven out their own Jewish populations, it might be easier for the Arabs to believe in the hook-nosed ghouls in the antisemitic broadsheets, and given their distance from the center of economic life, they can readily identify with the idea of a small but influential gang of Jews who are manipulating everything that happens in the world. After all, there are so few Jews and so many Muslims, then how could the former be so successful in their actions unless they used devious and conspiratorial methods? This is especially the case where the injustice of Zionism is so evident, as it is to those dispossessed by the Zionists, and as a result conspiracy theories abound in the Muslim world. When this is combined with the idea that Muslims are always victims, and that they previously treated the Jews in their midst so liberally, a potent brew of hatred is easily produced. But it is worth pointing out that this recent form of antagonism has everything to do with politics and nothing to do with the religions themselves.

The falsification of the Torah

What makes the relationship between Islam and Judaism difficult is the claim that the Torah as we now have it is not really an earlier message from God. God did send messengers to the Jews, but they tended to ignore them or even kill them, and they disliked the message, replacing it with one they preferred (although this presumably does not apply to the dietary laws which are said to be divine punishment). So the conclusion can only be that the main religious text of the Jews is corrupt and inaccurate, and does not really represent an earlier revelation from God. As with Christianity, the Jews are often seen as stubbornly rejecting a more successful and efficient approach to God, and the consequences are hardly to be wondered at. If someone refuses to do what he obviously should then it is no surprise that there is a resulting lack of success. It is rather like preferring an older machine to a newer machine and being surprised at the former being less reliable than the latter. Of course, this is not always the case with machinery, but if we are rational and are offered the choice between an older model and a more modern model of the same thing, we are likely to choose the modern version. There is no doubt that a lot of Jews throughout history, and even today, quite willingly embraced Islam, no doubt impressed by what they took to be the contrast between Judaism and the newer and perhaps rather less complicated faith.

Muhammad and the Jews

The Qur'an accepts the Jews (Banu Isra'il) as having a covenant with God, and classifies them as People of the Book. But as we have seen, the charge is that they have repeatedly broken their covenant, they have changed (tahrif) the Torah from what God gave them to what is convenient, and they have tended to oppose God's prophets. This opposition has even gone to the extremes of the Jews killing, or trying to kill, their prophets.

It is clear that some of the positive and negative comments have a background in Muhammad's experiences of living in an environment with significant Jewish tribes in the political framework. Initially he may have thought that they would be interested in his message, and the early favorable comments perhaps reflect this optimism. He was soon disillusioned, and the Jewish tribes in the Medinah area often allied themselves with the opponents of the new religion, so the Qur'an reflects this with many bitter attacks on the Jews and their treachery. The final defeat of the Jews of Khaybar in CE 628 and the massacre of the male population with the enslavement of the women and children brought to an end the active opposition of the local Jews. This event needs to be put within its context if we are to understand why it might seem to be justifiable in Islamic terms.

It was when 'A'isha was married to the Prophet that the Jews are said to have plotted and tried to kill the Prophet on more than one occasion, without success, and were punished for this. First, Jewish tribes such as the Banu Qayunqa and the Banu Nadhir were expelled from Medina. Then the Banu Qurayza—who we are told had broken their agreement with the Muslims during the battle of al-Khandaq and conspired to destroy them— were subjected to the punishment that was decided by the man whom they themselves had chosen to judge their actions, or so we are told, Sa'id ibn Mu'adh. It is explained that in accordance with the commands contained in their own book, the Torah, almost all the men were killed. One cannot find in the Torah such a law, but on the other hand there are instances where the Israelites acted in just such a way, so perhaps that is the relevant reference. All the men were killed, with the exception of four who accepted Islam, and all the women and children were enslaved.

Jews and the Qur'an

As the Islamic Empire expanded, it incorporated significant Jewish minorities and initiated a *dhimmi* system according to which the Jews would be a protected minority if they paid a specific tax for non-Muslims. The Qur'an sometimes treats the Jews as equivalent to Christians as People of the Book, but often as worse than the Christians. God punished them for their disobedience by giving them burdensome laws of acceptable food, what is *haram* for them or forbidden (6.146). One source of their punishment was their *zulm* or wrongdoing (4.160–161) which was usury, something they were strictly forbidden to do. Many of them compete with each other as sinners (5.62), not a very pleasant image, and in the second sura the Jews are roundly criticized for arguing ceaselessly about the precise way in which they are supposed to carry out a sacrifice, because they wished to avoid the sacrifice altogether. This perhaps represents an attack on the legalism of Jewish tradition that was so often criticized by Christians also. The behavior of the Jews leads the Qur'an sometimes to link them more with the polytheists than with the other People of the Book, since the claim is that they are not really believers and have a propensity to lead believers astray if left to act freely. Finally, Muslims are warned against being friends with the Jews and trusting them.

The Isra'iliyat

There are significant Islamic texts that are known in Arabic as the Isra'iliyyat, the stories that entered Islam from all the Jewish converts who brought along with them their traditions. This eventually led to various campaigns to cleanse Islam from too close an identification with Judaism, a campaign which can sail rather too close to the winds of antisemitism, of course. Then in parallel with the Isra'iliyat are the many stories in the Traditions of the Prophet and those close to him about the treachery of the Jews, together with similar stories in the various histories and popular sayings from the Islamic world. The persistence of Israel in surviving and indeed in dominating the Middle East is deeply frustrating to those who see the Jews as perpetually hostile to Islam and at the same time as often successful in plotting to pull the wool over the eyes of the world, especially the Christian world.

The "Isra'iliyyat" are the transmissions which originate with Israelite sources such as the Bible or are transmitted on the authority of Jews. The term is also used to denote traditions about the Israelites and Jews which are transmitted on the authority of the Prophet Muhammad or related in the Qur'an. Accounts of the Israelites, especially under the leadership of Moses, are frequent and widespread throughout the Qur'an. In addition to the detailed passages referring to Moses and the Israelites in Egypt, the Qur'an contains stories of the Israelites' time in the wilderness of wandering (manna and quails, Golden Calf, Torah, water from rock), their entrance into the holy land, the early kings of Israel (Saul, David, and Solomon), and stories of later prophets (Jeremiah, Ezekiel, and Ezra). The Qur'an in 2.67–73 tells the story of the Israelites' refusal to obey God's command to perform a simple sacrifice and in 7.163–166 narrates the story of a city by the sea whose inhabitants transgressed the Sabbath.

Muslim tradition also identifies the bulk of the prophets mentioned by name in the Qur'an as Israelite prophets, beginning with Jacob and culminating with Jesus (7.157 and 61.6). The Israelites are unique in being sent numerous prophets and given numerous opportunities to accept the messages revealed by God. Other peoples are only sent one prophet and given one chance before they are punished by God with destruction when they reject his revelation. This could be seen as having rather negative implications in that the Jews are given far more chances than anyone else to behave well and despite this they remain incorrigibly evil.

Muslim commentators refer to a number of passages from the Qur'an in which the Torah is said to have been revealed to the Israelites as a punishment for their disobedience. Much of this can be related to the exegesis of 3.93 in which the Prophet Muhammad is reported to have challenged the Jews of Medinah to deny that God had imposed food prohibitions upon the Israelites before the revelation of the Torah. The imposition of food prohibitions with the revelation of the Torah being put upon the Israelites for their disobedience is mentioned in 6.146. The Qur'an in 4.18 refers to a "painful chastisement" and in 4.160 says that God forbade the Israelites the "good things" which used to be allowed. The two times Jerusalem was destroyed are referred to in 17.4 which Muslim exegetes take as a reference to its destruction under the Babylonians and the Romans. The Qur'an in 2.47–8 warns that the Israelites will be punished on the Day of Judgment and no prophet will be able to intercede on their behalf.

In contemporary non-Muslim scholarship, the relationship and possible influence of Jewish and Christian sources upon the Qur'an and Muslim exegesis, and vice versa, is a hot issue. The parallels between the Qur'an and the Bible suggest to some the reliance of Islam upon Judaism and Christianity. On the other hand, Islam does declare itself not to be in conflict with (genuine) Judaism and Christianity, but a completion of them, and as we have seen accepts many of the same figures as prophets from biblical history. So any similarity does not in itself prove dependence. One would expect a later religion which sees itself as confirming the best aspects of prior religions to be linked with them. Pointing to such linkage as a proof of dependency is just wrong.

Jews and the attempted murder of Jesus

The apparent death of Jesus and his second coming plays a particularly interesting role in the Qur'an. Whereas many Christians today are hesitant in ascribing responsibility for the death of Jesus on the Jews, the Qur'an does not prevaricate on the issue. The text says, referring to Jesus' Jewish enemies "And they made a move, and God made a move. And God is the best of those who make moves" (3.54). The report continues, When God said:

> O 'Isa, I am to take you in full and raise you towards myself, and cleanse you of those who disbelieve, and place those who follow you above those who disbelieve, up to the Day of Doom. Then you will all return to me, whereupon I shall judge between you on what has been a matter of dispute.
>
> (3.55)

In these verses "and they made a move" refers to the evil designs of the Jews who planned to arrest him and to get him crucified. The next sentence "and Allah made a move" refers to the plan designed by God to save his prophet 'Isa from their ill designs. The Jews sent someone to Jesus to arrest him and God changed his appearance totally and made him resemble Jesus, who he in fact raised to heaven, while that person was crucified under the false identity.

The Jews started working on a series of conspiracies and schemes against Jesus going to the extent of convincing the ruler of the time that he was guilty of a crime. The ruler ordered the arrest of Jesus. While this was going on, God countered their plans by working out a way of rescuing Jesus, and at the same time providing a test for believers. God said two things to comfort Jesus at a time when the Jews were intent on killing him. God said that his death would come not at their hands but that it would be a natural death. In order to rescue him from the Jews, God promised to raise Jesus to heaven. The saving of Jesus by raising him would not last forever, it would be temporary since Jesus is only a human being and then he would return to the mortal world and prevail over the enemies of God at the appropriate time. Later on, death will come to him in a natural sort of way. This raising of Jesus to the heavens to allow him to escape the threatening designs of the Jews was really an act of emigration in its own way, similar to those in the past of Abraham (Ibrahim) and Musa (Moses), following which he would return to this world and achieve complete victory over the Jews.

God made five promises to Jesus: The first promise was that his death will not come at the hands of the Jews. It will be a natural death coming at its appointed time and that appointed time will come close to the Day of Judgment when 'Isa will come down from heaven to earth. The second promise was to raise him to heaven and so save him from violent death at the hands of his enemies. This happened as it was supposed to and his fate is a test for believers (4.159). Those who think he died, and those who think he died and was raised from the dead are both wrong, and they will suffer for it on the Day of Judgment.

The third promise was to have him cleansed of false accusations brought against him by his enemies. That promise was fulfilled when someone of the status of the Prophet Muhammad refuted all the false accusations of the Jews. For instance, the Jews slandered his parentage because of his having been born without a father. The Qur'an refuted this slander by declaring that he was born without a father because such was the power and will of God. We should not be surprised at this, after all Adam was born without either father or mother, and anything that God sets out to do he accomplishes. The Qur'an is replete with examples of what extraordinary things God can do. It is important to see God as at the heart of everything that happens, not a human being like Jesus. The Jews falsely accused Jesus of claiming to be God. There are many verses in the Qur'an in which, contrary to this accusation, Jesus has been reported to have publicly confessed his being human and a servant of God.

The fourth promise appears in "and placed those who follow you above those who disbelieve" which means that his followers will be made to overcome those who deny and oppose him. This promise was fulfilled in the sense that the belief in and confession of the prophethood of 'Isa is accepted by both Christians and Muslims. This does not necessarily mean that both Christians and Muslims will find salvation, though, since salvation depends on believing in all the teachings of 'Isa. The Christians did not accept that they should believe and have faith in the last of the Prophets who would come after Jesus departs, that is, the Prophet Muhammad. The Christians did not follow this instruction and so they may have deprived themselves of salvation, while Muslims by contrast acted in accordance with 'Isa's real words and intentions and so can confidently expect to be rewarded eventually. An interpretation of the promise which relates to having a dominant position over the Jews is connected to the prophethood of 'Isa. Christians and Muslims have always been more powerful than the Jews and always will be right up to the Day of Judgment.

The fifth promise, that of giving a decision about such conflicts in faith on the Day of Judgment will be fulfilled at the appointed time. The Jews are the only people in the world who say that 'Isa was crucified, killed and buried following which he never returned to life. What actually happened is reported in the Qur'an. God outwitted his enemies. God changed a person to look just like 'Isa and he was the person they thought they had killed (he is often taken to be one of those intent on killing Jesus, so hoist on his own petard in effect). The words of the verse (4.157) are as follows: "And they did not kill him and they did not crucify him, but they were taken in by appearance."

The Christians said that Jesus was killed on the cross but was brought back to life once again and raised to heaven. The verse has refuted this notion as well. It is said here that like the Jews who were rejoicing after their own coreligionist was killed, the Christians fell victim to the same mistaken belief in the identity of the crucified individual by believing that it was Jesus who got killed on the cross. The Christians also became the victims of mistaken identity, just like the Jews, since even the Christians did not acknowledge that God would never allow one of his prophets to suffer death at the hands of his enemies.

The sword verse

Those who want to argue that Islam sets itself in permanent conflict with other religions such as Judaism often point to the so-called sword verse. The "sword verse" at 9.5 states: "And when the sacred months are over, slay the polytheists wherever you find them, and take them captive, and besiege them, and lie in wait for them at every conceivable place." Another verse (9.29) is often conjoined to the above, which runs:

> Fight against those who—despite having been given revelation before—do not believe in God nor in the Last Day, and do not consider forbidden that which God and His messenger have forbidden, and do not follow the religion of the truth, until they pay the *jizya* with willing hand, having been subdued.

The first of the "sword verses," (9.5) with its internal reference to the polytheists who may be fought after the end of the sacred months, might well limit its applicability to only the pagan Arabs of Muhammad's time. The second of the "sword verses" is seemingly directed at the People of the Book, that is, Jews and Christians, but again, a careful reading of the verse suggests that it does not refer to all the People of the Book but only those from among them who do not, in contravention of their own laws, believe in God and the Last Day and, in a hostile manner, impede the propagation of Islam. Of course, a lot could be brought under the latter description.

The Qur'an in another verse (2.193) makes clear, however, that should hostile behavior on the part of the foes of Islam cease, then the reason for engaging them in war also lapses. This verse states: "And fight them until there is no chaos (*fitna*) and religion is only for God, but if they cease, let there be no hostility except to those who practice oppression." The harshness of the two "sword verses" is thus considerably mitigated and their general applicability significantly restricted by juxtaposing with them conciliatory verses, such as the one cited immediately above and other such verses. Among other such verses is the one that has been characterized as the "peace verse" (8.61): "If they incline toward peace, incline you toward it, and trust in God. Indeed, He alone is all-hearing, all-knowing." And "Slay them wherever you catch them, and turn them out from where they have turned you out; for persecution is worse than slaughter. But if they cease, God is Oft-forgiving, Most Merciful (2.191–92)." Also: "God does not forbid you from being kind and equitable to those who have neither made war on you on account of your religion nor driven you from your homes. God loves those who are equitable (60.8)."

These verses make warring against those who oppose the propagation of the message of Islam and consequently resort to persecution of Muslims contingent upon their continuing hostility. Should they desist from such hostile persecution and sue for peace instead, the Muslims are commanded to accede to their request. Qur'an 60.8 further makes clear that non-Muslims of good will and pacific nature cannot be the targets of war simply on account of their different religious background. However, a number of jurists came to privilege the "sword verses" over the conciliatory verses in specific historical circumstances, and in modern times they are often used by those such as 'Usama bin Laden to justify constant war against the Jews and those he calls the Crusaders. Even the more pacific verses can be given a militant interpretation. For example, the phrase "those who incline towards peace" may be read instead as "those who are or become Muslims," which gives these passages an entirely different complexion, of course.

"There is no compulsion in religion; the truth stands out clearly from error," affirms the Qur'an (2.256). Another verse (10.99) states, "If your Lord had so willed, all those who are on earth would have believed; will you then compel mankind to believe against their will?" The Qur'an, according to these two verses, does not seem to advocate the forcible conversion of non-Muslims to Islam since the diversity of humankind is part of the divine plan. "And of His signs," the Qur'an says, "is the creation of the heavens and the earth and the diversity of your tongues and colours. Surely there are signs in this for the intelligent!" (30.22). It has to be said though that the doctrine of abrogation (*naskh*) always leaves open the question of which verses are to be regarded as no longer viable given the impact of others. For example, the ban on compulsion in religion may only have been valid when the Muslims were not powerful enough to compel acceptance of their faith. Similarly, with the diversity of mankind, perhaps this is something established by God which he expects Muslims to change when they are strong enough to do so. As with all religions, there is no definite and final reading of the text that provides a clear interpretation of how Jews and other non-Muslims should be treated.

Can Muslims and Jews be friends?

There are verses in the Qur'an which suggest a negative answer to this question. The first verse appears in 5. 51 of the Qur'an and says "O, you who believe [in the message of Muhammad], do not take Jews and Christians as *awliya'*. They are *awliya'* to one another, and the one among you who turns to them is of them. Truly, God does not guide wrongdoing people"(5.51).The word *awliya'* (sing. *wali*), is commonly translated as "friends" The verse appears to be a very clear statement opposing friendly relations between Muslims, on the one hand, and Jews and Christians, on the other. However, while it is true that one of the meanings of *awliya'* is friends, it also means "guardians" and "protectors." According to many of the traditional commentaries on the Qur'an we are told that this verse was revealed at a particularly difficult moment in the life of the early Muslim community, and here it is necessary to describe the situation of the Muslims at this time in Arabia to put verse 5.51 within the right context. Qur'anic commentators do normally link verses with the particular context in which they were revealed, since it is this that gives them a guide to how they should be interpreted.

Before 5.51 was revealed, Muhammad and the Muslims had just migrated as a community from Mecca to Medinah. They had done so, according to the Islamic account, because of the persecution to which they were subjected at the hands of their fellow tribesmen and relatives in Mecca. Most Meccans worshipped various idols as gods and were concerned at what would happen to the idol business given the rise of interest in the message of Muhammad within the city, even though Muhammad was himself from Mecca. Islam threatened to disrupt the economic benefits of the annual pilgrimage season when people from all over the Arabian peninsula would come to worship the many idols at the Ka'ba—a cubical structure which the Qur'an claims was originally built by Abraham and his son, Ishmael, as a temple to the one God, before the corruption of religion in Arabia hid the monotheist message of Abraham and his successors. The prospect of the bottom falling out of the idol business could not have enthused those who made their living in it, so it is hardly surprising that Muhammad faced considerable resistance at the beginning.

Muhammad and his small band of followers were eventually expelled from Mecca and found sanctuary in Medinah. According to the commentaries, it was not long after this migration to Medinah that verse 5.51 was revealed. Specifically, we are told that this verse came down around the time of the battle of Badr (3.123) or perhaps after the battle of Uhud (3.152–3). In these early days, even though the Muslim community constituted no more than perhaps a few hundred people and had already left Mecca, the Meccans continued to challenge them militarily, and these two early battles, as well as others, were crucial events in the history of the early Islamic community.

The Meccans were a far more powerful force than the Muslims, and in addition, the Meccans had allies throughout Arabia. Given the small numbers of the Muslims, the Prophet and his fledgling community faced the real possibility of utter annihilation should they lose any of these early conflicts. Within this highly charged environment some members of the Muslim community wanted to make individual alliances with other non-Muslim tribes in the region. Within the city of Medinah, there were Jewish tribes who constituted a powerful presence in the town and who were on good terms with the Meccans, and to the north of the city there were also numerous Christian Arab tribes. Some Muslims thought it would be a good idea to make alliances with one or more of these groups as a way of preserving themselves should the Meccan armies ultimately triumph.

The view might have been that a young community, in such dire straits, could not allow dissension in the ranks of the faithful as would be created by various individuals linking themselves with non-Islamic groups. So we can see that the translation of *awliya'* as "friends" is misleading and that it should be rendered perhaps as "protectors" or "guardians" in the strict military sense of these terms. The verse should be read as, "Do not take Christians and Jews as your protectors. They are protectors to one another." This is the message of the verse, and the appropriateness of this interpretation is supported not only by the historical context of its revelation but also by the fact that nowhere does the Qur'an oppose simple kindness between peoples, as is clear from other Qur'anic verses. On the other hand, if we do not pay close attention to the historical circumstances of the revelation of this verse, one can see how it might be used to advocate constant hostility of Muslims to Jews and others. Especially when other verses are cited such as "And fight them until persecution is no more, and religion is for Allah" (2.193). There are several bellicose verses of this nature: "When you meet the unbelievers, strike their necks; finally, when you have thoroughly subdued them, restrain them firmly" (47.4; see also 8.12 and of course the sword verse at 9.5).

Jerusalem

The status of Jerusalem in the Qur'an needs to be linked with the status of a number of important figures in the Jewish Bible and Gospels. Abraham, Moses, David, Solomon, Zechariah, John the Baptist, and Jesus are among the prophets and messengers of God according to Islam. Jews and Christians also recognize David and Solomon as great kings and patriarchs of ancient Israel, but not as prophets. However, in Islam they are regarded as prophets. The Qur'an sees itself as recounting their stories and also restoring their status by removing some of the charges and allegations that were made against their characters by earlier and deceitful authors, in particular the Jews who are regarded as not only defaming their prophets but even trying to kill them when they have the chance.

David was accused in the Bible of committing adultery (2 Samuel:11–12) and Solomon was accused of idolatry (1 Kings:11). The Qur'an absolved them from all these charges (38.30). This suggests that David and Solomon are more revered and respected in Islam than in the Jewish and Christian traditions, and indeed the city associated with them, Jerusalem, is also given a high status in Islam. The city of Jerusalem is historically associated with these prophets, and so naturally is a city sacred to Muslims since Islam considers itself a continuation of the same spiritual and ethical movement that began with the earlier prophets. Historically and theologically it believes itself to be the true inheritor of the earlier traditions of the prophets and messengers of Allah. It is for this reason that the Qur'an called what is often taken to be Palestine—the land associated with the lives of many of God's prophets—the Sacred Land (5.21) and called its surroundings God's blessed precincts at 17.1.

The sacredness of the city of Jerusalem, according to Islam, lies in its historical religious reality. This is the city that witnessed the life and works of the greatest prophets and messengers of God. Here divine grace was at work for a long time. Mecca and Medinah are blessed cities in Islam because of their association with the Prophets Abraham, Ishmael, and Muhammad. In a similar way, Jerusalem is blessed and important in Islam because of its association with other prophets of God, namely David, Solomon, and Jesus. Jews and Christians do not recognize Ishmael and Mohammad as God's prophets and messengers, so they do not consider Mecca and Medinah as sacred cities. By contrast, Muslims believe in the Prophets Moses, David, Solomon, and Jesus, and so they must recognize the sacredness and importance of Jerusalem in Islam.

In the year 620 almost one-and-a-half years before his *hijra* (migration) from Mecca to Medinah the Night Journey and Ascension occurred. One night, in a miraculous way, the Prophet was taken on a journey from Mecca to Jerusalem, and then from there to heaven. The Night Journey was a great miracle that Muslims believe represented an honor for Muhammad and a confirmation of Mecca's spiritual link with Jerusalem. Both of these events took place on the same night. The angel Gabriel took the Prophet from Mecca to Jerusalem. There it is reported that the Prophet stood at the Sacred Rock, went to the heavens, returned to Jerusalem, and met with many prophets and messengers who were gathered together to meet him and he led them in prayers. After these experiences the Prophet was taken back to Mecca. It serves as an example of every Muslim's deep devotion and spiritual connection with Jerusalem.

During the trip, the Prophet is reported to have received from God the command about the five daily prayers that all Muslims are to perform. Upon his return to Mecca, the Prophet instituted these prayers. It is worth noting that Jerusalem was made the direction (al-qibla) which Muslims at first were told to face while praying. Jerusalem is thus called *ula al-qiblatayn* (the first *qibla*). The Prophet and the early community of Islam worshipped toward the direction of Jerusalem, during their stay in Mecca. After the Hijra (migration), Muslims in Medinah also continued to pray facing Jerusalem, for almost seventeen months. Then came God's command to change the direction of prayer from Jerusalem to Mecca (2.142–150). Muslim commentators of the Qur'an and historians have explained the meaning and purpose of this change. The change of the *qibla* in no way diminished the status of Jerusalem in Islam.

However, if we examine the wording of the Qur'an we find no explicit references to Jerusalem by name or by any of its names such as al-Quds, Bayt al-Muqaddas or Ursalim. There is only one reference to the masjid al-aqsa ("most distant mosque") figuring in the account of Muhammad's miraculous night journey that contains a reference to the holiness of what is taken to be a site in Jerusalem. The passage is "Praise be He who at night bore aloft His servant from the Sacred Mosque to the most remote mosque, whose surroundings we blessed, so that We might show him some of Our signs (17.1)." It is sometimes claimed that it was only after the Islamic conquest of Jerusalem in 637 that the view became established that the mosque called the most remote one was the Temple of Jerusalem, and that Muhammad had experienced a transmigration to heaven while standing upon the rock around which the Dome of the Rock was erected. There was in fact quite a controversy about whether Jerusalem was the site of the masjid al-aqsa, particularly as the reference in the Qur'an that may well be to Palestine describes it as near ("the Greeks [i.e. the Byzantines] have been vanquished in the nearby land" (30.2–3)). This would suggest that the distant mosque could not be the one in Jerusalem. It could also be claimed that Jerusalem was not even the first direction of prayer for Muslims. The Qur'an (2.142) does mention an earlier normal direction of prayer (*qiblati-himi 'llati kanu 'alayha*) prior to their being commanded to face the (Meccan) "Sacred Mosque" (al-masjid al-haram), and this is often taken to be Jerusalem, but there has been no explicit claim that the former or first direction of prayer was in fact Jerusalem. Today, and for some time, however, there has been no doubt among Muslims that Jerusalem was the first direction of prayer and that the mosque described as distant in the Qur'an has its site in that city.

Chapter 6

Written Law versus Oral Law

Rabbis often insist that they be given preference in their interpretation of Scripture, as sole spokesmen for the oral tradition, a tradition that was given on Mount Sinai alongside the ten commandments. It is the rabbis, and not the Bible, that fix the giving of the Torah on Shavuot on the 6th and 7th of Sivan, the festival that commemorates the giving of the law on Mount Sinai. Though there is a scriptural basis in Exodus 19, the Torah never explicitly states that this was the actual date. There are some unusual features linked to the festival. It is uniquely lacking in a biblically established date, a fact that led to the Karaite schism. The Karaites argued that we should follow the Torah by taking it to be literally true, and they argued that the festival was held 50 days after the end of Passover and not, as the rabbis argued, 50 days after the conclusion of the first day of Passover. They claim that the time to bring the Omer offering and to start the 49-day countdown to Shavuot is the day after the first Shabbat after Passover, rather than the day after Passover. This might seem a small disagreement that could not really provide a reason to split a community. But behind the debate over a text is one dealing with power and the issue of who determines these issues.

The confusion over the festival's date is replicated in the events accompanying the giving of the Torah, when the people "saw the voices"(Ex 20: 15). Rashi suggests that this remark reflects the confusion of the time: "they saw what was heard and heard what they saw." It was an event of such amazing significance that the senses of those there were confused. On Sinai, the Almighty pronounces ten "commandments" (literally words). According to the Midrash or story about the event, the children of Israel were so overwhelmed by the words that after only three (I am the Lord your God) they asked Moses to receive the rest on his own (Ex Rabba 89). It is sometimes argued that the uncertainty over the date reflects the passion with which the Jews linked themselves to God, noticing neither the date nor the place. Hence the lack of significance of the location, perhaps surprising given the importance in which other places are held. Mount Sinai has never been considered an important place by Jews, and there were no theological objections to returning the site to the Egyptians after it was captured in two of Israel's wars with Egypt.

The significance of forgetting

In the book of Ruth, the scope is widened from the history of the Israelites. It deals with the daughter of a despised race, the Moabites, in order to show that the Torah is not limited. It can reach anyone and anywhere, a point which is heartily endorsed by Levinas. There is a kabbalistic source that identifies the souls of Ruth and Abraham.

Both came from homes of idol worshippers. In shifting from one mode to another both had to forget their past. Abraham was ordered to leave his house, his country, and his birthplace for an unidentified destination. He immediately obeyed this command. Similarly with Ruth. One of the key points of her story happens when her mother-in-law directs her to the field of her relation, Boaz, in order to collect the sheaf left behind by the harvesters. Although this is only the harvest leavings, it is the very same "forgotten sheaf" of which the Torah commands an owner of a field to leave for the poor (Deut 24:19).

There are normally so many positive references to remember in the Torah—the Sabbath, Amalek, the Exodus from Egypt, and the creation. God is often brought back into the narrative with a reference to his remembering someone or something. Yet here we have a virtue made out of forgetting, not in the usual sense, but rather a deliberate not remembering. This preserves the dignity of those who can benefit from what we forget and do not see happen. In his remarks on charity, Maimonides puts on a high level giving money without knowing who receives it, and there are references to people leaving money in the Temple for others to collect, and to holding it behind one's back to be taken by those who need it. In all these cases, the dignity of the poor person is preserved through anonymity.

On the other hand, the reference to Amalek here is interesting. We are told in the Bible to "remember what Amalek did to you on the way out of Egypt...he attacked the weakest of you and you were tired and weary... Erase the memory of Amalek from under the heavens. Do not forget" (Deut 25:17–19). We are told to do two contradictory things here, both to remember and forget at the same time, unless the meaning is that we should not forget to erase the memory of Amalek. But once we have erased that memory, there is nothing to forget, so the demand is still problematic. It is worth noting that God himself much earlier said that "I shall surely erase the memory of Amalek from under the heavens" (Ex 17:14), although as we can see having a sentence like that in the Bible is not a good idea if one wants to erase a memory. Even if we thought that we should wipe out the Amalekites, the issue would arise as to who they are. According to BT *Yoma* 54a, the Assyrian King Sennaherib mixed up all the nations, so we cannot work out who the Amalekites are today. One might get around this by identifying them with whoever the current enemy of the Jews might be, but that seems a bit harsh when it is a matter of annihilation. The Amalekites attacked the Israelites at their weakest moment and at that time constituted an existential threat. That sets a high standard for enemies to count as potentially Amelekites, although there has been in the past and there is today no lack of plausible candidates.

Consulting the Bible

How do we settle the question of who the Amalekites are today? After consulting the Bible we might well feel that we require more guidance. This points to the significance of the dispute between the Karaites and the Rabbanites which seriously divided the Jewish community in the past, and a similar dispute seriously divides it today. There were many points of disagreement then, but the major focus of debate was on the Oral Law. The Written Law is not controversial since it is written down and accessible by everyone, and this suggests the question: why not just be satisfied with the Written Law? The answer seems to be that the Written Law is hardly perspicuous, despite God's description of it as "not in heaven"(Deut 30:12). It may not be in heaven but any system of law is ripe for reinterpretation because it always requires interpretation, and Jewish law is no different from any other kind of law. It could be argued that a perfect legal system would not require this sort of interpretation since it would be written in such a clear and obvious manner that everyone would perfectly understand how they were to apply it. Here we might distinguish between civil and religious law. It is hardly surprising that civil law is confusing and open to different views since it is the product of imperfect human beings. It is not just our imperfection intellectually, but often we are confused in what we are trying to do and so our legislation is similarly imperfect. Some of those who are affected by the legislation may wish to wriggle out of their obligations, or even deny that they have them at all, and this all goes to making law a fuzzy and confused activity.

But this is only a problem for human law, surely. God cannot have varying purposes for his law, and he would not phrase it in such a way that there would be argument about it, or so one might think. Yet we do argue over religious law in just the same way as we argue over civil law, and it is interesting to speculate why this is the case. This is not such an enigma as one might think, since the law could be perfect in its structure and meaning yet still be amenable to interpretation by us. We also need to grasp it and that requires us to reformulate it in the language of human beings. It is no criticism of divine law that we have to grasp it in our own way, since anything that we can understand is going to be affected by our way of understanding. What we can be sure of is that the purpose and framing of divine law is perfect, but that is all, and the perfection of the law does not translate into its being easy to use. So all Jews would probably agree that the understanding of what the Torah means requires a certain amount of discussion and analysis rather than just a quick read. If that was not the case, one might ask, why read it every year and think about it so much?

Oral Law

The Oral Law in the shape of the Mishnah, Talmud, and many other works is the real object of interest of many Jews. For one thing, it is much tougher than the Bible, consisting of difficult legal issues and disputed topics that are not resolved in the books themselves, so the reader has to gather together different passages and work out for himself what the solution might be. The Oral Law is much longer than the Bible, even including the Prophets and the Writings, and requires at least in the case of the Talmud a knowledge of both Hebrew and Aramaic. It was this explosion of commentary that so annoyed the Karaites. Would it not be possible, they asked, for the Bible to be consulted as the source of information on how to live without also studying this enormous range of additional material? The trouble with the commentaries is that they take on a life of their own. The Talmud actually quite often pokes fun at itself in this way. It constantly criticizes the greatest rabbi of them all, Rabbi Akiva, who is at one stage forced to admit that he is so stupid he is not fit to look after goats, apparently an easier option than looking after sheep which was his profession. There is a story of Moses returning to earth to listen to Akiva teach a group of students about the Five Books of Moses, and Moses cannot understand at all what Akiva is saying about what are after all the works that he received on Mount Sinai. Akiva managed to find meaning in even the tips of the decoration on the letters in the text.

There are at least two ways of reading this passage. One is that Moses approves of the close reading that Akiva is giving the text and the elaboration that Akiva manages to apply to it. On the other hand, it can also be read as critical of this process as overelaboration, a process that results in a new text bearing no relationship at all to the old one. It would then be a creative process designed more to display the hermeneutical talent of the interpreter than for any real intention to help understand the original better. The Karaites argue that all Oral Law is like this and that we are better off without it and for a period it looked very much as though they were going to become the dominant voice in Judaism.

The assault on the Oral Law

The creator of Karaism, Anan ben David (eighth century CE), appears to have been a candidate for head of the Jewish community in Babylonia, and was not successful in getting the job, on which he promptly decided to set up a rival organization. The movement certainly flourished in the Islamic world and then quite successfully moved on to Eastern Europe. Like some Islamic reform movements it criticized sharply what in Arabic is called *taqlid*, sometimes translated as blind imitation. It is one of those movements that are intent at getting back to the original principles of religion, to the thought of the basic text and not paying respect to the accretion of commentary and tradition that has built up around the text over time. Two comments have often been made about this movement. One is that the legislation that it produced was often far more stringent than that within the rabbinic tradition. The other is that it itself produced a sort of shadow rabbinic series of institutions, albeit with a different set of principles and these were to consciously set itself against the very detailed conclusions specified by the Oral Law.

The ethos of Karaism led to a great deal of diversity. This is hardly surprising, as it set itself up to pursue what in Arabic is called *ray* or personal opinion. It is no accident that the movement arose in the Islamic world, since these debates about the role of personal opinion and law were very much live issues in Islam in its early centuries and became formalized in the system of different schools of orthodox law, the *madhdhab*, and also the distinction between different approaches to Islam, both Sunni and Shi'i, and their various subgroups. It is often said today that Muslims do not want to end up encouraging the sort of disunity in belief and practice that is common among Jews and Christians. This is a frequent reaction to a proposed change in practice or custom. But fairly early on Islam validated a whole range of different interpretations of the Qur'an and law and differences were at least formally respected as being valid attempts at understanding how to act and what to believe. It was this trend that Karaism fed off, since it suggested that the law as it had arisen over time was some way off the original scriptural meaning that served as its nominal source and that it needed to be restructured in order to bring it back to the origins. This is the slogan of religious reformers everywhere, to bring back the original principles or intentions of the faith, to restore the clear and perfect axioms from which the faith grew, and to reject the sediment that had been deposited over the years on the pure source.

Karaism was thoroughly defeated in the Jewish world, although it continued a shadowy existence right up to today and it is not clear why it lost out to rabbinism. It may have been the fact that the laws that the Karaites produced were even stricter than those of their opponents, and the personal intellectual commitments that Karaism called upon may also have been felt to be too demanding by many. Although Karaism lost to what has become traditional Judaism, it has in a different form undoubtedly become the most popular version of Judaism today, if it is linked with the various reform movements in Judaism. Apart from a minority who continue to base their lives on the Oral Law, the majority of Jews today are thoroughly imbued with the values of Karaism if this means the imposition of personal opinion on how to live a Jewish life. If this means that they are intent on studying the original texts of Judaism in order to work out what the original meanings of those texts are then Karaism does not even exist in this sense. There is no reason to think that most Jews know much about the Bible or are interested in it as a guide to how to live, despite what their rabbis might hope. What led to Karaism was its opposition to what was then the majority approach, that based on commentary and tradition, and modern Jews who reject tradition have the same rather contemptuous attitude to the lifestyle of those who based their practice on the authority of others, those whom traditional Jews acknowledged as having the right to determine their interpretation of Judaism.

The Karaites and language

One of the characteristic features of Karaism is a fascination with language. The Karaites were famous for the quality of their work on language, especially the Hebrew language, which of course for them was the vital source of information about God's purposes in the Torah. They were also renowned for their skill in Arabic, the lingua franca of the Jewish community in much of the Islamic world, and this emphasis on language has persisted today in the Reform movement. For the Karaites, only a careful study of language was capable of deriving the clear meaning of the text itself, and to a degree, they had to argue that the text was clear since otherwise this would allow the rabbanites to insert their wedge that brought with it the whole of the Oral Law tradition. We need Oral Law, the rabbanites argued, since the text needs to be interpreted and explicated. However clear a text may be, there are always aspects of it that are left undetermined, and for that we require the help of commentary. For the Karaites, by contrast, skill linguistically will reveal the underlying clarity of the language of the text and so the lack of necessity for the sort of commentary that the Oral Law represents. Again, while there is nothing in the Hebrew text of the Bible that claims it does not require interpretation, the Qur'an does frequently refer to itself as written in clear and simple Arabic, thus offering for the Karaites a model of how a religious language might operate.

This enthusiasm for language persists today among the Reform movement since it typically widens the texts that can be called on to give us information about how to live or what to believe. So while for example many Reform rabbis will refer to a Jewish text, especially the Bible, they will often refer to other nonreligious texts, or even Christian texts, as providing us with useful information. Whereas Oral Law restricts interpretation to a relatively finite number of Jewish texts, Karaism today implies the use of any and all texts as sources of how to live and what to believe, and this can only work if one has in mind a clear approach to how language is to operate.

All these disparate texts can only be interlinked if there is a theory of how they all are based on the same ideas or reflect a common approach, and this involves a theory of language.

It is often said that the world in which Karaism emerged was one in which the *bab al-ijtihad*, the door of interpretation, was closed. Muslims decided at a certain stage that they had arrived at a fixed interpretation of their texts and they were not going to continue with the interpretative process any more. Some argue that this explains the relative lack of success of Muslim culture vis-à-vis Western culture that continued to explore and develop different religious interpretations. It makes Islam sound as though it were a fixed and authoritarian faith which in turn led to a society in which people could not think for themselves and develop an interest in science and technology. Yet we know that the opposite is the case and that frequently the Islamic world saw extraordinary cultural and scientific developments despite the so-called rigid line on religious interpretation. The door of interpretation was never really closed, Muslims continued to argue and debate about the interpretation of the Qur'an and as we have seen much of the earlier debate was formalized in the creation of the different legal schools. What refreshes debate is this attempt at getting back to the origins, to where the faith started, to the basic intentions of the main characters in the religious drama. That is what is so impressive about the modern Jew who adheres to virtually no special religious rituals or beliefs but acknowledges that they are Jewish and represents what is surely the majority of Jews today. For the Orthodox Jew, this individual is probably regarded with despair as a shirker. He or she may well not even be a member of a synagogue, not even a Reform synagogue or temple. Yet such an individual is living what surely we find in the Bible is a normal Jewish life. The people in the Bible do not allow religion to dominate their lives, and their religious beliefs and allegiances are in the main linked with their families and their nationalities. Of course the Temple no longer exists, and it is unsure what practices outside of the temple ritual took place. It might be said with Maimonides that prayer now replaces sacrifices, but this surely does not mean that it should take place at the same times or in the same way as the previous rituals. The very frequent prayers that exist today in the orthodox community are not at all representative of the sacrifice rituals that exist in the biblical and later periods. Maimonides would argue that the absence of the Temple and the priestly hierarchy now means that Jews have to rely on the rabbis and the commentaries to work out what their religious obligations are. Many Jews today would side with the Karaites in rejecting the Oral Law. The trouble is, from the Karaite point of view, that these Jews are also quite likely to reject the Written Law also.

Chapter 7

Philosophers versus kabbalists

At the annual conferences of the Association of Jewish Studies (AJS) in the United States there are so many lectures and papers that the program is broken up into different streams. One of the streams is Jewish philosophy and another is kabbalah. This distinction is interesting since it might be thought that Jewish philosophy, which after all makes some reference in its very name to religion, is linked with mysticism at least to some degree. Yet the differentiation that takes place at the AJS acknowledges an interesting historical fact that philosophers and kabbalists tend to be in distinct camps. When it was suggested at the conference that the two groups might be brought together and constitute one stream, the suggestion was received with dubious glances and a total lack of support. Philosophers and kabbalists do not see themselves as engaged in the same sort of process at all.

We cannot of course really talk about philosophers and kabbalists since both systems of thought are vast and cannot be easily defined. One distinction that is often made is between rationalists (the philosophers) and mystics (kabbalists) but it is misleading, since a lot of kabbalah is itself highly intellectual and indeed difficult to work out unless one is capable of operating at a high level of rationality. Another rather confusing observation is that Jewish thinkers, like their Islamic peers, often combined mysticism with philosophy, arguing that there are levels of knowledge which can be best accessed through mysticism and other types of knowledge for which rational thought is sufficient. In most cases, the mystical understanding of Judaism had no difficulty in linking up with the rational and legal approach, and this can be observed when we look at aspects of the institution of the Sabbath, a potent site of spiritual strength according to the kabbalists and an opportunity for Jews to thank God for his creation of the world according to those understanding it literally.

As Judaism developed, the rules about what constituted work and so cannot be done on the Sabbath became more and more complex. The rule against kindling a fire has been taken to mean that cars ought not to be driven since the spark plug works as a result of ignition and might be regarded as a fire, or so it has been interpreted within traditional Judaism. Most Jews today happily ignore the rules of the Sabbath and treat the day like any other day of the week. Yet the Sabbath has a huge significance in the traditional community and its meaning has been much discussed, especially in relation to mystical understandings of Judaism. One of the most popular synagogue songs on the eve of the Sabbath, *Lekhah dodi* ("Come my beloved") was itself composed by a kabbalist, Solomon Alkabetz, and refers to the Sabbath as like a bride, and the people of Israel as like the bridegroom waiting to greet her. As the Sabbath comes in, as the bride enters, so the spirit of the divine, the Shekhinah, descends also, and the Jews who celebrate the day prepare for a special and distinct period of time, a day in which they devote themselves to activities other than their normal business and apply themselves to God and more spiritual concerns. This can be taken in two ways, though. One is to see the Sabbath as fulfilling a commandment that we rest one day a week, with all that that entails, while another approach is to argue that the special nature of the day has huge spiritual consequences and possibilities for us that transcend the significance of mere rest and carrying out a commandment. These contrasting approaches were to replicate different ways in which Judaism came to be understood.

Mystery

One of the main differences between philosophy and mysticism is that the latter is based on a strong belief in the mystery of existence. Philosophy by contrast often sees the world as a place that can be usefully interrogated by the use of reason and God is assigned to the role of the most rational person in a world based on reason. So, for example, we should differentiate between a mystical belief in the underlying benevolence of the world and the philosophical arguments that seek to establish such a level of benevolence. When someone dies in tragic circumstances a mystic will often rejects the idea that that death can be described as merely part of the divine plan, since why things like that happen may be due to conditions about which we only vaguely know. Perhaps a mistake has been made in a prayer, or some sequence of great religious significance has been interrupted, and the microcosm will affect the macrocosm, a small event may have consequences for much larger congeries of action. This is because of the idea that everything is connected to everything else, which has the implication, dangerously radical from a theological point of view, that God is affected by us, since our prayers and actions serve to either repair or damage the connections between this world and the higher world.

It is often pointed out that much kabbalistic language is Neoplatonic, but this does not bring it any closer to philosophy. Neoplatonism is the philosophy that persisted in the Greek-speaking world for many centuries well after the deaths of Plato and Aristotle and came to wield a considerable influence on the Islamic and Jewish philosophical and theological worlds also. Neoplatonic language is indeed used, yet not in accordance with Neoplatonism itself. One of the themes of Neoplatonism is the doctrine of emanation, according to which God's grace overflows and brings about a range of degrees of reality, ending up with our world and indeed us. This process happens automatically, so we should not think of God as intending what happens as a consequence, it just happens as a result of his thinking. Kabbalah takes on this model but reinterprets it radically so that the direction of creation goes both ways, not only from God to us but also from us to God. It is rather like Jacob's dream of the ladder connecting heaven and earth, with angels both ascending and descending. Some kabbalists for example spoke of the desirability of acting very badly because they thought this might upset the balance between good and evil in existence and thus force God to intervene and send the Messiah. One might suspect that this sort of reasoning is rather self-serving, in that the immoral action which one contemplated with some eagerness could then become perfectly acceptable, albeit not in itself but for what it would produce. But the logic of such a position is intriguing and does present something of a moral argument for bad behavior, which in itself might make us question the credentials of kabbalah as a useful approach. The idea that it is bad to be good, and good to be bad, involves such a high risk of self-deception that it is surely not something we can seriously consider as a moral and religious option.

Shabbetai Zvi

A good example of the sort of confusion that this theory leads to comes in the example of the greatest false messiah of them all, Shabbetai Zvi, a figure whom we have already discussed briefly. A kabbalist of great repute, he gathered many followers from the Jewish community and led them in the direction of the Holy Land, getting no further than Turkey where his attempts at recruiting the local Jews met resistance from the Turkish authorities. Offered a choice between conversion to Islam and death he promptly chose the former, which did not exactly do much for his credentials as a Messiah among the Jewish community. On the other hand, his followers argued that his conversion was only superficial and he remained a Jew, yet why in that case did he not lay down his life *kiddush ha-shem*, for the glorification of the divine name, as so many Jewish martyrs in the past had done? The reason they gave was that his understanding of the cosmic balance of forces between good and evil was so advanced that he realized why the right decision in this particular situation was what looked to everyone else to be the wrong decision. Access to the secret structure of reality enabled him to align himself with the progressive forces that relied on his staying alive to carry out his redemptive task, and his apparent conversion should not be taken seriously, but only as a temporary allocation of physical matter in order to bring about a far more beneficial end result. Interestingly, at the start of the twenty-first century the existence of a few thousand Muslim descendants of the Shabbetai Zvi groups in Turkey, the Dönmeh, has been taken to represent a Jewish conspiracy intent on controlling the economy and society at large. The secrecy so prevalent in the much earlier group is taken to explain their apparent Islamic behavior and in typical antisemitic language they are accused of working together with Jews everywhere to undermine Islam.

Devekut

The kabbalists have a notion they call *devekut* and this involves cleaving to God, coming close to him or as close as we human beings can. All mystical systems have a similar sort of concept, and we can see its inspiration right at the start of the bible. We are told: "In the beginning God created the heaven and the earth...and God divided the light from darkness. And God called the light day and the darkness he called night" (Gen. 1:5). Here we have the breaking of one thing into two, and the idea that things exist in contrasting and related pairs. This of course includes us, for "God created man in his own image, in the image of God created he him. Male and female created he them" (Gen 1:27). The kabbalah states that God, in the form of the *Ayn Sof* or infinite, acts to create the world via emanation, whereby the one is broken into two as part of an eternal and constant process. The root of *devekut* is *dabak* and this literally means gluing and is an effective term for the idea that the things that have been separated want to be reunited again. They all want to return to the one, to repair the break caused by creation and the consequent loss of authenticity. The important thing to note about this theory is that it is dynamic, the process of creation through emanation is eternal and does not start or end at a particular time.

The mystery of naming

One aspect of the dynamic theory of the world is the linked notion that God's name is itself not finished but is still unraveling through time. The letters for the Hebrew word for nothingness, *ayin*, (*alef, yad, nun*) and the word for "I" are the same (*alef nun yad*). The growing participation of God in the world allows him to expand the notion of the divine subject and become fully himself. The way he does this is through the words of the Hebrew alphabet, and language makes up the building blocks of the universe. Adam walks around Eden naming what he sees, moving from silence to speech, and God does something similar when he creates the world and moves from nothingness to enjoying some sort of reciprocal relationship with his creatures. The importance of the Hebrew alphabet and language cannot be overemphasized here in the thought of the kabbalah. God moves from silence and isolation to entering into a relationship with his creation, and one of the first things that Adam does is name the animals, names that God himself gives him for them.

If we need another argument that connects us with God we might reflect on the point that the words for God (Yhvh) and for Adam (Adam) have the same numerical value. Hence the explanation in the Zohar of how the human being is made up of the ten sefirot or modes, thus reflecting within himself the basic structure of the universe. The idea of the microcosm reflecting the macrocosm is familiar in mysticism and especially prevalent in kabbalah. It provides a comforting sense that the gap between us and God is not so huge since we can affect the universe through our actions if we reflect the structure of the universe. This account provides space for *tikkun olam*, repairing the world through our actions and the performance of religious duties since what we do has an impact on much wider issues and relationships in the universe. The linked ideas of *tzimtzum* and *kelipot*, the withdrawal of God from the universe and the broken channels of communication between one world and the next, also leave open the possibility of coming into closer contact with the deity by repairing the channels and causing God to bring his withdrawal from the world and his hiding of this face to an end.

This seems very mysterious and questionable, in the sense that there is not much in the way of evidence to support such a theory, although one can always push biblical passages in a direction that might make it seem plausible. But there is more that can be said for such an account than that one has to accept it as a matter of faith. We are aware that our actions have implications for others, as their actions have for us, so the idea of an interconnected universe of beings is far from obscure. The idea that we could affect God might seem to interfere with the principle of God's perfection and unity, but on the other hand it might be an appropriate way of injecting some reciprocity into a religion that places God on such a pedestal that he might appear to be unapproachable. What is the point of having a deity in one's religion if one cannot affect him in any way? This does not mean that he has to be treatable along the familiar lines of one's friends, but it does mean that there should be some sort of relationship between God and the world. This is where the kabbalah is helpful, it stresses the significance of connections. There is an interesting grammatical feature in the Hebrew Bible, the repetition of the construction "*ve-zot*" at the start of sentences, where this means "And this." The question might arise as to why we need to start a sentence with a conjunction, something that is considered beyond the pale stylistically. The reason could be to emphasize the links between that part of the Bible and an earlier passage and indeed to bring out how everything in both the Bible and the world that it seeks to describe are linked in some way. It is only if we can understand the principles behind such linkage that we can understand the world of which we are a part.

Coming close to God

So the kabbalah is a very understandable series of doctrines, whose complexity really presents a confusing picture of a simple feature of religion. Religions consist of rules and regulations, and these have a very objective nature. This is something that Martin Buber comments on in his description of the difference between the Thou and the You, playing on the difference in languages like German that have a familiar second person singular and a polite form, in this case "du" and "Sie." How should we address God? Well, the Bible tends to address him in a very polite form, and as we know, he is so special that we are not even allowed to know his real name. The way we address him also is via prayer and the carrying out of his commandments, and in the case of traditional Judaism this is very much through the observance of law. Not only are we to follow the law, but we are also to spend a lot of time working out what it is, since we do not always receive it in perspicuous ways. The Talmud, as we have seen, is not a list of legal directives but more a series of legal arguments that leave us to construct for ourselves out of what we find an adequate understanding of what we should do and where our duty lies in a particular situation.

Buber contrasts this with the sort of second person relationship we have with people to whom we are close, where principles become of little or no importance and where the personal rules at the expense of the general. For example someone may commit a terrible action and yet we may still feel great (even more?) affection for them. It is this personal relationship that Buber saw encapsulated in Hasidism, in a simple, direct, and natural relationship with God that some Jews managed to establish. He does not accurately describe the real nature of Hasidism; he obviously has in mind a romantic notion of the movement. But that is irrelevant. What he has in mind as important in religion is the relationship between the human being and the deity which should take the form of a relationship that human beings could have with each other. At the heart of kabbalah is the desire for such a relationship, although the system itself replicates much of the complexity of halakhah or religious law that is characteristic of traditional Judaism. It is the validation of the subjective and the personal and the relationship as aspects of Judaism placed in a systematic process that give kabbalah its pull with many of its followers. The fact that working out how to resolve theological problems using the system is just as, if not more, complicated than any other approach to Judaism has more to say perhaps about the Jewish genius for superfluity than it does about mysticism. Yet as an attempt at lifting subjectivity from its previously lowly role in Judaism kabbalah has a very important function to perform, and we should not be surprised that some of its practitioners tend to stress too wildly the subjective at the expense of what might be regarded as basic features of Judaism.

It is this sort of reasoning that gives mysticism a bad name, of course, and that leads it to falling into suspicion as a doctrine that justifies one in pursuing whatever path one fancies. One is reminded of how determined believers in any faith or political party may accept anything their leaders do provided they can find some sort of possible, albeit not plausible, justification. What is even more problematic about many varieties of mysticism, including kabbalah, is that they may pursue an antinomian policy, that is, they do not think the pursuit of law is important. In fact, today most kabbalists are Orthodox Jews who do think the laws of their religion are very important, but there is a temptation for kabbalists to think that once they are possessed of the secret blueprint behind the construction and operation of the world, they require nothing else to know how they ought to behave. Halakhah, Jewish law, might become regarded as only appropriate for the ordinary believers, those who do not appreciate the secret meanings to which the kabbalist is privy, and for them, this would be their route to coming as close as they can to God. The kabbalist, by contrast, can hope to achieve ever-greater levels of closeness to God since he is as it were on the direct or fast stream, unlike the plodders in the rest of the community who must make do with the letter of the law and a fairly naive interpretation of it.

Interestingly, on this point the kabbalist and the philosopher have rather similar views. Many philosophers thought that their ability to manipulate rational thought gave them privileged access to reality, something that ordinary believers can only approach more distantly through their obedience to religion. This comes out clearly for example in Maimonides' parable of the court, where different levels of people get closer to the king or indeed are destined to remain at some distance from him. According to Maimonides, it is the philosophers and the scientists who really come close since they are aware theoretically of the nature of things and so aware of the nature of the deity, in so far as we can know God. The ordinary believer, the person who takes the stories in the Bible at face value, is obliged to remain at some distance from the king and is unable to move any closer so long as he believes literally in the imaginative representations of religion.

The ordinary Jew's beliefs

Does this mean that the philosophers thought that ordinary believers adhered to false beliefs, while more educated people could discover the truth? Some have held this theory but it seems far from accurate. The theory of Maimonides and many within the context of Islamic and Jewish thought in the middle ages is that both ordinary people and the intellectual elite are aware of the truth but in different ways. Those gifted intellectually understand it quickly and directly; they do not need an embroidered view which skirts around the truth. There is no need to think that the philosophers really understand the truth and that the others do not, but there is no doubt that the former are regarded by themselves as having an unalloyed view of how things really are, a view restricted to them since the rest of the community would not be able to make use of such knowledge. It is a bit like an exercise class, both strong and weak people can exercise, and yet it would be a waste of time giving a weak person heavy weights to lift, and equally pointless giving a strong person weak weights to lift. They are both exercising and benefiting themselves, and they are doing it each in different ways.

This seems not to be a very appropriate example, since exercise is a practice without any particularly significant intellectual content, so that we can readily understand how different sorts of people with different bodies might practice differently. Someone who does the wrong sort of exercise is not necessarily making any claim about how the world is, and she may be under- or overambitious in what she thinks she can do, but this hardly seems very relevant. It is not like the contrast between a religious believer who has a naive attitude to the nature of his faith and someone who is sophisticated in what he knows, or thinks he knows. Yet the comparison is quite apt in some ways; the knowledgeable exerciser has a theory on which he bases his actions, and he understands the links between what he does and physiology, or at least has a theory to which he adheres. The theory may be scientifically respectable or it may not, but at the very least it represents a thoughtful approach to what is being done. Religion is the same. There are practitioners who take a considered approach to what they do, by contrast to many others who just base their actions on imitation and tradition. Not that there is anything wrong with the latter or particularly praiseworthy about the former. Maimonides often talks about the ordinary believer with something approaching contempt, and in the parable of those approaching the king in his palace, these are the people who are well outside the walls of the palace (GP II, 51; 618–20). It is a bit like passing an examination, only those who are intellectually successful can come close to the king. This seems wrong, though, since many of those outside the walls are good and faithful religious believers, and they should also be allowed to come close to the real, here represented as the king. Otherwise we have a model of a religious community like an army, with the infantry who are just in the role of taking orders and an officer class who give the orders and actually understand why they are given. This may work for an army but it is hardly an appropriate model for a religious community, since one expects that from a religious point of view promotion is given on the basis of spiritual merit, not the ability to use theoretical concepts or give orders.

What Maimonides might well have had in mind are the very apposite comments of thinkers like al-Ghazali which are critical of *taqlid* or imitation in religion. Al-Ghazali died in 1111 and made a considerable impact on the Islamic intellectual world with his critique of philosophy and defense of Sufism or mysticism. Those critical of tradition would argue that there is not much merit in doing something just because one has always done it, or because someone else tells you to, or because one just follows tradition. Both Maimonides and al-Ghazali were very enthusiastic on the significance of tradition and basing our actions on it, but only basing our actions on tradition they regarded as unsatisfactory. For those actions to be worthwhile, Maimonides and al-Ghazali argue, they have to be understood for what they are, and to do this one has to grasp the intellectual context which provides them with their rationale. Here they go off in different directions, since for al-Ghazali, in the latest stage of his thought, the main way of preserving religious authenticity was to embrace a mystical interpretation of religion. For Maimonides, as opposed to his sons, the route to understanding is intellectual and involves attaining a high degree of scientific and theoretical awareness. Both thinkers seem to rule out of consideration as serious religious participants the mass of believers, the people who just live their religion without really thinking about what is behind it, why it is as it is, or whether any changes should be instituted. The military analogy works well here; these are the believers who are the foot soldiers of religion, the participants whose role is "not to reason why, just to do and die."

It has to be said yet again that this will not do for a religion, since each believer is entitled to think that his contribution is significant and he has the opportunity to relate to God in a genuine and meaningful way. God may be like a general, but a much more accessible general than one in the army, since God is addressed several times a day by believers, and is expected to be in contact with them. He can hardly respond that he will only listen to those who attain a certain level of intellectual and spiritual growth.

For Maimonides and al-Ghazali religions are very serious institutions. Most people just take them for granted, and they act in terms of their upbringing, but this is to misunderstand the nature of religious commitment. It has to be an individual declaration of faith based on intellect or personal feeling, and the believer has to build his life around it. The fact that that is not how most people experience religion is irrelevant to their claim, since they are arguing that despite what most people do, this is what they should do. This is an entirely reasonable argument, but what we need to establish here is whether it is valid. There are grounds for thinking that it is not. For one thing, people may often treat seriously activities that they do fairly automatically or with a degree of insouciance. The Jew who is wrapped in his *tallit* (prayer shawl) and *tefilin* (phylacteries) swaying as he prays in the synagogue may seem more serious about what he is doing than someone else who contemplates a rainbow and thinks of Noah. But how can we say? The *kavaneh* or direction of their prayer, or what comes close to prayer, may be the same or very different from each other, but what will persist as an issue is how they orient themselves toward God. It is not settled by their behavior and no amount of behavior will be enough to be sure.

This is an important point. We have asked already how serious one ought to be in one's attitude toward God. Some would say that God must be the most important thing in our lives if we really believe in him, since he represents the main principle of truth and reality and how could we be expected to pay much attention to anything else? Surely everything else is petty and unimportant by comparison. That does not seem to be what most Jewish thinkers suggest is the case, though, since as we have seen Judaism often insists on the significance of combining one's religious role with carrying out our ordinary duties. Maimonides and the kabbalists cannot really think that people would be better off ignoring their ordinary activities for science and mystical contemplation since a vitally significant part of out lives, our divinely established lives, is represented by those very ordinary tasks. Those who are outside the palace are not just those who follow the law, they are those who follow the law blindly. They are not interested in the reasons for the law, they just follow it, in so far as they can, given their lack of access to its internal workings. They are like students who work stolidly at their essays and exams but never get a high grade, and this is because they are never able to extend their argument, seek alternative points of view, or place the subject of the task within a wider theoretical context. They are the students who come and question their tutors as to their low grades, and are surprised to find that they were expected to write more than a paragraph or two. They are the students who follow the text or the lectures faithfully and leave it at that. Maimonides is not ridiculing religious belief and practice when he assigns the blind followers of Judaism to the outskirts of the palace. He is just pointing out that if all you do is follow those whom you regard as authoritative, then this can only go so far. It is the first step, an important first step, but will not be productive if it is also the last step.

Is this to insist on a too strict account of what it is to be a believer? Must one always go further than the rudiments of religion? Maimonides is often called an intellectualist, but he does not argue that we can only achieve salvation through using our intellect, nor that those reluctant to think much about what they are doing are necessarily leading unsatisfactory lives from the point of view of religion.

A central complaint that the mystics made of the philosophers in the middle ages was that the latter insisted that the highest level of thought possible for human beings was to reach the level of the active intellect. This is the principle of abstract thought which is sometimes identified with the moon in the cosmic system, something that is linked to our form of existence and yet is also celestial. This level of abstract thought is crucially abstract, and so impersonal, and seems to be a poor alternative to coming close to God. It also seems to restrict that sort of access, which does not go very far, to an intellectual elite, whereas we normally hold out as possible the elevation of absolutely anyone to the divine presence, should he be wiling to admit that person. In the story of Bontshe Shveig we have the example of someone who is simple and even rather stupid, yet his presence in heaven causes tumult because he is so famous there for his virtue and patience. Bontshe leads a life of extraordinary suffering and is totally unnoticed in our world, but his exemplary behavior gives him a huge status in the next world. Even when he is there and asked what he would like, he requests only a warm roll and butter for breakfast each day! It would indeed be unfair of a deity, who made everyone different, to reward them on the basis of their intellectual differences, and so the good person like Bontshe should stand just as much chance, if not more, of coming close to God as the intelligent person.

This criticism can be sidestepped if we take seriously the idea that both the stupid and the intelligent person have an opportunity to come close to God, albeit in different ways. What might be a problem is the insistence of the philosophers that intellectual achievement can be translated into coming close to God and is the best we can do. God is an abstract thinker, indeed the most abstract of thinkers, and so coming close to him is only possible through reaching some level of abstract thought. The abstract gets in the way of the personal, of course, yet we do precisely hold out as a possibility a personal relationship with God. That seems to be involved in prayer, and right throughout the Bible we find instances of people speaking to God and God responding to them, conscious as he appears to be of them as individuals who are in a personal relationship with him.

As Maimonides points out, this idea which is so persistent in Judaism, and other faiths, is problematic. How can God who is perfect know imperfect things? If he is really aware of us as individuals, how would we ever be free to sin since we would be aware that he was constantly checking up on our behavior and would this not place us under too much coercion? If God knows everything we do and will punish or reward us accordingly, would we have any scope for action outside of what God wants us to do? This is why the criticism of the active intellect as the peak of human knowledge was so effective. If all we can do to come close to God is be good at mathematics and physics, then this is hard to make coherent with what we think of as religion. It is both too demanding intellectually and too undemanding spiritually.

The idea that reason is sufficient to make sense of the world can also be a difficult principle to accept. When Moses Mendelssohn's very young daughter died he accepted this as in no way offending the eighteenth-century Enlightenment principle that the world is a rational place well-organized by a benevolent deity. Mendelssohn is a thinker who did much to integrate the German Jewish population into civil society, coming at a time when that sort of integration became feasible. He argued that it was time for the Jews to abandon their own language (Yiddish) and the ghetto, and move into the cities and live like everyone else. Mendelssohn had two audiences, the Jews and also the German gentiles whom he sought to woo with his excellent German and precise arguments as to why his community should become part of the body politic. He argued that Judaism would continue to be practiced by those Jews who entered normal German society since the religion was after all in line with reason anyway and so did not at all clash with the principles of civil government and cooperation. There was nothing the Jews had to fear about integration in civil society since their religion was perfectly compatible with that society, and with this argument he tried to allay the fears of those hesitant about what awaited them beyond the walls of their imposed isolation.

When his daughter died, Mendelssohn reasoned that she had lived as long as she was supposed to live, and so it would be a mistake to think that her death in any way suggested that anything inexplicable or terrible had happened. This sounds like a normal religious resignation in the face of the divine will, but this is not how Mendelssohn puts it. The point of religious resignation is that one thinks that God has a reason for what happens, but this is a reason that we cannot grasp or even contemplate, so we just accept whatever he does. Mendelssohn does not take this line, here he suggests that people have appropriate lengths of life and they all differ, and someone who dies young just lived as long as the length of life that is appropriate for them. It is not clear what his argument is for such a conclusion, but he is probably right in thinking that it follows from the general principle that the world is rationally organized by a benevolent being. If such a being allows people to die at different times then this must be because they were supposed to die at those times, in the sense that the universe is best organized in that way. That presumably is why flies live on average for a shorter time than we do. Precisely why different age spans are appropriate is not something we need know if we are rational, but we do need to appreciate that there is a reasonable answer to why it happens. This might seem a rather bloodless response, but it gains strength from the way in which human beings are often profoundly surprised and shocked when things go wrong in entirely predictable ways. We know that machines do not last forever, yet we are perpetually surprised when a car does not start in the morning, since every other morning it did start. Yet we know that sooner or later everything stops, including us, and at the same time as we have this knowledge we know that when things break down we shall be surprised, even amazed, despite what we know.

Kabbalah and rationality

This brings us back to the observation that kabbalah is not noticeably less rational than any other form of theoretical approach to religion. Indeed, it is often constructed in such a way that it involves even more complex thinking processes than philosophy. What is important is its claim about knowledge. Philosophers typically worry about how much human beings can know, given our material structure and the limited intellects that we possess. For mystics, though, there are ways in which they can acquire huge amounts of knowledge, and very important knowledge at that, rather similar to the ways in which God himself comes to know.

Like many radical doctrines, kabbalah portrays itself as traditional, indeed the word itself means "tradition." It is not clear precisely when and where it arose, although it is clear that it often represented itself as much older than it really was. According to Scholem, a plausible starting point is to be found in the book *Bahir* which circulated in Provence in the late twelfth century but which probably came from further east a century or so earlier. Whatever its precise date there is no doubt about its not being as old as second century CE, as it represents itself to be. The later kabbalistic works, and in particular the *Zohar*, develops and extends many of the notions discussed in the *Bahir*, but the latter work does include the main principles of kabbalah. The most ambitious claim is that although God himself is the *Ayn Sof*, the limitless, we can come to know his sefirot or characteristics which represent his unfolding as an active being.

One of the unusual aspects of the language describing these potentialities of God is the use of gender language. The tenth sefira is explicitly identified with the feminine, the Shechinah, the divine presence. Why is this presence identified with the female? The image which occurs most often is that of a vessel, and a very significant vessel at that, since it is precisely through that vessel that all the forces of the other sefirot flow. Sometimes God is compared to a king, and the Shekhinah to a queen, or to a royal daughter. She is clearly the vessel through which divine power enters the world, and as such a vital part of the structure of reality. The Shekhinah is very much identified with the Oral Law, and hence her importance, since the Oral Law represents our ability to use the divine law in the first place, since it brings that law down to earth, as it were, and makes it user friendly. When we obey the law we please her, but the reverse is also true, and she is made unhappy by our poor behavior. As the tenth sefira, the Shekhinah looks like the lowest and least important, since the sefirot are generally ranked, yet in some ways she is the most important, since it is through her that all the other sefirot have the possibility of being united and enter the world. It is only through her that the Jews have the opportunity to come close to God, and if they do what they ought to then she herself comes close to God, in just the way that a wife comes closer to her husband when both are pleased by the behavior of their children. Something that is feminine and so classified as rather lowly comes out as being very important, and that is surely one of the exciting things about the kabbalah; it often resists the ordinary interpretations of classical dichotomies such as low/high, female/male, poor/rich.

This playing about with opposites gives kabbalah its often paradoxical style, but it has to be admitted that it is really trying to do two things at once. On the one hand it is determined to come close to God, to understand the nature of the divine essence, while at the same time it is convinced of the difficulty of this. The way to achieve understanding, we are told, is by using kabbalistic techniques to understand biblical texts and thereby grasp how the world is really organized. Yet, this is a difficult and technically sophisticated task, the very mechanics of which might be suspected of taking the practitioner away from contact with God in much the same way as was said to have occurred in the case of the philosophers. As so often in intellectual life, something that is supposed to make life easier and less complicated ends up being just as difficult and complex as what it was supposed to replace.

Chapter 8

The ideal versus the real

The conflict between the ideal and the real is about how far a religion is based on a realistic understanding of the way things are and how far it insists on pursuing what it sees as ideal, as a perfect state of affairs. For example, there is a notion of physical love which represents what is for us our normal idea of the emotion, and then there is divine or perfect love, a relationship which is based on something stronger and more lasting than the desires of particular finite creatures. There is also the understanding that when human beings talk to each other they often do not tell the whole truth, and may have motives behind their shaping of the truth in order to reflect positively on themselves or negatively on others. Of course, we ought always to tell the whole truth, or so it might be thought, but the real position is that we tend to avoid the ideal. This conflict arises very much in political life when we consider the nature of peace, something that religions tend to advocate, yet in practical life is very difficult to pursue unreservedly. As we shall see, Judaism is quite clear on the necessity for violence to be employed in some instances, or so it might seem. On the other hand, it constantly sets out peace as an ideal, something that we should aim at and see as the culmination of our efforts. How does Judaism reconcile the pursuit of the ideal with the experience of practical life and the highly imperfect nature of the real world?

There is a long debate in many religions, including Judaism, about how far we should concentrate on our relationship with God and how far we should live an ordinary life full of normal social and personal commitments. We might think that our relationship with God is the most important thing about us, and, for example, when Abraham is told to sacrifice Isaac, he does not hesitate or argue. He immediately sets about his task, certain that once God had ordered it to be done, it had to be done. On the other hand, he might have argued that his relationship with Isaac was too important to be destroyed by murdering his own son. He might even have argued that he was not going to murder anyone regardless of what God wanted. We note surely here how weak Abraham was capable of being when he agreed to drive out Hagar and Ishmael at Sarah's request. God told him to accede to Sarah's wishes and that God would look after them, but even so one might have expected Abraham to wish to continue to participate in his older son's upbringing and not drive him and his mother out into the desert with just a jug of water and a loaf of bread. Ishmael grows up to be an archer and marries an Egyptian woman. Is this what Abraham wanted for him? We often have to make choices, and here he chose to side with God and Sarah and against Hagar and his other son Ishmael.

Although the Jews celebrate a festival of Passover or Pesach and thank God for having brought them out of Egypt, during the Exodus itself the Jews did not stop moaning and complaining. They frequently compared their present conditions unfavorably with their previous life in Egypt, and when Moses was delayed up Mount Sinai they promptly abandoned monotheism entirely for the Golden Calf. The Bible does not present them as nobly struggling faithfully to achieve the ideal, but on the contrary as largely concerned about everyday events and problems, and with only a vague commitment to anything more abstract. The Bible is a very realistic text and represents the ideal as something quite distant, important but only attainable briefly and with great difficulty.

How important is religion in our lives?

Should we devote our lives to God, or should we concentrate rather on pettier and more personal sorts or relationships? Perhaps there is no dichotomy here. God might want us to be concerned primarily with our social obligations. Judaism has little place for the sort of person who wants to dedicate his or her life entirely to God, since the everyday events of life are seen as lifted in their significance if they are done in the right spirit and in a worshipful manner. That is why there are so many blessings in the liturgy and why so many religious events take place at home. It is often said that after the destruction of the temples the main altar is now the table in the Jewish home, and this brings out the significance of everyday events carried out with affection by family members and friends for each other.

Loving God is a difficult thing to do in Judaism, since God is such an abstract figure. It is not clear how one can love something that is not physical and that is entirely different from everything else in the universe, as Maimonides might have put it. So loving God is often going to take a more indirect form, perhaps through an emphasis on worship or scholarship, or indeed on acting *tikkun olam*, to repair the world and make life for everyone a bit better, or a lot better in certain places. In much of the literature, this love for God is not seen as something to be abstracted from other aspects of Jewish life since it can best be carried out within the everyday structure of that life.

This notion that the mixed life, a life which has both a strong relationship with God and with other human beings, is what Jews should aim at, runs throughout much of the literature. There are certainly some philosophers and kabbalists who put on a pedestal the solitary life of reason or religious experience, but they are the exception rather than the rule, which is not of course to say that they do not better encapsulate the tradition. Yet there is so much in Judaism on the other side, the side of "Rabban Gamaliel, the son of Rabbi Judah the Prince [who] said it is an excellent thing to study the Torah together with some ordinary occupation" (*Ethics of the Fathers* 2.2). It is certainly true that we are told that the most eminent rabbis in the past were often manual laborers and earned their living variously as carpenters, builders, blacksmiths, farmers, tentmakers, watercarriers, woodcutters, and so on. Akiva was a shepherd, for example. Much of the classical literature emphasizes the significance of involving oneself in the affairs of the world at the same time as carrying out one's religious duties, and the Reform movement places a particularly strong concentration on what it calls *tikkun olam*, repairing the world. This kabbalistic expression which often means taking part in religious activities in order to repair the breach that exists between this world and the divine world has been reinterpreted by the Reform movement to mean social action, making the world a better place, and in this way to bring it closer to the next world. A perfectly reasonable reinterpretation, this reflects well the Reform movement's advocacy of a simpler form of religious ritual together with a desire for a broader notion of justice as described by many of the Jewish prophets. The only feasible strategy then is social action as a main route to performing one's duty of Jewish action.

Rather than asking how a Jew ought to behave, the Bible and later Jewish works tend to ask how human beings ought to behave. Psalm 15, for instance, provides a list of what human beings are supposed to do and it is a fairly uncontroversial list. It includes the pursuit of virtue, righteousness, and sincerity. We should abstain from slander and evil, and from shaming others. We should hate horrible people, honor those who respect God, and value oaths. Usury and bribes are both to be condemned, we are told. People who fulfill these conditions have hopes, the Psalmist suggests, of living in God's high mountain, with him. Yet most of these virtues and vices deal with our relationships with other people, not with God. Other formulations share this characteristic, as with Micah's "Do justice, love mercy and walk humbly with God" (6:8). In fact there was a real passion in Judaism to provide the most concise summary of the Torah, Rabbi Simlai referred to the 613 commandments given on Mount Sinai to Moses being distilled down to their essence by David in the above psalm into 11, by Micah into 3, by Amos into 2 and by Habakkuk into 1 (*Makkot* 23b). Amos puts them as "Seek me and live" (5:4), as spoken by God. The implication is that life with others in a community and approaching God are much the same sort of activity, or at the very least closely linked with each other. Finally, Habbakuk stated that "The righteous shall live by his faith" (2:4). Being faithful to God involves at the same time being faithful to the lives of social life that we find in the Bible and other works, and do not just describe the relationship between the solitary believer and her God. Awe in the presence of the deity is not just a feeling we are to have when praying, or thinking directly about God, or when in a religious environment, but it might be suggested should envelope our lives, since we are never out of the presence of the deity. It is appreciating the transcendental nature of the world as characterized by the divine presence that leads us to consider how we should behave with respect to others, or so Jewish works often argue. After all, if we do not see the world as having a divine basis we might conclude that we could behave in any way whatsoever since the meaning of the world is nothing higher than it.

Psalm 111:10 is often translated as "The fear of the Lord is the beginning of wisdom" but fear might be better expressed here as awe or respect. The idea is that if we see the world as an arena devised by divine authority then we are able to orient ourselves appropriately in it. Not all this orientation will be directly toward God, since given the distance that he maintains from the world, our immediate attention will have to be directed at our fellow human beings and the natural environment. It is only through them that we have any prospect of relating to God, and so there is not much point in following a policy of abandoning oneself to trying to establish a route to God which follows some sort of solitary and exclusive path. As is often said in the Jewish literature, the Torah is not sent down to replace life but to celebrate and sanctify it.

Slander

The Gemara says that Akiva's 24,000 students were killed by plague between the second night of Pesach and the 33 days of the counting of the Omer because they did not treat each other with respect, something that Akiva certainly tried to do, using the principle *veahavta l'reyacha kamocha*, loving his friend as himself. One character flaw that this story refers to is that of *lashon ha-ra*, slander, about which Jewish morality is very critical. *Tzara'at* or leprosy is often compared to punishment for human failures. Moses' hand becomes leprous when he expressed doubt about the willingness of the people to believe in his mission (Ex 4:6–7), Miriam was struck by leprosy when she spoke against Moses (Num 12:1–15) and so the leper or *metsorah* is compared to *a motzi shem ra*, a person who speaks ill of others. According to Maimonides, in *Hilkhot Deot* 7:3, *lashon ha-ra* or slander is like denying God, since it kills three people, the speaker, the hearer, and the person about whom it is said. By contrast with the prevalence of conflict and slander among some in the Jewish community, the school of Hillel were said to have been "gentle, modest, and taught the views of their opponents before their own" (*Eruvin* 13b). This expresses something of what is taken to be an ideal in social life, and is sharply contrasted with what are often regarded as the rather sharp and strict attitudes adopted by the School of Shammai, the great opponents of Hillel and his supporters.

Judaism and love

How does Judaism deal with ideal as compared with ordinary notions of love? There are two notable aspects of the *Song of Songs* and they both suggest that this book does not find a natural place in the Bible. It is unabashedly erotic, with two lovers, obviously unmarried, working themselves up into a lather describing each other's body and the effect it has on the other. This sort of enthusiasm suggests that they are young. Second, there is no reference to religion at all, and the poem is infused with a sort of pantheistic ethic, whereby the natural world becomes fused into the lovers' bodies or where their bodies are compared to nature. Both the man and the woman are described as strong and decisive, she is compared to a fortified building and he has things like marble pillars. When she wanted him she got up and searched for him, finally bringing him into her house, indeed into the room where she was conceived. Yet the course of love does not run smooth, she finally misses her lover and is actually beaten by the watchmen (5.2–8). Perhaps these are the same watchmen who found her when she was looking for her lover earlier and found him (3.1–4), and whom she seems to have brushed aside. The implication here is that when her search was successful she had a male companion, and so she was safe, but when he left her the watchmen stripped her of her shawl and beat her, since now she is defenseless. This rather gets in the way of the egalitarian analysis of the poem.

Love as strong as death

One of the most interesting and darkest passages occurs at 8.6 where she says:

> Stamp me as a seal upon your heart
> sear me upon your arm
> for love is as strong as death
> passion as harsh as the grave
> its sparks will spark a fire
> an all-consuming blaze.

This famous passage of Hebrew poetry is particularly effective when heard, and the English translation is much longer and heavier than the original, as is so often the case with translation. It is clear that a sort of parallelism is in operation here, with the lines operating in couples or even triples to emphasize progressively the point made in the first sentence.

Yet how could love be as strong as death? Does this mean it extends into the next world? There is nothing in the poem to suggest this, and the sort of love we find described here is definitely the very earthly love of physical beings. One cannot imagine what sort of relationship could exist between the lovers in a world without bodies, for example, or at least some sort of material environment. So the obvious response is to allegorize this passage, and here it can become part of a theodicy where Israel loves God to the point of death.

The poem was controversial from the beginning. The great Rabbi Akiva who lived in the second century CE is said to have criticized those who quoted it in the taverns (Mishnah *Yadayim* 3.5), while at the same time saying that the whole world is not worth the day on which the *Song of Songs* was given to Israel, and comparing the poem to the holy of holies, unlike the rest of the Bible which is by contrast only holy (Tosefta *Sanhedrin* 12.10). Commentators increasingly allegorized the work as describing the relationship between Israel (the woman) and God (the man). For Christians it was about the Church and God, or the individual and Jesus, or some other permutation. This is a familiar technique in religions, when it becomes difficult to understand a passage—allegorize it so that it means something quite different. Indeed, the initial difficulty is taken to be an indication of the need to allegorize, since how could there be a love poem in the Bible unless it referred to something much deeper than physical passion, loss, and emotional anguish? The *Song of Songs* like the Book of Esther does not refer to God, but the latter at least has some pretty important religious lessons in it about the survival of the Jewish community and their tendency to acquire enemies who need to be overcome. The *Song of Songs*, by contrast, has to be very thoroughly allegorized before it can be given any sort of religious meaning. Perhaps that is what Akiva meant when he said it was like the holy of holies, the fact that it makes no apparent religious claim means that really it is entirely about our relationship with God, since the whole poem has to be seen as having a new and transcendental meaning. Other books in the Bible have obviously religious passages and so these we can pay less attention to, since they require less in the way of interpretive work.

The philosopher Albo (*c*.1360–1444) raises the question whether someone falls in love for reasons or for no reason at all. He argues in his *Sefer ha-'Iqqarim* (Book of Principles) that we should follow Aristotle and distinguish between three kinds of love: love of the good, the pleasant, and the useful (NE VIII, 2, 1155b). He discusses an additional type of love that he calls not *ahava* but *heshek* which is passionate love and without reason. An example of such love is the love of God for Israel which is entirely based on a lack of reasons. Deut 7: 6–7 "The Lord your God has chosen (*bahar*) you to be his own special (*segula*) people...not because you were more in number...did the Lord love (*hashak*) you and choose you." God's choice was completely free, and whatever it was about the Jews that inspired him to love them, it was not an essential character that obliged him to love them.

"Go forth you daughters of Zion and gaze upon King Solomon wearing the crown with which his mother crowned him on the day of his wedding" (3.11) is explained in *Song of Songs* Rabbah 3.2 as like a king who has an only daughter who he loves so much that he describes her not only as a daughter, but also as a sister and eventually as a mother. God loves Israel so much that he encompasses every form of love, even love of a mother, which is regarded here as the highest form of love. In the *Bahir*, the Shekhinah is literally the divine embodiment in the world, and the female vehicle for God to enter the world. Solomon was crowned by his mother, the third sefira, with the crown of the Torah, the tenth. Clearly kabbalists had no difficulty using the language of the *Song of Songs*.

One of the interesting questions which arose quickly within Jewish thought is what the nature of love is in the *Song of Songs*. Is it a calm and rational sort of affection that two individuals feel for each other, or is it a passionate and arational, even irrational, kind of emotion? What hangs on it is that if the sort of love in the poem is indicative of the sort of relationship God has with humanity, and in particular perhaps the Jews, then we can use the *Song* to find out the nature of that affection. There are good arguments for both sides of the meaning of love. The more rational form of love might seem to be more appropriate for a God who is often seen as profoundly rational, calm, considered, and reflective. The idea of God displaying passion is not something that many accounts of religion would appreciate, given the very pure and abstract concept of God that they use. There is, to be sure, plenty of description in the Jewish Bible of God as jealous, angry, sad, and so on, but few commentators take this sort of language literally, arguing that here as elsewhere the Bible speaks in human language and this is not to be taken at face value.

God and the physical

To give an example of how careful we need to be in using physical language to describe God, let us look at the sacrificial rites in the Temple. A lot of things went on in the Temple, but sacrifices were very important. These sacrifices, we are told, should be "a pleasant aroma to the Lord." Yet surely God does not have a nose, and why should he care about the smell of sacrifices? After all, he does not seem in other places to be much interested in the sacrifices themselves, but more in what is behind them. "To what purpose are your sacrifices to Me?" (Isa 1:11) he says when he disapproves of the motives of those carrying out the ritual. Everyone who wishes to serve God should be aware that the ritual by itself is not enough, it has to point toward future good actions in the same way that a pleasant aroma suggests good future things to come. "Open Me a gate of repentance the size of the eye of a needle, and I will open for you large gates through which infinite light will enter" (*Song of Songs* Rabbah 5:3).

What the use of the very physical imagery in the *Song* might be taken to mean is that the relationship that God has with creation is the same sort of passionate and almost willful relationship that characterizes our emotional life. Is this an appropriate relationship for God to have? Don't we tend to think of him as more properly being calm and controlled in every situation, since after all he knows everything that has happened and everything that is going to happen. For us, passion and everything that goes with it is not entirely unrelated to the fact that there is a good deal about our environment and how it is going to develop of which we are very ignorant. This could well be true and yet does not rule out the use of passion on God's behalf. Here the passion would have to be seen as entirely free and not carried out for some ulterior motive, just a free choice about how to feel and what to do. Since God could do absolutely anything since he does not need us for anything, and since something has to move him from inaction to action, it might seem that passion is a plausible motive to get him going, in just the same way that for us it may represent a reason for us to do something rather than nothing.

The *Song of Songs* is read during the Sabbath in the week of Passover and one reason for this surely is all the spring imagery in the poem, and Passover does take place in the spring. Another reason is one of the themes of the text, the triumph of simplicity over sophistication. The young woman in the story resists the blandishments of the king's palace and all his inducements to submit to him and returns intact to her country lover, someone who addresses her in the most simple way and feels for her an uncomplicated and natural love. Passover is also a celebration of simplicity, something difficult to appreciate given the complex laws that have developed to ensure the distinction between bread (*hametz*) and unleavened bread (*matza*). After all, unleavened bread is simpler than leavened bread, it does not rise and is much flatter and more basic than its leavened equivalent. Restricting one's diet for the week to avoid anything that can be linked with ordinary bread might also be seen as simplifying one's life, although in practice the determination of many Jews to find alternatives that are kosher for Passover may make the festival a rather complicated period in the year. This is a good example of ways in which Jewish law may be used to oppose what might be thought of as the point of particular instances of Jewish law. To take another example, many minor fasts may be avoided by studying holy texts, and reading and perhaps discussing a small passage may obviate the need for the fast. Yet fasting also simplifies life, it gives us a period when we are not taken up with food and drink and allows us to use that space to concentrate on a more spiritual way of living, albeit for a limited period.

Simplicity in the Bible

Although the *Song of Songs* has been made out to be a very complex text, it does not really seem to fit such a bill. On the contrary, its simplicity is its very charm, and its lack of apparent religious relevance simplifies it still more.

Like the Book of Esther it includes no reference to God, but unlike Esther it seems to include nothing of relevance to the Jewish people at all. Esther at least details the travails and eventual success of the Jewish community in Persia and the very robust measures they take to survive in a world full of enemies. Yet, in the *Song of Songs* we do not have even that reference to the Jews, just a setting presumably in Israel, but a setting which could surely be in any rural spot.

It is this simplicity which perhaps expresses the religious nature of the text, not the elucidation of desire that we find in it. It is the idea that there is something healthy and right about love, the sort of earthly love and sex that is celebrated in the book. The frankness of the lovers, the apparent reciprocity with which they express their affection, these all serve as indicators of the desirability of a natural relationship of human beings with each other. It is worth adding that the liberal use of language linking their bodies with the natural world may also be seen as desirable, as expressing an easy relationship with the environment, with the natural world in which we live. The symbol of Passover is very much the humble matza, unleavened bread, since bread is such an important part of life and yet is often ignored because it is so ubiquitous. For the Jews leaving Egypt, bread represented their main means of survival at the start of the journey, since there was presumably very little else they could take with them to eat. Flat unleavened bread was also much less bulky than the ordinary kind and enabled more to be carried to provide food for longer than would otherwise be the case. There is also a sense in which allowing yeast to raise the flour in bread is a symbol of a stable society in which people can wait for the bread to prove and increase in bulk, a symbol that fails to make sense when lives are disrupted by emigration. Yet what do we need in a material sense in conditions like that? Like the lovers in the *Song of Songs*, all we need are natural ways of acting and relating to each other.

Or so one of the messages of the poem might suggest. And the ways in which Passover has become so complex might be seen as a bit of a parody of what it might have really been about, something which is not so unusual in religion. After all, Christians often criticize the direction in which Christmas has gone in Western culture, and this sort of criticism of the growth and expansion of religious and cultural ritual at the expense of the basic meaning of the ritual is surely entirely appropriate in the Jewish sphere also. It is what leads some Jews to abandon Judaism or seek new rituals to replace those that they see threatening to overwhelm it.

Peace and war

The Bible is often brutally realistic. When the Jews come to Samuel and suggest that the country become a kingdom he points out:

> This is what a king who will reign over you will do. He will take your sons and make them serve with his chariots and horses, and they will run in front of his chariots. Some he will assign to be

commanders...and others to plough his ground and reap his harvest, and still others to make weapons of war and equipment for his chariots. He will take your daughters to be perfumers and cooks and bakers. He will take the best of your fields and vineyards and olive groves and give them to his attendants.

(1 Samuel 8)

This is precisely what does happen when people set other people above them, the rulers are obliged to exaggerate the distinction between them and their subjects because they are rulers. There is no point being a ruler unless one is at a distance from the ruled.

Yet, the Bible also points to various ideal relationships between people such as are embodied in the principle of the Jubilee where every fiftieth year all debts will be cancelled and everyone will "proclaim liberty throughout all the land unto all the inhabitants thereof" (Lev. 25.10), the words inscribed on the Liberty Bell in Philadelphia. This is what rather annoyed Samuel—the fact that in choosing a king the people were not aware of their primary relationship with God, for "The land must not be sold permanently because the land is mine and you are but aliens and my tenants" (Lev. 25:23). In returning the land to its original owners at the behest of God one is acknowledging his ultimate ownership of everything. Yet there is no doubt that there is nothing wrong with possessions or enjoying those possessions. The enunciation of the messianic era is given in terms of possessions, where "Every man will sit under his own vine and his own fig tree and no-one will make them afraid" (Micah 4.4). What would they be afraid of? A plausible suggestion is being dispossessed of their property, something which we are entitled to own, albeit not permanently, and which we may see as part of a desirable goal of human behavior.

This distinction between the ideal and the real comes out nicely when discussing not only private property but also political issues such as war and peace. Within religion, the idea of dying for the sake of God, *kiddush ha-shem*, in sanctification of the divine name, often figures. Within Judaism, a caution has arisen about the concept of *milhamet mitzvah* or *hovah*, commanded or obligatory war, especially after the disasters of the revolt of CE 66 and the Bar Kochba rebellion of CE 132 (Mishnah Sotah 8.7). On the other hand, in his commentary on Maimonides' Book of Commandments (positive commandment 4), Nahmanides claims that "it is a positive commandment for all generations obligating each individual even during the period of exile" that the Land of Israel is conquered and settled.

When Adam and Eve are excluded from the Garden of Eden, God makes it clear that they would now experience both death and hardship. We should recall that they are excluded from the Garden for exercising free choice, for doing what they were forbidden to do. Later on, after the Flood, God acknowledges our evil nature and at the same time says despite this that he will never destroy the world with a flood again (Gen 9:15). Yet this does not mean that the world is going to take a gentler turn in the future. Some of the instructions by God to the Jews involve not only killing all the human beings in particular communities, but even their animals! By contrast, the messianic age is described as a time of perfect peace, with the lion lying down with the lamb, a period of complete justice, and is the state of affairs toward which history is working, however slowly. In the end, all conflicts will be resolved, by divine fiat, and some Jews are prepared to wait patiently for this time to arrive. For example, there are Jews who see their major function as studying and praying while awaiting the Messiah, and who take no realistic steps at all to resolve any conflicts which may persist between them and the gentile world (a position thoroughly satirized in Kafka's short story "Jackals and Arabs," where the Jews are the jackals who constantly complain but do nothing to help themselves).

The importance of peace

There is also an immense emphasis on the significance of peace. For example, in the courts in Israel which consider divorce there is often a great stress on the promotion of *shalom ha-bayit*, peace in the house, and wives will often be obliged to try yet again to put up with the objectionable behavior of their husbands and vice versa. Conflict resolution is frequently skewed in terms of serving particular interests, and the justice of an individual case may have to make way for what are taken to be wider issues of justice. These issues may be thoroughly unjust in what they think of as the normal relationships between individuals and groups of people.

In Isa 45:7 we read "who forms light and creates darkness, who makes peace and creates evil" thus linking peace or shalom with the opposite of evil, a role we would normally expect to be played by the concept of the good. This tends to suggest that peace is a good in itself regardless of how it is established or what goes along with it. But is it? Certainly there is a lot to be said for peace, especially after a period of extended conflict, but there are surely also circumstances in which it is right to fight for one's principles and where the pursuit of peace is unrestricted.

There is no one very general principle of conflict resolution in any religion, whatever may be said, and certainly not in Judaism. People often think there must be some final and all-encompassing rule about how issues in this area should be resolved. There are indeed a variety of principles, and these often point in separate directions, and have to be applied differently on distinct occasions, and this is what we would expect. A religion that is based on clear and distinct general principles would not be a religion worth having, it would not mesh with everyday experience nor with the very complicated messes which human beings get into from time to time. Religions require a system of conflict resolution that reflects the conflicts of everyday life, and Judaism certainly has this. An interesting question would be whether these systems are so flexible in their attempt at linking up with the facts of everyday life that they become incapable of embodying wider principles of justice and just become ways of bringing conflict to a temporary pause. That is, are they all about establishing ceasefires or about bringing into operation final arrangements for peace? It might be argued that the best we as human beings can do is to bring about a ceasefire, and leave the final arrangements to the Almighty, in whose hands all decisions are finally placed. On the other hand, a ceasefire may merely bring to a temporary halt a conflict and may even institutionalize it, so that the parties come to feel that the justice of the situation remains unresolved in favor of particular parties to the conflict. If a building is unsound, papering over the cracks will preserve the appearance of the building temporarily but will not preserve the building ultimately. The methods of conflict resolution in Judaism and Islam may be criticized for concentrating on the smaller and more manageable aspects of such conflicts, leaving the final issues and permanent arrangements to another and more ultimate authority, that is to God.

The significance of violence

Along with conflict resolution as an ideal, Judaism accepts that sometimes one has to act violently, even in the sense of getting one's retaliation in first. The Book of Esther, for example, positively gloats over the number of Persians killed when the Jews attack them before they attack the Jews. What is interesting about this book is that the name of God does not figure even once in it, and the implication might be that when God is not directly involved, then strenuous measures are perfectly acceptable with the aim of self-preservation. But there are also plenty of casualties even when God is directly involved, and in part of the daily morning service Jews recite a song which celebrates the overcoming of the Egyptians and their drowning with the words, "God is a man of war" (Ex. 15.2). There is a Midrash according to which the angels in heaven cheered at the defeat and destruction of the Egyptian army, and the Almighty is supposed to have chided them at their pleasure over the death of some of his creatures.

But it has to be said that God did destroy a large number of his creatures in Egypt even before this event, the death of the firstborn, presumably the vast majority of whom were entirely innocent of any persecution of the Israelites and involvement in Pharaoh's policy toward them, so it is not clear what is meant by this midrash. Perhaps God was suggesting that all human life is valuable even when it needs to be taken, and this is an action that should be carried out reluctantly and certainly not made into an event to be celebrated. Islam also is a hard-nosed religion; it recognizes that there are people in the world who need to be resisted and insists that when appropriate they are resisted.

Pursuing peace and war

The Jewish Bible often links peace with justice. In the 34th Psalm, there is the verse: "Depart from evil and do good. Seek peace and pursue it" (15). The link between peace and justice is often made, and in this passage an interesting term is used for "pursue." *Radfehu* is the verb which has as its cognate noun *rodef*, pursuer or aggressor. A *rodef* is someone who disturbs the peace, who seeks to harm us, and who may perfectly legally be resisted. This verse works by contrasting notions like good and evil, peace and aggression, and suggests that peace should be sought as aggressively as its enemies are resisted. It does not actually suggest that one should never be violent, only that peace is the eventual outcome for our actions. We are familiar with people arguing that they only use force in order to bring about peace.

There are times when enemies do need to be identified and vanquished. There is a discussion in Jewish theology about why the Bible starts with the account of the creation of the world and not with a list of the commandments. For the rabbis it might seem to be the commandments which are more significant. The answer is, or an answer is, that the creation of the world and the commandments are linked. Rashi's commentary at the start of Bereshit (Genesis) on Bereshit Rabbah 1.2 links the creation of the world with the displacing of the original inhabitants of the Land, the Amorites, since the creator of the world could give whatever he wanted to whomever he wanted. This act of violence is apparently linked with justice, a relationship that as we have seen is repeated rhetorically time and time again. Derrida made the point that violence and justice are part of what we mean by God. This has for thousands of years been very much a theme of Judaism and provides some indications as to the route by which any form of plausible conflict resolution acceptable to Judaism will take place.

God in Genesis is at first not that involved in the wars of the chosen people, as we can see when Abraham sets out by military means to rescue his nephew Lot and enters into an alliance with some of the local kings to carry out this end (Gen 14). By the time of Exodus, the situation has completely changed and God's intervention is decisive. Moses tells the people, no doubt much to their relief, that God will fight for them (Ex 14:14) against the Egyptians, although we are told that they were armed when they left Egypt (Ex 13:18). As we have seen, the famous Song of the Sea that is part of the Morning Service in Judaism describes God as a man of war (Ex 15:3; see also Josh 17:1, Judg 20:17, I Sam 17:33, 2 Sam 17:8, Ezek 39:20). There are many military references to God. The messenger of God to Joshua comes as a soldier with drawn sword and describes himself as a general in God's army (Josh 5:13–14). God's violence against the Egyptians takes on the form of a campaign, the systematic destruction of the country, the firstborn in it, and eventually the army in the Sea of Reeds.

Does this mean that the Israelites are not supposed to do anything in their own defense? It looks like it, when God says "The Lord will battle for you, you hold your peace" (Ex 14:14), yet this verse is immediately followed by "Why do you cry out to me? Tell the Israelites to advance" (14:15). There is a Midrash which says that it was only when the first Israelite went into the sea until his head was covered that the waters parted, for that represented an exercise in perfect faith in God's providence. Once they escape the Egyptians, they are confronted by Amalek (whom they will have to fight in each generation—Ex 17:16) and are now very much on their own, having to fight this indefatigable enemy. When later on Joshua selects fighters and goes out with them to battle, Moses holds his hands up, and while they are up the Israelites win, and when they come down they lose. In the end his hands are actually propped up, and so victory results. What this is often taken to mean is that the people have to take their own future into their own hands and can no longer depend absolutely on the direct participation of God in their affairs. Not only is war permissible on outsiders but also after the event of the Golden Calf Moses asks the tribe of Levi to kill those who took part in the revolt against God and Moses' authority (Ex 32: 25–28). It is hardly surprising that out of this retelling of history the issue of how wars are to be fought and peace established became an important source of law in Judaism. It is quite possible for a religion to value peace and also to be realistic with regard to it. Even when the Gibeonites deceived Joshua into signing a peace treaty with them, Joshua nonetheless adhered to its terms, and much later the Israelite attack on the Gibeonites in violation of the pact was regretted by King David. His regret was translated materially in the form of compensation. Oaths and treaties should be respected, and if they are broken that is a crime to be assessed for which payment is due.

Peace and justice

The Prophets and the Writings, which together with the Five Books of Moses constitute the Jewish Bible, really emphasize the significance of peace. Justice and peace come to represent God's plan for his world (Isa 2:1–4, 11:6, 45:7; Job 25:2; Micah 4:1–5, Pss:96, 98). The Book of Amos is very critical of war and it has often been pointed out that this is a repetition of Jacob's critique of Simeon and Levi (Gen 49:5–7) when they used violence against Shechem (Gen 34:30). Peace becomes the ideal state toward which history is marching; the implements of war will be converted into tools of peace. Even King David, who is often represented as the paradigm of royalty, is condemned for his involvement in violence (1Chron 22:8).

As we have seen, this is not to say that there is anything pacifist about the Jewish tradition. War is acceptable, if it is obligatory, permissible, or carried out in self-defense, especially when used to frustrate someone who is intent on causing one harm, a *rodef* or pursuer. On the other hand, one is not permitted to kill the pursuer once his act is over in order to punish him, he may only be killed to prevent more violent actions on his part. Force must be proportional, and no innocent third party should be killed, even were this to be part of a policy of saving life in general. As one might imagine, these rules have been cited recently in criticism of the legal basis of actions of the Israel Defense Forces (IDF). Even in Deut 20:10 we are told that when besieging a city you should start by calling for peace and only if that is rejected can the siege start. Once the siege is underway, the civilian inhabitants should be given the opportunity to leave, and this applies even to the soldiers. But once this offer is rejected then the civilians need no longer be seen as civilians, because they have decided to stay and be part of the resistance to the siege. If they are then killed, provided that there is no primary intention to kill them, this is legally acceptable. This has been much cited recently in accounts of what follows from the IDF's blockade of Palestinian cities. On the other hand, both Maimonides and Nahmanides argue that behind all the rules is a blanket ban on cruelty to the enemy, and it has been argued that the treatment of the civilian population is liable to increase their suffering. On the other hand, the IDF says that they are acting on the basis that peace was first offered to the other side and was rejected. Civilians were given the opportunity to leave the area of fighting and were not intentionally targeted. The IDF would also point out that since the start of the al-Aqsa intifada less than 3 percent of the Palestinian casualties are women, whereas almost 30 percent of the Jewish casualties are female.

According to Leviticus Rabbah 9.9 "Great is peace, for all blessings are contained in it...God's name is peace" and "The whole Torah was given for the sake of peace, and it is said 'all her paths are peace' [Prov 3:17]" (Gittin 59b), and Numbers Rabbah 19.27 "It is written 'Seek peace and pursue it' (Ps 34:15). The Law does not command you to run after or pursue the other commandments, but to fulfill them on the right occasions." By contrast, peace has to be pursued on every occasion and in every place. As the wife of Rabbi Meir pointed out, we should not pray for the death of sinners but of their sins. Beruria (Berakhot 10a) refers to the end of the verse in Ps 104: 35 where it says "and let the wicked be no more" and suggests that once they repent they will no longer be wicked. Rabbi Meir then prays for their repentance and they repented, and he goes on to refer to stories about Aaron, who is famous in Jewish tradition for his love of peace. Aaron is supposed to have been pleasant to evil people and intimidates them as a result, leading them to improve their behavior. As Hillel recommends, "Be of the disciples of Aaron, loving peace and pursuing peace" (*Ethics of the Fathers* 1.12). There is another passage in Genesis Rabbah 76:2 where the phrase "Then Jacob was greatly afraid and distressed" is considered, where it is asked why there is this repetition, since is not fear and distress the same? The explanation is that he was afraid that he would be killed and distressed that he would kill Esau. It is also worth pointing out that some of the most important prayers in the repertoire such as the Amidah, the kaddish, the grace after meals, and the priestly blessing (in some synagogues terminating the service) all conclude with an invocation of peace.

The word in Hebrew for war, *milhama*, is actually related to the word for bread, *lehem*, and it is often thought that there is a connection between (lack of) bread and violence. In *Pirkei Avot* (Ethics of the Fathers) we read "The sword comes into the world because of justice delayed, justice perverted and because of those who render wrong decisions" (5.11). And there is also "Not by might nor by power but by my spirit says the Lord" (Zech 4: 6). This is part of the Shabat Chanukah haftorah, the passage read after the main reading from the Five Books of Moses on the Sabbath during the Chanukah festival. Chanukah is the holiday that celebrates the victory of the Jews who wished to preserve their distinctiveness over their enemies. The reference here to divine influence suggests that the military victory of the Maccabees is not what is important about the festival. It is not as though their victory came about through their own actions; it came about only through the participation of God on their side. On the other hand, this passage should not be taken to be critical of violence. It could mean that might and power are not sufficient conditions of success, only God fulfills that category, but they could still be necessary conditions and as such essential. Indeed, it could be that power will only be successful if it is motivated by the divine spirit. Once God is with you then you will prevail, and there is nothing wrong with violent struggle provided that it is sanctioned by God.

I criticized earlier the idea that there are principles in Judaism, and a good example of why the search for such principles is misguided can be found when examining what might pass for a Jewish conception of peace. In what we can now see was the buildup to the murder of the Israeli Prime Minister Yitzhak Rabin there was a lively correspondence in some circles as to whether he should be regarded as a *rodef* or aggressor given his peace agreements with the Arabs, and as we know, a *rodef* is an acceptable target, or may even be a target one is obligated to attack. What might have been regarded as especially serious was Rabin's contemplation of returning land given by God to the Jews to someone else. If the creator of the universe says that the Jews should have this land, as he does say on several occasions, then anyone who goes against this gift is intent on frustrating God and his chosen people. Such a person sets himself against God and the Jews, and a violent response to him might well be appropriate, or so it was argued. It is worth remembering this event and what led up to it, whenever people are critical of theology as merely talk without any significant impact on the world.

The Jewish approach to peace and violence

Was the murder of Rabin in accordance with Jewish principles of justice? Are there principles of justice and violence in Judaism? No, in just the same way that there are no principles of Judaism itself. In the contemporary politics of the Middle East, some Israelis regard the actions of the IDF as perfectly proper, as satisfying the rules of dealing with an enemy. Peace was offered and rejected, civilians are not targeted directly, people have the opportunity to leave cities when there is heavy fighting, and the overall motivation of the soldiers is to pursue justice. The Arabs are intent on destroying the Jewish state and individual Jews, and they have the status of aggressors and Jews are entitled, indeed obligated, to resist them.

Others would find this legal analysis misleading. The peace that was offered was not a just peace, since it involved a Palestinian state that would always be at the mercy of a more powerful Israeli entity. Although the Israelis claim not to target civilians, they are prepared to target combatants with reckless regard for civilian life. It is not true that civilians can escape from a siege, in fact the main Palestinian cities are often equivalent to prisons. Finally, the ban against a besieging army destroying fruit trees, because these represent the continuity of economic life for the local population, has been violated by the destruction of the local economy by the Israelis, both directly and indirectly, and so it cannot really be argued that their actions are in accordance with the halakhic principles of conflict. The sort of peace that Israel has in mind is one where their enemy is totally overwhelmed and humiliated, and this does not accord with the respect that Jewish law applies to the enemy during war.

Which is the Jewish view? It has to be said, neither and both, and a vast variety of other views can also be justified legally. That is how religious law works, it is flexible enough to interpret a situation in various ways, and so in court the prosecution and the defense both have room to argue. There is a well-known story about a rabbi being visited by a man and his wife. The man tells the rabbi about the terrible things that his wife got up to, and the rabbi nodded his head and agreed with him. Then the wife told the rabbi a totally contrary story about how she had done none of those things, and the rabbi agreed with her. The husband became exasperated and said to the rabbi "But we cannot both be right!" The rabbi replied by saying "You're right too." This brings out what might be called a highly realistic attitude to peace in Judaism. There are plenty of wars in the Bible, and the rules of war are pretty pragmatic. The whole basis to God's support for Israel is the latter's observation of the covenant, the obedience to God's commandments. Once the Israelites abandon these rules, disaster follows, as Moses predicts toward the end of Deuteronomy. But the covenant persists, so that if the Jewish people return to their previous state of good behavior, God will restore them to their land.

Peace and the messianic age

This brings in what might be called the more metaphysical aspects of peace, what it is about peace that makes it so desirable. The Hebrew term is closely linked with the term for completeness and wholeness, and there is the idea that a state of peace is valuable because it brings about a state of affairs in which one is fully oneself, as it were. The descriptions of the messianic age must have seemed delightful to communities of Jews who were suffering greatly at the hands of hostile countries in which they were such unwelcome inhabitants. On the other hand, the desire for a Messiah often lead to mistaken enthusiasms bringing about yet more disasters, and this inspired Maimonides to argue that the messianic age would be little different from an ordinary state of affairs, with the sole difference that the Jewish people would once more be living in their own land. As against this, some commentators such as Isaac Abravanel (1437–1508) interpreted the messianic age as an entirely different form of life as compared with the present state of affairs. It is not just a matter of a Jewish state, but a re-evaluation of life as we know it, and a change in the whole nature of international relations. Interestingly, that debate has brought about a linked debate in Zionist philosophy over the nature of the State of Israel. Some follow Maimonides and say that what is important about it is that it is a Jewish state, and it does not have any function apart from that (although Maimonides would no doubt insist on messianic intervention to bring it about in the first place, he would probably argue that the Zionists had jumped the gun). Others would argue that the State of Israel can never be just another state among many others, it has to be a light to the nations and can only survive if it is the precursor to a new way of living both internally and externally.

Another thinker who argues like Abravanel that the peace of the messianic age must prefigure an entirely different form of human life and action is Levinas. Violence is the negation of action, according to Levinas, because it suspends morality and alienates human beings from each other. As a result what we often see as being a period of frantic action is in fact its reverse, since what is done bears no relation to what we are, how we could be and the basis in our nature to bring about significant and positive change in the world. He focuses on the way in which violence destroys us not so much physically as morally, and since morality is the whole context within which we are who we are, the absence of peace defines us as incapable of living authentic lives. Peace is not a matter of ceasefires and temporary agreements, nor of the absence of conflict because of the mutual threat of force. This is not peace, this is the (temporary)cessation of violence, and it brings with it the inability of human beings to live the lives they should be experiencing. Only in a radically different future can we genuinely experience peace, and whatever form that future takes, it must be very different from our present. As with Abravanel he sees real peace as not a continuation of the sort of life to which we have become accustomed, only a bit better. It is an entirely different sort of life altogether.

Maimonides is not convinced of this. He agrees that peace has a defining relationship to the way in which we live our lives. Maimonides comments on the story of the four Jewish sages who entered Paradise (Hagigah 2.3–4), where only Rabbi Akiva emerged unscathed. According to Maimonides, Akiva entered, but was not really affected by what he saw there, since his soul was already so calm, as a result of his having reached the heights of moral and intellectual enlightenment. Similar accounts are provided by the kabbalists of Abraham entering Egypt (seen as a demonic realm) and Noah living safely through the flood. Maimonides also refers to Moses' death being equivalent to a kiss, in that the distance between his life and his death was as slight as a kiss and the transition was as easy. These individuals were all at peace, and as such they found it easy to survive any difficulties in which they might find themselves. It is important to note, though, that their state of being at peace was founded on a solid basis of knowledge and virtuous behavior. This was not just an attitude or mental state that they managed to adopt, it came about as a result of their having achieved a balance in their lives by orienting themselves appropriately with respect to the nature of reality. This as we shall see is very much of a theme in Jewish accounts of peace. Peace by itself is not of great significance, it has to be linked with other aims. This comes out in the story of the four sages entering Paradise, they all had different experiences because they had each achieved different levels of understanding and perfection. Akiva who had really perfected himself was able to enter in peace and leave in peace, and the impression one gets is that it is only possible to leave in peace if one can enter in peace. Of the other sages, one died, one became a heretic and one went mad!

Peace as boring

Let us concentrate here on the nature of life in a state of peace. Would it not be very boring? One of the features of many of the novels and films about utopian life is that it often comes over as tedious, in that life no longer has much flavor if it is entirely safe and regulated, and if ordinary antagonisms are dissipated. Of course, it might be preferable to live a peaceful and risk-free life to a bellicose and dangerous life, but the advocates of peace do not argue that this is a better state of affairs than its contrary; they argue that this is the perfect state of affairs where we live a complete and wholesome life, where we become who we really are, as it were. They could argue that perhaps we should get used to a level of boredom, that this is natural and is a small price to pay for safety. Yet, it is difficult to think of oneself being charged a price at all during the messianic age, and were a charge to arise then in what respects is the age messianic at all?

Maimonides' account of the messianic age has the advantage of being about a society that we can all recognize, since it is so much like our society. The laws of nature are all the same, the laws of religion remain the same also. All that has changed is that the Jews have returned to their country. The peace that would eventuate is then a peace that we can understand, since it is precisely the same sort of peace with which we are currently familiar. It is coming home from a hard day at work and relaxing in front of the fire or TV, it is looking forward to the annual vacation, it is the quiet in the evening when the children are in bed and the road outside is not busy for a while. The sort of perfect peace that Abravanel advocates is difficult to understand and make agreeable. It involves such a radical change in human nature and the corresponding practice of politics that we do not really know what it would mean. More importantly, would it leave enough of the trials and excitement of everyday life to make the resulting respite desirable? We often say that it would be wonderful if people stopped fighting and cooperated totally. There is a Hebrew song with the lines "Wouldn't it be pleasant if everyone acted as though they were brothers?" Of course, brothers do not make a particularly good account of themselves in the Bible, one thinks of Jacob and Esau, of Joseph and his brothers, of Cain and Abel (the first brothers), even of the later relationships between the descendents of Ishmael and Isaac. But putting this to one side, suppose that human relations were characterized by love and harmony at every stage. Would this be desirable as part of a state of total peace? It might well be better than a state of nature in which everyone was violently opposed to everyone else, and yet the opposite of that state is not necessarily an environment in which everyone loves everyone else. A bit of antagonism in public and private life, like a pinch of salt in one's food, often adds spice and flavor to human affairs.

This suggests that as so often Maimonides has a more appropriate grasp of the topic than many of his critics. The idea that the messianic age is going to be rather similar to our age does reflect what might be regarded as the realism of Judaism. Maimonides is particularly clear on a criterion for a false messiah as being someone who advocates even a tiny change in halakhah, Jewish law. Halakhah will persist in its present form in the messianic period since the basis of relationships between human beings, and between us and God, will remain the same. So peace in the messianic period will maintain its connections with states of affairs that are conflictual, and preserve its status as being a contrast with those states. The sort of wholeness involved in peace is not then a total state of perfect wholeness; this presumably is not attainable in ordinary human society, but will always be partial and imperfect. But its imperfection is what makes it have the characteristics it does have, and so we have to see peace as really having a relative rather than absolute status.

Like many religions, Judaism places a lot of emphasis on distinctions, distinctions between the sacred and the profane, between the Sabbath and

the rest of the week, between the Jew and the Gentile, and between peace
and conflict. What is interesting about distinctions like this is that each
polarity relies on the other to work. That is, if there are no ordinary days
of the week, then there is no Sabbath. The whole point of the Sabbath is to
contrast with the other days of the week. Even the study of Torah itself is
not supposed to be the exclusive activity of those who wish to live a worthwhile life, they are encouraged to combine that study with earning one's living through ordinary activities. The study of Torah should be *lishmah*, done
for its own sake and not carried out in order to earn money or a living. Why
is this? Surely if the Torah is such an important source of information and
spiritual guidance Jews would be best advised to spend all their time concentrating on it. What could be more important that studying it, and why
should one do anything else? Studying the Torah is of course important, but
it is not all-important. If one studies it to the exclusion of everything else
one will not really understand it, because one needs to understand the
world that it describes in order to appreciate it fully. To understand that
world one has to participate in its daily activities, one has to involve oneself
in what ordinarily takes place in that world.

One might say the same sort of thing about peace. Peace is important, but
it is not all-important. There are other significant aims of human activity
apart from peace, and one would not be able to understand or appreciate
peace if that is the only guiding principle of one's life. A state of perfect
peace would not be agreeable unless it contrasted with periods of conflict,
just as the Sabbath would lose its flavor unless it contrasted with ordinary
days of the week. So while Judaism values peace, it adopts a realistic attitude to its implementation and to its role in the notion of the worthwhile
life. There are certainly claims that look ambitious. For example, there
are these passages "Great is peace, for God is called peace" (Judges 6:24),
"The Messiah is called peace"(Isa 9:5), and "Israel is called peace"
(Zech 8:12). But we are also told: "The world rests on three things; on
justice, on truth, and on peace" (*Pirkei Avot* (Ethics of the Fathers)1.12).
Notice the links between these three concepts. Peace without justice and
truth is not worth having, hence the three principles are conjoined. It is this
trend of realism that runs throughout much of the thinking in Judaism
about peace, and it is a trend that we should bear in mind when trying to
understand the various claims that are made on this topic. Like other religions Judaism values peace, but it does not value peace exclusively and it
connects the value of peace with other important values. When we discuss
the views of a religion on peace surely this is the way forward, to forego the
lofty sentiments and empty phrases and instead to concentrate on linking
peace with other realistic human goals. Only in that way will our thinking
on the topic have real content.

Chapter 9

The intellectual versus the natural

Large Jewish communities were established in Eastern Europe from the fifteenth century until they were destroyed by the Nazis in the twentieth century, a disaster from which the Jewish world has never fully recovered. It is not only the loss of so many people but also the powerhouse of Jewish tradition and learning that was based in Eastern Europe that is now entirely gone from there. To a degree, it has survived in different and more welcoming locations, but these have not really managed to recreate what was lost, merely providing a weak taste of what was a powerful cultural liquor. But an argument from eighteenth-century Eastern Europe has continued today in one form or another, and this argument is linked with the attitude we are to have toward religion. Is religion something to be treated very seriously and described as a difficult and technical process that has to be undergone because it is important? Or is it less of an intellectual task but more of an emotional commitment and something that we can acquire and follow quite naturally? There is today in many religions, including Judaism, a basic divide between those who find in the traditional forms of prayer and practice a fulfilling spiritual path as against those who seek to develop new ways of being religious, new ceremonies and rituals which reflect what they see as a smoother and less artificial form of worship.

Together with this debate is the question of what it is to be religious. This might seem not to be much of an issue, since one either is or is not religious, but in fact it is a significant issue in Judaism, since some argue that only a very committed attitude to piety is acceptable, while others support a more relaxed attitude. What is interesting in this discussion is how it helps us define the nature of piety and bring out its problematic status in religion. A very high standard of religious behavior might serve to denigrate the practice of others and also be seen as a sign of self-satisfaction. On the other hand, we might well expect Jews to exhibit some form of religiosity, especially if they claim some enthusiasm for their religion. How to get the balance right here remains a potent issue for debate, and it has a significant historical source.

A controversy arose between two groups of East European Jews, the Mitnagdim and the Hasidim. This controversy is worth discussing since it has remained persistent in Jewish culture in one form or another. The Mitnagdim were supporters of the Vilna Gaon (1720–97), a thinker of forbidding solemnity, who developed what can only be called a pietist form of Judaism. This called for a minute examination of personal morality combined with the strict enforcement of halakhah, interpreted in what is often described as a narrow way. The Hasidim were supporters of the Besht, whose real name was Israel ben Eleazar (1700–60). Besht stands for Baal Shem Tov, master of the good name literally, and he was a charismatic figure who advocated a more mystical and emotional interpretation of Judaism. In its initial stages Hasidism was even quite antinomian, critical at least of some of the traditional laws and regulations as they were currently interpreted. Later on it became much more like other forms of orthodoxy, although still combined with some of its original distinctive features. This antinomian tendency was overemphasized in his many books on the Hasidim, by Martin Buber who saw it as important counterbalances for what he regarded as the cold and formal version of religion that represented Orthodox Judaism in Central Europe in the twentieth century. This is exemplified in a delightful story of Hasidic life according to which Rabbi Schmelke of Nickolsburg, it was said, never learnt anything from his teacher the Maggid of Mezritch, since whenever the latter quoted the Bible and said "and the Lord spoke" Schmelke would begin shouting in amazement "The Lord spoke, the Lord spoke" and had to be carried out of the room because he would not stop shouting.

The town versus the country

Jewish life had changed a lot from the eighteenth to the twentieth century. In earlier times, communities in Eastern Europe were still largely rurally based, and one of the things that Hasidism stressed was closeness to nature and the celebration of nature. The Vilna Gaon, as his name suggests, represented the propriety of the city as opposed to the wild frontier, the stately values of an urban community as opposed to the folk beliefs of their rural coreligionists. Jews living in small and self-contained country communities could develop feelings of unity and fraternity that are less easy to acquire in the city, and Hasidism is full of stories of how whole communities were imbued with a particular form of religiosity, since all aspects of everyday social life were carried out within a relatively isolated village (shtetl) environment. In such a context, it is not difficult for everyone in a community to go around asking everyone else for forgiveness before the Day of Atonement, for example, or for a particular religious issue to energize and dominate an isolated community, as we read in the accounts of Hasidism.

The Jewish calendar is lunar and comes from an agricultural tradition in early Israel. Some of its festivals are quite strange in an urban context since they involve so much agricultural imagery. Sukkot for example, the festival of Tabernacles, commemorates the way in which the Jews leaving Egypt for the Promised Land lived in huts or booths (tabernacles). Jews in the diaspora are familiar with the experience of shivering in their sukkahs, if they live in northern climes. Most Jews in Europe and North America are very far from a rural lifestyle and from the sort of intimate community that existed in the past when opportunities for alternative lifestyles were few and far between. It was in this atmosphere that Hasidism flourished, and it is an interesting question whether it can really survive in its full sense anywhere else, since that closeness to nature might be thought to be so important to at least its original constitution.

Hasidism

What is Hasidism? *Hasid* in Hebrew means righteous and the early Hasidim devised for themselves a form of worship which they felt brought them closer to God and also closer to nature. They would sometimes pray in the open, and would emphasize the significance of dance and movement in general in their devotions. Rather redolent of Islamic Sufism, and Paul Fenton has argued that one can link the two movements, Hasidism established a more direct route to God, one that could be initiated without an immense amount of legal knowledge or learning. This is not to say that there is anything wrong with such education, but it could get in the way of the development of our emotional side, and this is perhaps more important for us in our search for proximity to God than is satisfying some academic standard.

This contrast exists in all religions, of course, and not only in religion, but in other aspects of cultural life also, like art, literature, and especially sport. One wants to say that there should be some mean between the passion of the Hasid and the cold logic of the Mitnag, but it is difficult to define such a position. Certainly there is much in Judaism to support such a compromise, in particular the insistence on a mixture of legality and personal enthusiasm for the enterprise of addressing and approaching God. There are many Hasidic stories in which the Hasid warns his family that he does not know whether he will survive saying his prayers, since any form of possible contact with the deity could result in anything at all happening, even disaster. This is certainly not the attitude of someone saying his prayers just out of habit or tradition. Yet this remarkable attitude could hardly be our customary attitude when praying, since surely for most of us it would completely drain our spiritual reserves. In some ways praying as an activity militates against this sort of enthusiasm for thinking about God, something that Buber talks of often in his disinclination to participate in the rituals of Judaism.

Prayer might be compared to the institution of marriage. As we know, people who are married may enjoy a passionate relationship, and one would hope that at some stage at least passion would exist. But as we also know from bitter experience of how human beings wane in their affections, marriages often end and love with them. It would be wrong to expect a marriage to continue for many decades at the same level of passion at which it started, but some do. Yet it has to be said also that marriages may continue for many years at a different level of affection, not perhaps passionate love any more, but rather companionship, mutual consideration, and a pleasant familiarity. Those romantically inclined may despise this sort of relationship, in just the same way that they may disapprove of the ways in which someone who prays frequently may sink into the familiarity and comfort of the prayer ritual without perhaps achieving a passionate attitude toward God in his devotions. In fact, it may be the companionship of his friends and companions while praying, the tea afterwards and the conversation about the news that brings them together more than anything else. These are not diversions from prayer, but activities of which the Almighty might well approve.

Piety

There is an interesting text in the Talmud (*Berakhot* 4a): "A prayer of David...Keep my soul, for I am pious (*ki hasid ani*)" [Ps 86:1–1]. Levi and R. Isaac [comment]. The one says: Thus spoke David before the Holy One blessed be He: "Master of the universe, am I not pious (*hasid*)? All the kings of the East and West sleep to the third hour [of the day], but I, at midnight I rise to give thanks unto You." We might think that David is being a bit presumptuous here, by contrasting himself favorably with other kinds with respect to God. This is an essential ingredient in genuine piety. It is said of David that "No man in Israel abased himself for the sake of the commandments more than David...like the baby that has just come out of its mother's womb and is not too proud to suck at his mother's breasts, so is my [David's] soul within me, for I am not ashamed to learn Torah even from the least in Israel" (*Numbers Rabbah* 4.20, p. 137). David is often portrayed as an ideal since he tries always to be modest— "Neither do I exercise myself in things too great or things too marvellous for me" (Ps. 131:1). Here he follows the principle, much approved of in the Talmud, "Do not enquire into things that are too wonderful for you, do not investigate what is hidden from you, enquire into things that are permitted to you, you have no concern with wonders" (the discussion in *Numbers Rabbah* illustrates this advice by pointing to aspects of David's life). David is supposed to have got up every night at midnight to study Torah until the break of dawn when he would attend to affairs of state (*Berakhot* 3, already mentioned).

David proves his piety by the fact that all other kings insist on pomp and ceremony, while he is different. He deals with complicated halakhic questions, very technical issues that involve the laws of ritual purity and impurity. He was the king, and David could have ordered his underlings to attend to such questions. He was pious or *hasid* because he did not think it was beneath his dignity to serve his people, even in troublesome issues of ritual purity. This Talmudic passage suggests that the criteria of genuine piety or love of God are humility, the assumption of personal responsibility, and commitment to truth, a willingness to learn from others whatever our rank in society. We should avoid at all costs *yuharah*, presumptuousness. Often religion can serve as an arena for personal wealth and self-importance, and this must be avoided at all costs. Hence the emphasis on the significance of combining secular work with Torah.

False piety and self-deception

There are differences in the forms of prayer and rituals of the Jews who originate in Europe (the Ashkenazim) and those from the Middle East and North Africa (the Sefardim). It is customary in most Sefardic congregations for congregants to remain seated when the Ten Commandments are read as part of the morning's Torah reading. The logic of this custom is that the entire Torah is holy; to stand up for this particular section would imply that the rest of the Torah is of lesser status. On the other hand, the usual custom among Ashkenazim is for the congregation to rise for the reading of the Ten Commandments. This custom calls for the symbolic reenactment of the original revelation at Mount Sinai, when the people of Israel were standing. Both customs are perfectly legitimate and deeply rooted in Jewish tradition. Suppose some congregants decided to stand up for the reading of the Ten Commandments, even though the congregation's custom was to remain seated. Those who stood felt they were demonstrating respect for the Torah. Some legal authorities would say that these individuals were guilty of haughtiness and disrespect for the congregation. This is an exhibition of false piety.

If we could ask those who stood whether they had intended to demonstrate false piety or show disrespect to the congregation, they would surely reply in the negative. They would say that they were simply trying to perform a pious deed, honoring the Ten Commandments by rising to their feet. But in disregarding the community's custom, they were saying (through their action) that they showed more respect to the Ten Commandments than did everyone else in the synagogue, that they knew better and were more religiously observant than the rabbis and sages of all the communities that remained seated for the reading of the Decalogue. Their motives could not really be for the sake of Heaven. They were driven by the desire to display their piety. This is often called *yuharah*. This might seem harsh, since the individuals concerned may say that they are merely obeying the law as they see it. However, from a legal point of view, for example, on Sukkot, when it is a mitzvah for Jews to eat and sleep in the sukkah, one should desist if it is raining or cold. The roof is not supposed to cover the inside completely, it should have enough holes in it for the stars to be visible, and there is an exemption on sitting in it if the rain comes in. To ignore the exemption and still sit in the sukkah is presumptuous and is likely to lead to arrogance. If one wishes to adopt a practice that the law does not require, then he should do so privately. To display in public one's extreme piety in this way is thoroughly objectionable.

In the rabbinic literature there is a spirited discussion recognizing the dangers of excessive piety, but wondering whether one could practice a higher standard in private. The general answer is that one can, but here one has to be careful of self-delusion. Is the additional practice genuinely done out of an attitude of humility and devotion to God or to make one feel better about oneself? According to Scholem, many kabbalists maintain that the Sabbath is the day when "the light of the upper world bursts into the profane world in which man lives during the six days of the week" (1970 p. 139). This is reflected in Buber's account of the Hasid who fasted from sabbath/Shabat to Shabat in order to increase his pleasure in the Shabat, and who felt great satisfaction in managing to hang on one Friday afternoon before breaking his fast. His rabbi said "Patchwork" when he heard about this, implying that his life was not unified in terms of ritual and feeling. It is only right to point out that in the story the Hasid himself realized what was wrong with his practice, since as soon as he felt that sense of satisfaction he drank, even though it was not yet Shabat.

This brings us to another intriguing issue, whether it would be acceptable to do something forbidden by the law if it was for the right motive. During the civil rights campaign in the United States, some Orthodox rabbis were placed in difficulties when offered food that might be kosher, but might not, by their black friends. They could explain that they were not permitted to eat food that was not clearly kosher, but this could shame the giver, and that is something one is forbidden to do. It might even be that sharing food with an oppressed group would be a powerful political signal that one acknowledged their equality, since perhaps their opponents did not feel comfortable accepting their food or even eating with them. Yet how could an Orthodox Jew intend to do the right thing politically while doing the wrong thing halakhically? Reform Jews would have little difficulty here, since for them the intention is far more significant than the legal ruling, and this brings out the rather one-dimensional life of the Reform Jew.

It is for this reason that Maimonides disagreed with Aristotle on the appropriate attitude toward humility. Aristotle argued that one should adopt a moderate attitude to feelings of self-importance, and if one is really important then it is certainly permissible to express this and feel this. Of course, one should not take that attitude too far, since then it would become ridiculous and inappropriate, but we should feel pleasure in our accomplishments, if we have any. This leaves out God, though, and we should appreciate from the theocentric point of view that whatever we have we have because of God, and our efforts at doing the right thing are a pale reflection of divine action. Therefore we cannot be humble enough if we are to take an accurate view of our position in reality, however *hasid* or pious we might take ourselves to be. In fact, being extreme in our humility, like David, avoids the danger of extremism in the pursuit of religion, since we will never feel that we have achieved everything that we could, and will question our motives and our interpretation of our duty frequently. This ensures that we would find it difficult to insist on a particular rendering of how we should live, or indeed whether someone should live at all, which would produce the sort of religion that ends up with extreme actions like murdering people or violently insisting on a particular form of religious observance. On the other hand, we really should avoid extremes in every other aspect of our lives: "You shall faithfully observe my commandments. I am the Lord. You shall not profane my holy name, that I may be sanctified (Lev 22:31–32)." This includes not going to extremes and acting in ways that reflect badly on the community. It is important for people to consider the impact that their behavior has on God, especially in the case of the Jews. "You are My servant, O Israel, in whom I will be glorified" (Isa 49:3) implies that the actions of the Jews can affect the way in which God is regarded and so those actions have to be considered and appropriate.

The difficulty of being Jewish

This brings out a significant difference between the Mitnagdim and the Hasidim of the past, although the distinction between them takes on a much subtler form today. The Hasidim might be called the optimists when it came to the links between our moral stature and our actions, since they emphasized the intent that we have when we act and the links that exist between us and a God who is basically on our side. This link comes out nicely in the many stories of how God forgives and rewards us for doing things for the right reason but perhaps not in precisely the right way. There is the story of the simple Jew who went to synagogue and could not pray because he did not know how to read or how to say his prayers. So he addressed God in his heart with this information and just recited the alphabet, leaving it to God to arrange the letters as he wishes. God is said in the story to have appreciated that prayer more than all the other more proper prayers that were said in the synagogue service that day. There are some examinations where students are rewarded for getting the technique right even though the result is wrong. Here the worshipper gets the result right but the technique wrong, or so it might seem. But if you see prayer as intimately tied in with the mental processes of the worshipper, as Judaism certainly does, then the worshipper in the story got the technique right and the result wrong, since he only knew how to do something very basic and had no hopes of attaining the formal end that everyone else could.

The Mitnagdim disapproved of this sort of story. Surely, they would say, it is not difficult to learn how to pray properly, many people of unimpressive intellectual capacity manage to learn how to pray. Some people pray but do not really understand what the words mean, and some people understand what the words mean but do not think of them while they are reciting them. Still others understand what the words mean and think about them as they use them but do not agree with them. The Vilna Gaon took a very serious attitude to prayer and followed what might be regarded as a rather severe line, which was popular at that time in the German Protestant Church, and this implies that we have to examine ourselves very thoroughly before we can be satisfied, or even get on the path of being satisfied, with our approach to prayer. Both intent and practice have to be synchronized, so that we not only think the right thing but also do it, and we frequently examine ourselves to ensure that we are getting it right. One of the features of frequent and substantial prayer is that it does encourage this sort of attitude of self-examination, in the sense that if we think that we are communicating with God many times in the day then we will want to be doing the right things and have the appropriate thoughts. Of course, there is the danger of self-deception and false pride, to which we have already alluded, in getting things right, especially difficult things, which a simpler lifestyle might have avoided. A simpler lifestyle might be thought to include just going through the ordinary rituals of traditional Jewish prayer without the sorts of introspection that might otherwise be involved.

Reviving ritual

It might seem harsh to criticize the Hasid who fasts from Sabbath to Sabbath. After all he has taken special steps to establish his credentials as a hasid, his actions are supererogatory and so surely especially deserving of praise. It is quite common for observant Jews to make a special fuss over the Sabbath, to wear particular clothes and eat off certain dishes, and similarly for the various festivals, since they need to be marked in some way that emphasizes their special nature. We have already seen how people who try to emphasize their piety are sometimes criticized for lacking humility and wishing to set themselves up above others. There are Orthodox Jews, for example, who vie with each other on the time that they wait after eating meat products before they consume milk products in order to observe the law on not mixing meat and milk, which itself is a derivation on the instruction in the Bible to the Jews not to cook a kid in its mother's milk. Some wait two hours, some four, some six, and so on, as though one's piety increases proportionately with the time of the gap. It might be argued that one ought to follow the rule of the community of which one is a member, in just the same way that it is appropriate to speak the language of the country in which one resides, since this represents the local way of doing things. Why should one set oneself up as better than everyone else by doing something different?

This brings us to an interesting point, the question of how far we are morally obliged to understand ourselves if we are to act well. The attempt at being as pure as possible in one's performance of duty leads to the danger of being unbalanced in life, since ritual might be seen as embodying the rules of balance. When we seek to go beyond ritual, or create our own rituals, we perhaps run the risk of going too far in one direction or another. The beauty of ritual is that it takes over our life and enables us not to think about how we do what we do, but frees our mind up to think about why we do it. That is, it allows us to concentrate on more important things, since the less important things are already taken care of. One also has to accept, for this sort of argument to work, that ritual is devised by someone who understands how to align our spiritual and physical needs, not difficult to argue if one accepts that it has an ultimately divine source.

An issue with ritual, and one that the early Hasidim latched onto, is that it can become automatic and unthinking in a negative way, so that it merely validates a feeling of customary action and a degree of self-satisfaction, and nothing more. There is not much merit in this from a religious point of view or so it might seem. Judaism in many texts stresses the importance of understanding what we do while we are doing it, especially prayer. The idea of saying a prayer on almost every occasion is the idea of keeping God in one's mind throughout everything, surely a highly desirable religious aim. But it can become an empty formula and the more involved the ritual, the more formulaic it might become. This is because the more involved one is in thinking about how to perform the ritual, the less attention one might spend on other topics. One thinks in particular about the long rituals in the Gormenghast novels by Mervyn Peake which seem to have no point except that they represented tradition.

To a lot of Jews today, and no doubt in the past also, much Jewish ritual has a Gormenghast connotation. It was to a certain extent for this reason that the Hasidic movement arose in the first place and it might be regarded as the ultimate irony that it has devolved very much into the school of its enemies, the Mitnagdim, in modern times. This is something that often happens with revolutions, however, in that they become what they have been fighting, as the original spirit of the movement settles down and becomes subject to the same forces of stability as the original way of doing things. Nonetheless, the issue of what in Jewish life counts as piety remains a very live issue, and we have examined here a range of approaches to it.

Chapter 10

The "norm" versus the "deviant"

Sex and gender in Judaism

Like many religions, Judaism is often very negative in its comments on those it sees as the other. Sometimes the Other are non-Jews, but often they are Jews but nonmales or nonheterosexuals. There is no doubt but that the Bible and the major Jewish commentaries are very critical of homosexuality, and also place women in an entirely different role in Jewish society than men. In traditional Judaism there is a horror, for example, regarding menstruation and the fact that women periodically bleed is taken to be a good reason for excluding them from a wide range of public religious tasks and responsibilities. Women's religious role is taken to be primarily domestic, so that if she spends most of her time bringing up the children and looking after the home and husband, she has done what she ought to do. This does not mean that she need not pray, but these prayers can be abbreviated as compared with those said by men and can be based in the home since she has no obligation to go to the synagogue. And of course it goes without saying that women have not participated on the whole in running Jewish organizations in the past like synagogues, yeshivas (colleges), and religious courts (the beth din which exists in most parts of the Jewish world and adjudicates on issues of halakhah or Jewish law).

This is not to say that women have not been important, though, since there is no lack of evidence that they have played a very visible role in Jewish history. The Bible, for example, gives an important role to a range of powerful women, who played a decisive role, in so far as they could, in Jewish history. It is also worth saying that despite the legal penalties under which they found themselves Jewish women have been playing a significant role in the past and present. It is worth agreeing also, as apologists of traditional roles for women in religion always urge, that the position of running the family is by no means a minor role, and might easily be regarded as the most important thing to do in society. After all, the family is the locus of future generations and through their work here women are at the very heart of Judaism as a living and continuing tradition. All this is true, but nonetheless it has to be said that women in traditional Judaism play what can only be described as a secondary role. In the more modern versions of Conservative and Reform Judaism, women play very much an equal role with men, with women rabbis, women called up to read the Torah in synagogue, indeed, women given precisely the same role as men. The issue really relates now only to traditional Judaism. Even here some women are seeking to maintain the traditions while making the change that women are to be regarded as having no essential differences from men as far as their religious functions extend or at least less differences than was thought to be the case in tradition.

Similar remarks might be made about homosexuality. Within traditional Judaism this is still regarded as a sin, and there are of course explicit passages in the Bible condemning nonheterosexual practices. Within nontraditional Judaism there is a general acceptance that gay lifestyles are perfectly compatible with Judaism, and there are openly gay rabbis, synagogue members, and so on. Even within traditional Judaism there are individuals who are gay and who at the same time regard themselves as Orthodox Jews, and yet who also acknowledge their gayness as not necessarily something to suppress and hide. They ask the question, and it is a similar question that Jewish feminists raise, as to the importance of the ban on homosexuality. Suppose one accepted everything else about the religion except the rules dealing with women or with gay people, what would be lost?

Centrality of gender and sexuality roles in Judaism

One problem with the approach being followed in this book is that the idea of an essence to Judaism is not being used normatively to establish the boundaries of the religion. The normal way of assessing a potential change in a religion is to ask how it relates to the essence of the religion, and we can see that by taking it out of the religion, and seeing what really changes as a result. Whatever might be thought to be the main principles of Judaism are really unaffected by a more egalitarian approach to gender and sexuality or so it might seem. So women are called up to read the Torah in synagogues (only men receive *aliyot* or invitations to go up to read the Torah in traditional Judaism), girls have bat mitzvah (precisely equivalent to bar mitzvah, but not celebrated in that form at all in traditional Judaism), and there are women rabbis. Then the traditional texts are purged of their sexist references to women, and the Bible's references to the penalties for homosexual acts (stoning) are toned down or reinterpreted. Gay men and women are welcomed into the rabbinate, and into congregations, and the priority given to marriage and children in the religious literature is emphasized less. Finally, the rules for divorce are equalized for men and women so that the role of the *agunah*, the wife chained to a husband who refuses to give her a *get* (Jewish divorce) and who as a result cannot remarry becomes a thing of history. Would that solve the situation and establish a new way of living, a Jewish life that recognizes more adequately different kinds of individuals in the community?

It is tempting to agree and suggest that there is no good reason for the future to represent the past faithfully if we decide that the past was based on an objectionable patriarchy. On the other hand, it should not be forgotten that the very different roles of men and women in Judaism did not presumably come about just by chance. It was very beneficial for men if their wives saw their own domestic role as preeminent, since then the men could concentrate on what they found most valuable, Jewish learning. In Eastern Europe it was even the case in some communities that wives would devote their lives not only to looking after their husbands and children, but they would also run stores and small businesses in order to free their spouses up for the real business of life, studying. Persuading women that their real role was outside of the synagogue and the yeshiva (college) was excellent for those who could then co-opt the effort of those women to preserve their advantage. As a result of the years of unfair treatment Jewish women are participants in a system in which the main roles have predominantly gone to men and this played and continues to play a huge part in defining the expectations of both men and women in every level and variety of Judaism.

Whether traditional Jewish texts can continue to be used is a very real question if we are to take seriously the notion of Jewish feminism. Those texts are often predicated on the absence of women, or their absence from an active role in their own history, and so they might be seen as reflecting men's attitudes to what happened, rather than the attitude of human beings, Jewish or otherwise. It is difficult not to hear the tetchy male response in much that we read in the Mishnah and Talmud. Perhaps more significantly the main biblical characters are nearly all male. There are of course important women in the Bible, but they are generally acted upon rather than being the main characters and as such might seem to predicate a general lack of power and authority in the female role.

Different and equal?

There are two ways around this apparent difficulty and neither is very successful. One is to push the different but equal line and suggest that although men and women in the Bible do not do the same sorts of things both are important and indeed complementary, and both carry out important tasks, which could not succeed unless we all stuck to our different activities. It is certainly true that if one had to choose between the competing importance of going to synagogue to say morning prayers and staying at home to look after children, it seems quite clearly to be the latter. After all, morning prayers can be said anywhere, but children have to be looked after precisely where they are and when they require the care. The consequences of missing prayers pales into insignificance compared to the consequences of neglecting children, an inaction that may result in their harm or even death. Yet as has often been pointed out, there is an inverse relationship between the importance of an activity and how we regard the people who do it. The "equal but different" slogan might work if we really treated people equally for doing different things, but we do not. In apartheid South Africa, it might have made sense to use that slogan if in fact the segregated services and facilities between the races were equal or similar to each other but of course they were not.

The group which benefits from an unequal distribution of resources is usually most likely to defend it and point to a specious kind of equality which is supposed to justify the relationship. One way of assessing whether equality really can involve different roles is to think about role reversal. So for example were a husband to stay at home to look after the children and the wife go to synagogue in his stead, he could do almost everything she could do with the children. But she could do very little in a traditional synagogue. She could not sit with the men, she could not be called up to read the Torah, she would be largely an observer in what went on in the synagogue. "Different and unequal" is a far better slogan to describe this sort of situation. In the traditional series of morning blessings there is a prayer recited by men which thanks God for not having made him a woman, while the female equivalent is to thank God for having made her in accordance with his will. It is clear what is going on in these prayers, and it is telling that both men and women do not thank God for having made them in accordance with his will, which would of course be entirely appropriate. If God is thanked for not having done something then the implication surely is that what he has not done is better not done.

There are other ways to take this passage in the *siddur* (prayerbook), however. When she blesses God for having made her in accordance with his will (*ratzon*) this could mean that he makes her like him, like his will or personality. When a man thanks God for having not made him a woman, this could be a reference to the fact that he is less close to God and will have to control himself as well as the world outside of himself, whereas women are seen as naturally coming close to the divine style of nurturing and care. This is a possible interpretation of those blessings, but not the most obvious one. In any case, it sets up men as active and very much in the public world, while women are consigned to the nurturing role. Perhaps the latter should be regarded more highly than the former, but generally they are not, and so yet again the idea of gender equality is seen as very distant from traditional Judaism.

The direction of change

Yet, if the old ways and texts are hopelessly compromised, what can we do? We could produce entirely new texts, but it is not clear what that would involve in a religion that sees itself as centered around a particular ancient book. Or we could tweak the existing texts and bowdlerize them to produce more progressive forms of what already exists. So, for example, we could replace those parts of the Bible which do not display much of an egalitarian spirit with others that are better, or less bad, from a progressive point of view.

Let us take some examples here. As we saw in the chapter on kabbalah, the term Shekhinah is feminine and reflects a notion of the holy that involves the female side of the divine. One could construct a new language about God which really portrays him as not male, but as having no gender, or even as predominantly female. One can construct new rituals surrounding the Passover Seder, for example, the service which takes place in Jewish homes to commemorate the escape from Egypt. Such new rituals may give women more of a role in the event, perhaps by including new prayers and readings that reflect women in particular. Ritual does change all the time, of course, and there seems no particular reason why changing sensibilities of the roles of men and women, and of queer lifestyles, should not impact on ritual and the prayer book. As has often been pointed out, many of the most traditional Jews today wear the clothing of eighteenth-century Polish nobility, which can hardly be said to have much antiquity. One of the entertaining sights in Israel is people in the heat of the day on the Sabbath walking in Jerusalem in long black coats and fur hats, while other Jews are on the beach on the coast in very few clothes indeed. Which ritual is the more traditional? Well, perhaps long ago in the past people still lay around in the open enjoying the sun with few clothes on, whereas it is doubtful whether anyone walked around with a fur hat on his head! Rituals change and have to change if religions are to survive, and there is nothing as variable as what counts as tradition. So this looks like a powerful argument for the feminist. rewriting of texts and rituals to make them more inclusive and the gay reevaluation of laws and biblical readings to ensure that sexual orientation does not make some members of the community feel excluded.

Correcting Judaism?

We should be careful before we go down this road, however. We do not necessarily want to sanitize the texts we use until they accord entirely with our own views on things. One of the delightful aspects of dealing with texts is working with texts that are difficult to accept, let alone understand. Why does the Bible make explicit demands that Jews not participate in homosexual acts? Perhaps it was because they were identified with idolatrous practices, or perhaps because homosexual sex does nothing to increase the size of the population, quite the reverse. Perhaps it is because such practices are seen as unnatural and offend against some notion of how sex ought to take place. The link with idolaters is clear in some of Maimonides' discussion of lesbianism, which he links with Egypt in *Sefer Mitzvot* quoting Sifra parsha 5, halacha 8.2. The expression *nashim ha-mesolleot zu b'zu* which we find in *Yevamot* 76a and which could be translated as "women writhing around together" is clearly meant to describe a sexual act.

It is worth remembering that when Lot's angelic guests were assaulted by the Sodomites intent no doubt on having their evil way with them, Lot offers the mob his two virginal daughters to no effect. The Sodomites seemed to have other targets in mind. Lot's offer was not just to preserve the sanctity of hospitality, something which we are often told was disregarded in Sodom and the other cities of the plain that came to be destroyed but presumably also to prevent this highly unwelcome form of sexual intercourse. This is a difficult text. Lot appears to be very weak in offering his daughters to the crowd, although at that time they were probably regarded as just part of his property and so easily disposed of in this way. That also is hardly a pleasant notion, and for some the violent end of the cities of the plain, including the small number of innocent people who might well have remained in their midst makes for rather grim reading. One can easily see how a reader might seek to substitute for these passages alternative passages that are more spiritually uplifting, positive or indeed inclusive in their references. On the other hand, we might want to reflect here on how we sometimes do use our families to save us from embarrassment, although Lot perhaps takes this principle rather far here. Yet, it is not entirely unknown even today for parents to use their children as ways of reflecting their own achievements or to compensate for their own lack of achievement, and this is something on which we might wish to meditate when reading about Lot and his relaxed way with his daughters' virginity.

This rather unappetizing story has an appropriate and equally unappetizing conclusion, when Lot's daughters seduce him while he is drunk, allegedly because they thought that otherwise humanity would be wiped out. Again, we might like to reflect on how if we try to exploit those weaker than us, they may return the favor when they become stronger and with interest. These may not seem to be very elevated topics for discussion, nor even especially religious, yet they reflect the very realistic nature of much that takes place in the Bible and the commentaries, where readers and hearers are encouraged to relate what scripture reports to their own lives. This can only be successfully done if the scripture contains everything, warts and all.

The Ben Bag Bag strategy

A popular saying is given by Ben Bag Bag in the *Sayings of the Fathers* 5.25. Referring to the Torah he says: "Turn it, and turn it over again, for everything is in it, and think about it, and become old and grey over it, and do not move from it, for you can have no better standard than it." One assumes that this might have been a popular saying, since it is quoted in the Mishnah in Aramaic, the lingua franca in Israel at that time. References to this passage frequently only quote the first part which suggests that we should look at the Torah from a variety of perspectives, which is surely true. But the rest of the quote is important too. Ben Bag Bag is pointing out that the study of this book is not a simple and limited task but could extend over a whole life and indeed a whole series of lifetimes, as the Jewish people, and not only they, study and reflect on the Torah. This could be taken to suggest that instead of ignoring difficult passages, as though we were politely ignoring someone who had made a rude noise, we should work with them and confront them directly. If we are going to pick and choose the passages we want to discuss then we might as well write our own scriptures and discuss them. The problem in such a case would be that of course there would be nothing to discuss, since anything that we produced would be lacking in the depth and difficulty of the Bible and the Talmud. Questions like "how could God have allowed that to happen?" "how could God have done that?," "how could passage A be reconciled with passage B?" and the vital question "What does that mean?" represent an aspect of our struggle with the text.

Growing up with Jewish texts is like growing up with a person, and indeed as a person. I remember being shocked one day when my young daughter told me in front of her friend Ruth, who is black, that she did not like Ruth because she was black. As one can imagine, this amazed her parents, who had never heard her utter a racist comment before in her life, and who also knew that Ruth was one of her best friends. There are ways of dealing with racist comments, and no consensus about the best strategy. Ignoring the comment and changing the subject is not generally recommended as helpful. Yet this is precisely what those who disapprove of aspects of the Bible and the other Jewish works do. When a person annoys us or does something we cannot justify we do not generally wipe him or her out of our lives.

Is the suggestion here that these inconvenient passages are really not so serious that we need stop reading them or discussing them? It might be said that it is only if we are not really horrified by inequalities that we do not get very excited or annoyed by them and continue to use the texts that describe them in favorable terms. Two points are worth making here. One is that what is most dangerous in the Bible as far as equality is concerned is not the explicit negative comments on women and gays, but the implicit establishing of the concept of normality that excludes both women and gays. For example, the *Sayings of the Fathers*, a title that was not selected by chance, repeats several times that gossip with women is to be avoided (1.5). What runs through this and so many other texts is the positing of an ideal of study and scholarship which is strictly male where space for the ideal is bought at the expense of other groups who labor to provide it. It is this largely invisible work force who toil away and are only occasionally referred to, and then in patronizing ways, who make possible the construction of the *hacham*, the sage. The division of labor is regarded as so natural that it does not even need discussing in most of the Jewish literature and it is this absence of discussion rather than the few explicit and negative remarks on women that have been so effective in preserving for men a favored role in Jewish life.

A second reason for doubting the strategy of picking and mixing our texts at will is the doctrine that the Torah came from heaven. If we see it as having been composed by a bunch of grumpy middle-aged men then we shall be much more likely to edit the text until we arrive at something acceptable. It is much more interesting though to take it as coming from heaven since then there must be good reasons, if we could only discover them, for the apparent inconsistencies and even immoralities in the text. We do not literally have to believe that the text came directly from heaven, but we need to think that it is important and has a foot at least in a deep grasp of how things really are. This is why when our friends behave disgracefully we do not necessarily reject them and cast them out of our lives, despite what we might threaten. We may have a deep relationship with a person, which will survive even shocking changes of personality and revelations along the way. This is not to say that the relationship will be unchanged nor that it could not come to an end, but it need not end just because of something that took place and does not fit in with our view of what should have happened. The relationship might have been deep enough to persist in one form or another despite the unfortunate behavior. One might even say that that is what makes relationships interesting and why we continue to read and find interest in the Bible.

A final argument for retaining and working with the passages in the Jewish writings that we find objectionable is that there are so many of them. The Bible is full of rape, murder, incest, cheating, and so on, and sometimes these acts are carried out by the heroes in the text. It is a very realistic text, people are presented with all their defects, and often it seems as if the more defects the better. As the Talmud puts it, "The world goes its normal way" (*Avodah Zarah* 54b). With reference to this passage Maimonides says that no one should imagine that the normal course of events will be transformed in the Messianic period or that there will be a change in the order of creation (*Laws of Kings* 12.1). If this is not going to happen in the messianic period then in the normal run of things we should expect what we are accustomed to happen to prevail. So we will find all sorts of human interaction described in the text, some approved and some condemned and we need to make sense of what we find there, in just the same way that we need to find sense in the world in which we find ourselves living.

This sounds very much like a recipe for just letting everything continue as it has in the past, since the suggestion is to leave the text as it is and study all of it as though it were all equally appropriate. Yet is not some of it rather objectionable, especially those parts that are clearly sexist and anti-gay?

One response is to reiterate what has already been argued, and that is that the most challenging parts of the Bible and other Jewish texts are not so much the explicit places in which objectionable remarks are made about groups of people but the general tone of the text which ignores or hides those same groups. We do not make things good again by removing some of the most obvious examples of what is difficult to accept but by going root and branch at the text itself. And that we can only do if we preserve the text and as Ben Bag Bag says, turn it and turn it again, so that we can in the end examine it carefully and decide what we are going to accept and what is going to be bracketed with conditions that makes it acceptable and comprehensible.

Respecting the text

But is this not to display a lack of respect to the text? Are we not saying here that if we dislike what the text says then we are going to change how we see it? How is that working with the text? Well, to take an example here from the Bible, there are a large number of capital offences in that text. Not keeping the Sabbath, engaging in homosexual acts, being a witch, and so on are all punishable by death. The Bible is very clear on this point. Yet, there is a Mishnaic saying that if a court carried out the death penalty even once in seven years they were regarded as murderers (*Makkot* 1.10). Two eminent rabbis, Tarfon and Akiva, say they would never condemn anyone to death. This remark is followed by another rabbi suggesting that such a lax policy would increase the number of murders in the country. Yet the general tone is to criticize the death penalty. Is this because the writers of the Talmud were contemptuous of the Bible and the penalties within it? Certainly not, but it does not follow from the respect they gave that text that they have to follow every rule and regulation blindly. It is for their unthinking acceptance of the platitudes of religion that Job's friends are criticized by God and only pardoned if Job himself will intercede for them, while Job himself with his direct challenge to God and the notion of divine justice is apparently approved of by heaven and rewarded greatly in the end. This might be taken as an indication that we should examine and interpret what we have before us, rather than tear it up and start again.

Chapter 11

Orthodoxy versus Reform

The changes that took place in Judaism in the nineteenth century onwards have their immediate origins in the Enlightenment movement that had such an impact on Europe and what became the United States in the eighteenth century. This movement in the Jewish world, the Haskalah (from the word *sekhel* or wisdom in Hebrew), based itself on taking a rational approach to everything, including religion. As we have seen when looking at the impact of Greek thought on Judaism, the application of rationality to Judaism is hardly a new phenomenon. The Enlightenment had such an impact because for the first time for many centuries Jews were brought into normal civil society and could think of themselves as citizens of individual states, with all the duties and rights that that involved, and so they could raise the issue of how much like everyone else they wanted to be. The stereotype of the Jew as someone speaking a strange language, dressing differently from others, and eating separately came to embarrass many Jews who saw themselves as modern. Would it not be possible, they asked, to make some changes to Judaism so that it fit into the modern world and its society, while of course holding onto the essentials?

The Reform movement bears some resemblances to the much earlier Karaites. The Karaites were critical of the Oral Law, and the Reform movement has very little time for it also, except for decorative reasons. As a result of that attitude they argue for a different approach to the Torah, actually a very different approach from the Karaites. The Karaites had no doubts about the validity of the Torah, and in fact their disapproval of the Oral Law was based on what they took to be its contrast with the Written Law. By contrast, many in the Reform movement were rather skeptical of the Written Law too and especially its status as *torah min ha-shamayim*, as being law from heaven. They tended to argue that although the Torah is no doubt divinely inspired, whether it is literally something that God gave to Moses on Mount Sinai is very dubious. Since it does not all come directly from God, we can discuss what parts we should keep and what parts we can abandon. Changing circumstances may even indicate that parts of the Torah are no longer relevant, and perhaps were only meant to apply to earlier times, while other parts are so general and total in their acceptability that there never could be a time when they would not apply.

Not surprisingly given this thesis the Reform thinkers tend to prefer many of the later works in the Bible as opposed to the Five Books of Moses, since the former tend to stress universal values like justice, sincerity, and monotheism. Some festivals like Purim and Chanukah were initially rather disapproved of by the Reform movement since they seemed not to embody any general desirable virtues apart from survival and it includes a worryingly enthusiastic attitude to revenge. Purim celebrates the survival of the Jews in Persia when Haman, the king's favorite at the time, was intent on destroying them. Chanukah represents the triumph of the Maccabees over the Syrian rulers of Israel and their Greek culture. The Five Books of Moses seem to be a good deal about the tribal rules of a particular group of people at a particular stage in their history, and one wonders why those rules should be regarded as unchanging since everything else in life changes over time. Perhaps at one stage dietary laws were important in defining a degree of separation between the Jews and the gentiles. Perhaps as Maimonides suggests the rule against seething a kid in its mother's milk is designed to break the Israelites of the customs of Egypt, in a slow and gradual way. This may have been an Egyptian custom that God wanted the Jews to drop to help them establish a new identity. But how far does any of this affect people thousands of years later? Not very far at all, the Reformers suggest, since the likelihood of people today being still in the thrall of Egyptian customs seems remote.

It would be said on the side of Orthodoxy that one cannot tell what non-Jewish customs might have a hold on the individual, and so it is safest to adhere to every jot and title of the law, which is after all a divine law, in order to eradicate in us any remaining character trait that does not accord with our role as faithful Jews. Bringing oneself under the authority of a sacred legislation is precisely to obey laws that have no other purpose but to define their observers as Jews intent on doing whatever God tells them. It is here that the main differences between the Reformers and the Orthodox really takes hold, since the Reformers are quite happy with Jews having characters that fit in with the contemporary ethos, provided that they also embody the particular universal values that they say are so essential to any civilized and humane form of behavior. In this, Reform does genuinely adopt a modernist attitude of not accepting anything as obligatory that does not display its rationale.

The roots of Judaism

Modern art seems fascinated by how things work. Many exhibits explain and display in detail how the finished product came about, what is inside it, and how it operates. We want to know how things are made, how they are repaired, what lies behind what we cannot see. In much modern architecture we get to see the apparent guts of the building, the cabling for example, the pipes, and so on, as though this were to bring to the surface what the building is really about and what it would otherwise conceal. Reform is like that—the idea of there being obligatory laws that impinge on our behavior and which we cannot really understand except that they have been commanded. This really offends the modern spirit that everything must be comprehensible and out in the open.

Maimonides said that if you vary a law even a little, then the law is destroyed, since once you start to ask why you do something in one way rather than another, the obvious next question is why you do it at all. He actually has a dynamic theory of ritual that raises this question since he describes a developing system of ritual starting with sacrifices, changing into prayer, and finally resolving itself into quiet and solitary meditation. How is one to know in which period one finds oneself? Reform seems to suggest that we are now at a stage which does not require the same sorts of ritual as persisted for many centuries in the past.

How could we know this? Orthodoxy suggests that we could never know that the right time has come to change the law since a divine law differs from a civil law in never requiring change. Civil law as we have seen is variable and imperfect, divine law is unchanging and perfect. Yet, if divine law is designed to change our character, could we not acknowledge that it has succeeded and move on? Yet, there would here be tremendous scope for self-deception, resulting perhaps in wishing to remove what might be regarded as burdensome by claiming that it was no longer needed. Reform would say that the possibility of self-deception is not enough to rule out change as such, and surely this is correct. Just because there is the possibility of our getting it wrong does not imply that we must change our behavior completely in order for this to become totally impossible. Or so the Reform would argue, but the Orthodox response is that in something so important as this it is vital to get it right and one has to take whatever steps are likely to be effective in preserving our alignment with God.

The roots of Reform

It is often rightly said that Reform owes a good deal to the Enlightenment, but the Romantic movement in Germany in the nineteenth century was also significant. This movement advanced the idea that religion has to involve passion and inspiration, and traditional Judaism was often seen as being formulaic and cold. Many traditional synagogues then as now must have seemed uninspiring to the reformers, people come and go when they want to, prayers are sometimes said in unison and sometimes not, people sometimes have conversations with friends when they come in and the service has little of the character of a church service, for instance, with its order and fixed repertoire. A service entirely in Hebrew is mysterious to those whose Hebrew is weak or nonexistent, and the variations on the prayers and the very length of the prayers makes even a weekday service quite onerous to those not used to the format. Prayers are said so quickly that perhaps the person reciting it has no thought of what it means, or since it is in a foreign language, if Hebrew is not his ordinary language, then he might just be repeating a long-learned sequence of words without really knowing what they mean. So traditional religion offended both the Enlightenment and the Romantic movements. The former were annoyed by their lack of a rational basis and their reliance on tradition. The latter were unhappy with their emphasis on law and custom and the possible abstraction of those features of religion from our emotional lives. Judaism was held to require a revival which is both rational and also resonates with the personal lives of modern Jews, and the Reform movement in Germany came about to answer these joint demands.

One interesting aspect of the movement was that it quickly came under trenchant opposition by forces that sympathized to a degree with the principles but could not accept the need for such a radical change. Samson Raphael Hirsch (1808–88) perceptively criticized the use of the expression "Orthodox" to describe traditional Jews, arguing that this was a means of suggesting that there existed a variety of ways of being Jewish and the traditional Jew was fulfilling only one way of that lifestyle. For Hirsch, there is only one way, and the Reform movement represented not a version of Judaism but a parody of it. As Hirsch put it, it is not the case that there are Orthodox Jews and Reform Jews, but rather that there are observant Jews and then there are bad Jews, Jews who are not interested in carrying out the full obligations of their faith. Yet, Hirsch himself is very much seen today as the creator of neo-Orthodoxy or modern Orthodoxy, since while he criticized Reform he did not turn his back on change and innovation, arguing quite plausibly that Judaism had always changed over time and would continue to do so, and had the resources to change while staying faithful to its main principles and practices. The question was, though, whether this degree of change was in line with the rapidity of change that was necessary in a Europe that was undergoing such a radical transformation. Of course, for Hirsch, the sorts of changes that are necessary are quite mild and do not address what was seen to be the disparity between the traditional way of doing things and modernity.

The Conservative movement

A more moderate line between traditional Judaism and Reform was taken by Zacharias Frankel who together with Solomon Schechter created what became in the United States the Conservative movement. As its name suggests, it was intent on conserving much of traditional religion while not entirely accepting that everything in the Bible came from heaven. Frankel actually wrote a text on the topic "On Changes in Judaism" and this does represent fairly the Conservative attitude to change, as something to be contemplated and possibly adopted if there is a very good argument for it, and if the change can be seen to reestablish some important principle which contemporary practice obscures. This is of course a difficult balancing act to achieve, since going too far in the Reform direction makes the Conservative seem radical, while leaning toward the traditional suggests a disinclination to take on board a wholesale examination of the roots and practices of Judaism. It is worth pointing out that in its early days at least the Conservative movement did emphasize the scientific study of Judaism, yet without suggesting that anything generally held to be important in the religion be changed even after the roots of the faith were examined closely.

Sitting on the fence

The Conservative movement's attempt at defining a role for itself in between Reform and Orthodoxy is today coming unstuck, and not entirely due to modern trends. It is often argued that the intellectual roots of the Conservative movement were basically incoherent, since it preserves a good deal of orthodox practice while rejecting the rationale for that practice. Being positioned in between Reform and Orthodoxy is not possible since there is no room between them. They see each other as the Other against which they define themselves, and Conservative Judaism tries to establish a form of religion out of the space between these two positions.

Let us take as an example the Conservative position on segregation of men and women in the synagogue. It is the custom in traditional synagogues for men and women to be separated either by a partition or to sit in different parts of the synagogue. The *mehitzah*, as it is called, is based on two principles. Men and women were separated in the Temple and so we should follow that practice. Also such separation is important not to allow anything improper to take place. Let us examine the evidence of temple practice. There was certainly an area called the Women's Court in the Second Temple, and as one might expect it was some way from the center or the Holy of Holies. Now, there is some evidence from the Tannaim (rabbinic teachers of the Mishnaic era) and the Amoraim (rabbinic teachers of the Talmudic period) that men were not excluded from this area, so we should not assume from the name that it was restricted to women. There is a reference in Mishnah *Midot* 2:5 to the building of a gallery in the Women's Court so that the women could watch a ceremony while the men were below, and it is said that the purpose of the balcony was to prevent mixing. In Tosefta *Sukkah* 4:1 there is a reference to three balconies all built to prevent mingling between the sexes. The issue is whether the separation of men and women is just a custom that arose or is it a biblical obligation?

The Talmud refers approvingly to a passage from Zechariah (BT *Sukkah* 51b–52a) which goes "And the land shall mourn, each family by itself and the house of David by themselves and their women by themselves and their wives apart" (12:12). We seem to be pulling together some evidence here of the historical basis at least to separation, but in her commentary on these passages Rabbi Monique Goldberg does state correctly that there is no direct biblical passage that orders either a balcony or separation or the necessity to prevent frivolous behavior. She suggests also that synagogues and the Temple are so different that it is invalid to argue from one to the other. Finally, she challenges the idea that mixed prayer and seating were regarded as unseemly (*ervat davar*) in the biblical and premedieval age. It is true that there is no direct order to that effect and so she takes it as not a compulsory requirement. In an aside, she adds that even if this was the practice in medieval times, we are entitled to change it now if circumstances have changed. Since now men and women are much more used to working and being together, they are not a distraction to each other in the synagogue. On the contrary, people like to pray with all the members of their family, and so the partition is no longer obligatory.

How plausible is this argument? It really does not work at all. We do not know whether the Women's Court in the Temple was exclusively for women, but it seems likely that its inhabitants were at least predominantly women. After all, the Bible and the commentaries on it do not exactly offer us an egalitarian message, and the idea of segregating women for prayer and the sacrificial rituals seems very likely to have taken place at that time. We have already seen in an earlier chapter what sorts of distinctions are traditionally made in Judaism between men and women. Are men and women prone to frivolous behavior if they are together? There is a good deal in the commentaries that suggests this is very much the view of the rabbis. Is the synagogue to be linked with the Temple? It is difficult to reply in the negative, so much of the liturgy at least in the traditional service refers to the Temple, as do so many of the prayers themselves. The partition in the traditional synagogue is solidly based on the past and on the legal understandings of the basic differences between men and women. We could decide to change our attitude to those texts that urge segregation and also be ready to abandon the past traditions when we feel they are wrong. That is the honest response of the Reform movement, and traditional Jews maintain what they take to be the past forms of life since they think they are based on eternal truths and so cannot be changed. There is no middle ground between these positions, and the Conservative movement reveals its intellectual vacuity by trying to defend such a middle ground.

The Pittsburgh Platform

A good way of looking at the principles of the Reform movement is to examine the Pittsburgh Platform, which is now a rather dated document (it was produced in 1885) but still a pretty good summary of the ethos of the whole movement when it was founded. It starts off by claiming that Judaism represents "the highest conception of the God-idea." So that is a positive announcement on which to begin. Then, this is balanced by a statement about the modern discoveries of science and their compatibility with Judaism, and here we learn that "the Bible reflect[s] the primitive ideas of its own age and at times cloth[es] its conception of divine providence and justice dealing with man in miraculous narratives." That is a pretty scathing description, it contrasts the Bible with science, the latter being accurate and up-to-date while the former is written in a way that made sense in the past but not necessarily today. So we are prepared for a skeptical reading of the Bible in the sense that that is the appropriate reading for modern scientific readers.

The third principle presents a criterion for accepting and rejecting law. We should accept that which is ethical and such ceremonies as elevate us, but reject those that do not fit into modern civilization. For example, we look to the fourth principle which specifies such laws and ceremonies we can do without as anything to do with priests, diet, and dress, and in fact everything that is Mosaic and rabbinical, in short the great mass of halakhah or Jewish traditional law as it has come down to us. The fifth principle is interesting and defines the Jews not as a nation but as a community, and the implication is that they are then citizens of the country in which they live and reject any political identity of their own. The sixth principle asserts the rationality and progressive nature of Judaism. The seventh that immortality can only be spiritual and not corporeal, and finally, the eighth directs the Jews to address social issues and to take as their exemplar "the spirit of Mosaic legislation," which is seen as rejecting poverty and advocating the pursuit of justice. Although the Platform does not mention Hegel, his spirit is alive in it, in the sense that the historical development of religion is taken to represent its growing rationality. The thought of Hegel was shown earlier to challenge many of the features of Judaism, and his ideas were taken as a challenge that had to be answered by nineteenth-century and later Jews. We can either fight this development and be excluded from the forces of progress or we can enthusiastically change our attitude to our faith and be part of history as it shapes our future or so the Hegelians would argue.

With its faith in science and confidence in progress, the Platform looks really rather oldfashioned in the twenty-first century, since we are today often skeptical of these Enlightenment ideas and especially about the rationality of religion. Indeed, the desirability of rationality has come in for a good deal of attack recently, so that calling religion rational is hardly to compliment it. The Enlightenment itself has been criticized for its uncritical acceptance of rationality as the supreme principle of human thought. These comments aside, the Platform does seem a fairly clear set of principles on which to base the reform of religion. It is actually very radical. It cuts through the great mass of ritual and law in Judaism, rejecting virtually everything not in the Bible, and most of what is in the Bible also. The principle of going along with the spirit of the law but not the letter is interesting, since it places on the individual the onus of working out what that spirit is and how to embody it in action, a problem that does not occur to his more traditional coreligionist in quite the same way. In practice, Reform rabbis do use halakhic works in coming to decisions about issues, but they use them in a more suggestive and loose way than do traditional Jews, often selecting a phrase that they like and find helpful, and ignoring the masses of alternative ways of exploring that issue. There is nothing distinctive about the Jews, the Reform movement argues; they are just a group who have become dissimilar from others as a result of the invidious position in which they have been placed by history and yet they are part of a common humanity which shares many of the same problems and possibilities.

Varieties of Jews

Over time, Reform has become less radical. In the Pittsburgh Platform, the idea of a return to Palestine is belittled, but most Reform Jews today are Zionists. Over the years, more and more Hebrew has come into the prayer service, and some traditional attire such as the yarmulka (skullcap) and the tallit (payer shawl) are worn, albeit not by everyone. There are movements which are even more radical than Reform. Reconstructionism, for example, has a more detailed prayer service than Reform, but constantly pours scorn on the idea that there is anything divine in what is behind the Bible or that the historical events in that book accurately represent the past. Then there is secular Judaism, a movement which rejects everything religious about Judaism but tries to hold onto some cultural connection with the past. Finally, Messianic Judaism ought to be mentioned, since its followers are sometimes former Jews or describe themselves as Jews. This is a group of people who believe that Jesus is the Messiah, and so the culmination of the Jewish Bible, but their services are like synagogue services with the exception obviously of favorable references to Jesus. Whether they should be called Jews is questionable, since they seem to deny what most Jews take to be an axiom of Judaism, namely, that the Messiah has not yet come.

It is very difficult to rule out beliefs and practices as incompatible with Judaism unless one believes that there are principles in religion, and it is the argument of this book that these do not exist. I was listening recently to a father of twins discussing the bat mizvah of his twin daughters and the difficulties of spending less than $1,000 on the event's final party for their friends. He decided to take all their friends out to eat crab. Yet, he obviously had not given a thought to the fact that crab and shellfish as a whole are forbidden to Jews in the Bible. Presumably, he was a Reform Jew and rejected those rules. They represented the thinking of an earlier time, and now we do not need to specify particular food as being forbidden or allowed, since we live as equals in a society that eats crab. If God did not want us to eat crab why did he make them so tasty? This might well be a Reform slogan. As might be the question as to why is it so important for Jews to have distinctive laws of what they eat. These are surely reasonable topics to raise, and the Reform and the traditional Jews will answer them in different ways.

How serious should we be about religion?

Can we say which answer is more plausible? If we think that religions have essences then we could adjudge between them, since we would just have to examine the principles of the religion and then see which alternative came closer. The trouble is though that it is the principles which are themselves in question, as can be clearly seen in the principles of the Pittsburgh Platform. They are clearly designed to replace what had up to then been regarded as the principles of Judaism. If we rule them out just because they are different then we are going to enthrone reaction in religion, and that itself requires some considerable argument. So it looks as though it is impossible to decide which version of Judaism is more Jewish or more in line with the religion than any other.

This might seem a very strange position to reach. Cannot we say that a Jew who prays three times a day, obeys all the halakhic rules, is a member of Daf Yomi (the worldwide group that studies a page of Talmud each day), and so on is more of a Jew or a better Jew (albeit not necessarily a better person) than someone who hardly ever prays, makes no attempt to follow the law, is uninterested or unaware of the Talmud, and so on? That is what Hirsch suggests, when arguing against the idea that there are Orthodox Jews and Reform Jews. For him there are just Jews and some are more conscientious than others while some are totally uncommitted to Judaism. There is a lot to be said for such a view in the sense that just because someone is doing something he thinks is an alternative way of acting does not in itself mean that it is an alternative. This comes out nicely in the story of Aaron's sons, Nadav and Avihu, who thought they were carrying out the right ceremony but were not and suffered the consequences. Spontaneity is dangerous when it tries to replace a ritual, rather than deepening and extending it. This might be said to reflect poorly on kabbalah and mysticism, since that process involves taking risks in coming close to God. When the four sages enter Pardes (Paradise) only Akiva returns serenely. The other three, Ben Azzai, Ben Zoma, and Akher all go in with Akiva but they are not capable of understanding what they see and returning with it to our world. It is sometimes said that it was because Akiva knew how to link what he saw with the mitzvot and laws of Judaism that he kept his feet on the ground, as it were, while the others did not maintain that link and so went awry.

This seems right; just because I think a ceremony is right does not make it right. On the other hand, just because someone thinks it is wrong does not make it wrong. So there is no nice way to distinguish between being a serious and observant Jew and being some other sort of Jew, as opposed to being a traditional Jew and a Reform (or one of its variants) Jew. There is an interesting objection to this line and that is that this does not work for distinctions in religion. In religion, there is an appropriate attitude to take toward one's faith, and that is a serious and committed attitude. After all, what can be more important than our relationship with God, and how can we treat that relationship as though it were not something we should be serious about? So the Jew who prays three times a day and who obeys all the injunctions has God constantly in mind, and identifies firmly throughout each day with his Jewishness, while the Reform Jew has a more casual relationship with God and his religion, and can be criticized for that. This is not after all a debate on how significant chess ought to be in one's life, with some people thinking it should be very important and others of little significance. One would normally expect the more serious chess players to be better players, but we could not debar those less enthusiastic as chess players also. Here is where the link with religion breaks down, since chess is just a game, but religion is about so much more, and anyone who does not take a serious attitude to religion is not regarding it in the right sort of way, not just in a different way. Games have rules and religions have rules, but it does not follow that they are the same sort of activity. The observant Jew then has the right attitude toward religion because he treats it as important and as something that defines him. The nonobservant Jew is not just observant in a different way, he just does not take on the responsibilities and commitments that are appropriate to his role. Like a driver of a car who has had too much to drink, he should not be taken to represent a different state of sobriety from a driver who has had nothing to drink. He is drunk, and that is how he should be described.

There are problems with this view, though. One is the longstanding issue of how we should live. This involves working out what the main aims we as human beings ought to have. And of course on this there is a lot of argument. Aristotle expressed it as the contrast between the life of intellect, which he seems to have prioritized, and the life of the secondary virtues, activities such as politics, social life, working for a living, and so on. Many Jewish thinkers like Maimonides took up this dichotomy and wondered how far we should value our religious lives experienced as intellectual and rational, and how far we should pursue them as an aspect of social life. He is often called an intellectualist in that he sometimes suggests that only those who can really understand the rational basis of what they are doing in being pious Jews can achieve ultimate happiness.

This seems to leave out the great mass of ordinary Jews who follow halakhah out of tradition but do not have much grasp of how it operates or why. Yet it seems a mistake to leave out these people, not only because they constitute the vast majority of the religious community. Since God has made us all differently, he could hardly have prevented some of us, indeed the majority, from reaching the heights of human spiritual growth just because they are not intelligent enough. Cannot an unsophisticated but genuine person have confidence in his or her ability to lead a significant spiritual life despite their intellectual limitations? Surely the answer is affirmative, since many intelligent people are evil and many unintelligent people seem to be good at the very least.

How seriously should we take religion? Is it just one aspect of our lives or the most important thing in our lives? It was suggested earlier that surely religion would have to be the most important thing in our lives, since this is after all a system of beliefs concerning the meaning of life, our salvation, how we should live, and so on. These can hardly be also-rans. On the other hand, there is a vast range of ways in which one can acknowledge the significance of something. It is rather like a funeral in which some people tear their hair out, scratch their faces, and throw themselves on the coffin, while other people hardly change their normal behavior at all. Must we say that the more demonstrative people are those who are most sad? This would surely be wrong and would fail to do justice to the mourning of those who are just not very obvious in the display of their emotions. Indeed, some would say that the more expressive people are, the sooner they will recover from their grief, and vice versa, so that in fact it is the more undemonstrative people who are going to feel grief for longer. Whatever the case here, one would not want to say that someone had to produce a certain sort of behavior for them to be counted as really feeling a particular emotion. One of the standard issues in philosophy is how to tell what someone else is thinking or feeling, since there is no clear link between what is inside us, as the expression goes, and our appearance.

This brings out the difficulty of distinguishing between the serious and the irreverent Jew. How can we tell whether the former is doing what he does out of anything more than habit? How can we tell that the latter while smoking and eating ham sandwiches on the Day of Atonement is not really having deep thoughts about God and his role in the life of the Jewish people? As we have seen throughout this book, many Jews are without anything in the way of faith or knowledge of how to practice their religion in any of the ways available to them among the varieties of Jewish religious practice and yet firmly hold onto their Jewish identity. Perhaps they are still waiting for God to demonstrate his existence to them or perhaps they are not yet convinced of the need to pray or carry out any of the other obligations. Are they bad Jews, or lazy Jews, as Hirsch would put it, or are they different kinds of Jews, Jews who have not made up their minds on lots of things and yet do not cut themselves off from the Jewish community as a whole. It might even be argued that many of the important figures in the Bible fit into this pattern of behavior.

Running away from God: the case of Jonah again

Jonah, one of the most successful prophets, immediately ran away when God told him to go east to Nineveh. He went west and was eventually disgorged by the fish in the right place. Even at the end of the book, when his mission has been so successful, he is complaining of its very success, and it is God who has to remind him of the significance of turning that huge city around. Jonah ran away from his task, he grudgingly carried out his task (it is difficult to explain in any other way his slogan "Nineveh will be destroyed in forty days"), and in the end he moaned about the Ninevites, whom God had gone to some effort to save. This is one of the books which is read on the solemn Day of Atonement when Jews are supposed to confront their sins to God and to others and repent, something which Jonah never seems to have done.

One of the things that annoys Jonah about his task is that he is sent to save gentiles and not only gentiles but people who are the natural enemies of the Jewish state. He could be contrasted here with Abraham who when called Abram tried to save the people of Sodom. He argued with God, saying "Shall not the Judge of all the earth do right?" (Gen 18:26). At the end of the Book of Jonah, the prophet complains to God for having caused the death of the gourd which had provided him with shade. In the last verse God rebukes Jonah. "Should I not be concerned for Nineveh, that great city in which 120,000 persons live that cannot discern between their right hand and their left and also much cattle" (Jon 4:11). God is here committed to the salvation of everyone, certainly not just the Jews. Even the cattle come in for a mention, but probably all that is meant by the ending is a phrase to emphasize the significance of the city.

Jonah buys a ticket and boards a ship headed for Tarshish, which is precisely in the wrong direction. God responds to Jonah's action by creating a storm, while Jonah is in deep sleep. This reflects his state throughout much of the action, he does not participate so much in the action as respond to things that happen to him. The sailors then make a sacrifice to God, perhaps through their local gods, and make vows. Jonah is soon identified as the source of the problem, and thrown into the sea. Jonah does not drown; he is devoured by a great fish. He prays from the belly of the fish. It takes these events to induce Jonah to pray, and the implication is very much that otherwise he would not bother. Chapter 2 is the prayer. Jonah is praying to the God, whose mission he has rejected and done his best to avoid. Jonah prays to God: "Out of my distress I cried to God and He heard me" (2:2). This prayer is in the past tense perhaps because although Jonah was able to pray in the past, in the present he finds prayer difficult. Then he asks: "Will I ever see the holy Temple again (2:5)...I shall sacrifice to you" (2:9). This reference to the Temple might be taken to reflect Jonah's hostility to the idea of God as the God of everyone and not of a specific people, those who have the Temple at the center of their service. It is this idea that Jonah struggles against in his rejection of the divine task he was set. In Chapter 2:1, the fish is twice referred to as a male fish—"*dag.*" In 2:2 the fish changes to a female fish—"*dagah.*" This is commented on in a midrash and it is suggested that Jonah was swallowed by a male fish. However, he does not pray, but simply sits passively in the belly of the fish. God vomits Jonah out of the male fish to a female and very pregnant fish. The unpleasant and cramped environment in which he then finds himself obliges Jonah at last to pray seriously. God reappears to Jonah and repeats the details of his prophetic task. This time Jonah accepts his mission.

He walks to Nineveh. The city is described as so large that it takes three days to cover its breadth and is inhabited by 120,000 persons. Jonah walks into the city, preaches only one sentence with the text: "Another forty days and Nineveh will be overthrown" (3:4). He does not refer to God here, perhaps because he is still annoyed at having to carry out this task, and despite this or perhaps because of it, everyone repents. A fast for an undetermined time is proclaimed for all persons and animals. All, including the animals, wear sackcloth (3:8) and receive the forgiveness of God, something which seems to annoy Jonah even more. Jonah is angry with God (4:1) for saving the people. The story ends with a scathing comment. Having protected Jonah from the heat of the sun, in the desert, with a bush, God then destroys the bush, leaving Jonah in the heat of the sun. When Jonah complains God criticizes him for being more concerned with his own comfort than with the inhabitants of the huge city of Nineveh. Jonah is an excellent example of someone who really does not take his relationship with God that seriously but despite this is very effective in doing what God wants him to do.

Bontshe the Silent

There are also cases outside the Bible worth examining, like the famous story Bontshe the Silent. In this Yiddish short story by I. L. Peretz, Bontsche dies and in the next world a huge fuss is made about him, while in this world he was one of the lowest of the low, a real *lamed vavnik*. The *lamed vavnik* is one of the 36 people (*lamed vav* represents 36 in Hebrew) whose goodness prevents God from destroying the world but who are widely ignored and often take up menial positions. The story about Bontshe goes on in detail on what he suffered throughout his life without complaining, and how everyone did him a bad turn but he never retaliated. Yet, there is nothing religious about him, not directly; we do not hear about how he prayed or paid particular attention to halakhah. Another Yiddish story, also by Peretz, "If not higher," tells of a rabbi who instead of going to the synagogue to pray the Selichot prayers before the New Year goes early each morning to help a widow and prays while cutting wood for her. At least he was praying, but whether one could really concentrate on one's prayers while carrying out such a task is questionable.

To give a last example, the painter Marc Chagall was thoroughly imbued with Judaism yet does not seem to have had any religious beliefs during his mature years. Many of his subjects are biblical, his language of choice was Yiddish, a large number of his friends and commitments were Jewish, yet he was entirely secular in his behavior. He actually came from the town Lubavitch that the Hasidic group today takes its name from and as a young man was in contact with the leaders of that movement. Clearly, when he grew older, he distanced himself from them; yet, if we compared him with a Lubavitcher hasid with his black clothes, large hat, religious fervor, and so on we clearly have two very different people. Could we say that Chagall was not Jewish enough, or that he could not represent a person who underwent a Jewish life? Many people if asked to name a twentieth century Jewish artist would choose Chagall. The conclusion has to be that it is not possible to rule out different ways of living Jewish lives a priori, that is, before examining them and seeing how far they might fit into Judaism.

Chapter 12

How special are the Jews?

There is a clerihew that used to be quite well known and it goes:

> How odd
> of God
> to choose
> the Jews.

The notion of the Jews as a chosen people does of course make them distinctive and an unusual community. It is not clear what this status as chosen is really supposed to represent for those without strong religious views, and even those who believe that God selected the Jews to have a special status might find it difficult to specify precisely what implications this has for the Jews. One response would be that it means that the Jews should be a holy nation, and so they should behave themselves and obey the laws that God gave them. Many Jews reject this however and are no more or less holy than anyone else; in the summer on Shabbat there are probably more men and women in skimpy swimming costumes on the beach in Israel than wearing more sober clothing and attending synagogue. Yet, even secular Jews often examine closely the names of people who are praised for doing good deeds, or blamed for bad ones, to see if they are Jewish, as though this reflected generally on the community as a whole. Not all ethnic groups do this, and perhaps it is a reflection on the sense that the Jews are different from everyone else, and that difference needs to be acknowledged.

When he was annoyed with the Jews, Amos has God saying: "To me, O Israelites, you are just like the Ethiopians, declared the Lord. True, I brought Israel up from the Land of Egypt, but also the Philistines from Caftor and the Arameans from Kir" (Amos 9:7). This comment is modified by a later promise to restore them to the land (9:15), but the Jews do seem to receive special treatment in the Bible, something that Muslims in particular very much criticized them for upholding. After all, in Exodus 19:5–6 we read: "Now, if you will obey me faithfully and keep my covenant you will be my treasured possession among all the peoples. In fact, all the earth is mine but you shall be for me a kingdom of priests and a holy nation." So God does seem to make no bones about the special status in which he holds the Jews. On the other hand, it is important to note the conditional nature of this remark, and as we saw in Chapter 1 there are many instances where the Jews certainly did not obey God faithfully, nor did they keep his covenant. Perhaps then the Jews have forfeited their special status as a result of their recalcitrant behavior. On the other hand, as we also saw in Chapter 1, God is capable of great patience on occasion, while sometimes he punishes with a ruthless speed and efficiency. It is not easy to conclude either that the Jews continue to play a special role in God's eyes or that they do not.

It is the ethnic sense of superiority that the Jews are held to possess that is often roundly criticized by Islam, and the role of being a chosen people might be taken to typify this. It stems to a degree from the experience of standing at the foot of Mount Sinai and hearing the law being given that had such a strong effect on those there and imposed obligations on their descendants, the Jews. It starts with the escape of the Jews from Egypt and continues with the giving of the law to them. This distinctiveness of the Jews is reflected in two references in the Bible to God not forsaking his people, in particular the Jewish people. One of those passages comes at Psalm 94:14 and mentions not only his people but also the land. The other verse is at I Sam 12:22, and here we are told that he will not forsake his people since this sanctifies his divine name.

A relevant point about these promises is that they are not conditional. When God establishes the covenant with Abraham at Gen 15:18 he announces that he gives him and his descendants the land of Canaan for ever and for nothing. Later on, Abraham does things that impress God and leads him to repeat the covenant, and further on in the Bible, Moses presents the Jews with a blessing and a curse, so there is obviously a degree of conditionality here. Yet the first covenant with Abraham is like the covenant that God makes with humanity after the flood not to send another one. That is despite the fact that God acknowledges the evil nature of humanity, but he says that however evil we become he will never send another flood, something that he indicates by the phenomenon of the rainbow. God's links with the Jewish people are certainly not because the Jews are better than anyone else, or more important, or large in size, or have any other rationale in the sense that they oblige him to choose them. He could have picked any people. Yet, the implication is sometimes drawn that there is something special about the Jews, and this sense of pride in being chosen by God may be a source of conflict with other groups who perceive God to link up with people on the basis of some other characteristic and not their nationality.

This debate about the Jews has persisted throughout history. The Jews in the desert who had escaped from Egypt constantly complain of their living conditions by contrast with life in Egypt, and instead of being grateful for being rescued, many of them seem to resent their expulsion from Egypt. When given the opportunity to assimilate, Jews have leapt at it, and so largely disappeared into the host community, until some persistent hostile force manages to extract them and eliminate them, such as the Nazis in Germany for example. Some have argued that the Jews are in themselves a distinct group and should preserve their differences, not to the extent perhaps of failing to make a contribution to social and economic life, but by maintaining a distinct religion and lifestyle. Others see in that distinctness something of greater moment. On the other hand, it is also worth pointing out that plenty of people disagree with the idea that Israel or Jews have a special mission, that of guiding the rest of the world appears to be triumphalist. The Jews do not have a mission but a task, that of "being a kingdom of priests and a holy nation" (Ex 19:6). After all, the high holyday prayers and many other prayers do not mention the Messiah and so we might think of God bringing all the nations to him, not the Jews or their Messiah.

How different are the Jews?

This argument came out nicely about a hundred years ago when Zionism was in its infancy. It was founded really by a secular Viennese journalist, Theodor Herzl, who was shocked out of his complacency as a European Jew by the Dreyfus Affair. This event occurred in the late nineteenth century in France. Captain Dreyfus, an Alsatian Jew in the army, had been accused of espionage and punished, yet the evidence for his conviction was weak and there was little doubt but that his ethnicity had much to do with his conviction. Yet, here was an assimilated Jew, a career soldier dedicated to the service of his country, and his country turned its back on him and framed him for a crime not of his making. The furious debate which then emerged in France was not so much on his guilt or innocence, but on whether a Jew could be trusted and allowed to join civil society. Herzl (1860–1904) with a remarkable prescience predicted that a Europe which could adopt such a negative attitude to Dreyfus would eventually turn its back on its Jews and kill them. The only alternative he saw as feasible was for the Jews to have their own homeland, where they could live independently of everyone else.

Why did Herzl pick Palestine? He was not in any way religious, and an offer of Uganda by the British was quite enthusiastically received by him, but it still seemed to him that the historical connection with the Holy Land was one worth pursuing in a new state (which he called *Altneuland* or "Old/new Land"). Yet, at the time Herzl was running around the world trying to develop support for his idea, he was certainly without any significant support from anyone. Many socialist Jews in Eastern Europe believed that solidarity with their gentile peers was the way forward, and their home was in Europe, not in what then was an obscure part of the Ottoman Empire. Many religious Jews argued that they would only return to Palestine when the Messiah appeared, since that was the only right time for such a return. Most Jews just felt that they were Europeans, or Americans, or citizens of the Ottoman Empire, and were distinctly unexcited at the prospect of giving everything up to establish a specifically Jewish political entity separate from other states. It might be regarded as a remarkable success of Herzl that in spite of this initial lack of enthusiasm a state did come about and has managed to stay in existence so far for over 50 years. We should not ignore the impact on the existence of the state of the Holocaust and the survival of the state owes much to poor Arab leadership. Nonetheless, the establishing of a state after two millennia, the rebirth of the Hebrew language as a secular channel of communication, and the continuing development of the State of Israel despite its many powerful enemies is a remarkable event in history.

Israel: an ordinary or extraordinary state

One of the interesting debates in Israel even before the creation of the state was whether the state should be just another state like any other in the world or whether it should be distinctive. Here we see the old debate about the Jews again, whether they are the same as everyone else or different. When the Jews demanded that Samuel present them with a king, their "argument" was "So that we can be like the other nations" (I Sam 8:20). There is no doubt that one of the motives behind some varieties of Zionism is for the Jews to become like everyone else, and one of the ways to be like everyone else is to have one's own state. This particularly reflects nineteenth-century thinking, of course, when the Germans, the Greeks, the Italians, and so on all campaigned and fought for their own states in order to provide an environment in which they could express themselves and conduct their own affairs. The Jews lived all over the world, often precariously and concentrated in certain professions, and as a result had become rather strange people in many cases (it is hardly a surprise that Sigmund Freud and many of his stranger patients were Jewish). Living as a minority does perhaps not allow an ethnic group to experience fully the variety of occupations and careers that the population as a whole can adopt. An illustration of this could be the dysfunctional families of most of the major biblical characters. Having one's own state obviates this problem, if it is a problem, and ensures a normal life for the community as a whole. Or so the theory goes. It has to be said, though, that they do not seem to become any less dysfunctional with a state, as evidenced perhaps by David and Absalom or the various other kings and leaders of Israel and Judah.

The argument that a people needs a state implies that there is nothing distinctive about the Jews, there are only distinctive social conditions, and once these are resolved they will live in just as normal a way as anyone else. Whether the State of Israel actually brings out the normalcy of the Jews is a moot point, especially as many roles in the State are carried out by Arabs or foreigners and not by Jews at all. A new approach to Israel has become popular in recent years and is called post-Zionism. Post-Zionism questions what it sees as the myths of Zionism, that it was the heroic winning of the land against huge odds and determined enemies and that right was obviously on the side of the Jews who in the role of David slew the Goliath of the Arab armies lined up against them. What is not normally discussed as part of this approach but is perhaps even more important about it is that it takes a more relaxed attitude to Israel than could exist in the past when the State was under constant threat of destruction. Now there is the feeling, justified or otherwise, that the State of Israel is powerful and in control of its future, and so Israelis and Jews can examine critically all aspects of its history and origins. This would suggest that the State has become to a degree like a normal state, since this indulgence in self-criticism is very much a function of such normalcy and self-confidence.

There are features of the State that militate against its normalcy. It is a secular state in which religious symbols are significant. For example, the flag is a combination of the prayer shawl and a Jewish symbol, the Star of David, and the national anthem, the *hatikvah*, exclusively refers to Jews, so it is an awkward anthem for the 20 percent of the population who are not Jewish. The *hatikvah* assumes that the Jews are in the West, since it refers to looking eastward, and this was not even true of many Jews who lived in the Arab world, the Sefardi or Mizrachi Jews who form something of an underclass in Jewish Israel, slightly higher in status to the Arabs. Then of course there is the fact that the State has been constantly at war with its neighbors and in a difficult relationship with a large number of countries who are either Islamic or linked with this powerful group of countries. People often appeal to these factors to suggest that Israel is such a strange and unusual state that it could not possibly hope to be regarded as normal.

Yet is any state normal? Virtually every country has something or indeed many features that are unusual about it, and many of the difficult problems that have arisen for Israel are hardly directly of its making. Perhaps the most important factor from a Zionist perspective is that Israel is a country where a majority of the population is Jewish and so inhabitants have the experience of growing up and developing in an environment in which, if they are Jews, they are not in a minority. This was in the past always counted as one of the main points of a Jewish state and an argument in favor of Zionism. It very much works from the principle that there is nothing very different about Judaism at all, it merely requires an environment in which it can flourish as the main or ordinary practice, however it is interpreted. It could even be argued that the reason why many Jews do not make *aliyah*, emigrate to Israel, is that they enjoy living in an environment in which they are a minority.

But isn't this perverse? So many prayers and festivals make reference to the desirability of living in Israel, and the Bible itself emphasizes the same thing, that one would have thought that Jews would, when given the opportunity, move there in large numbers. Yet, not only is this not the case, but large numbers of Israelis have moved out of the country, in the converse of *aliyah* (going up) called *yeridah* (going down). As relatively well-educated people, many Israelis can get better jobs and living conditions elsewhere, and so it is perfectly understandable why they leave, but it does not say much for the idea that Jews in general are seeking a life within a majority Jewish environment where they can experience and develop a specifically Jewish approach to how to live and so on. On the contrary, many Jews enjoy living as a minority and often assimilate completely with the host population. They do not see themselves as Jews in any way that makes serious demands on them to be different from anyone else.

But are they authentic Jews? Some would say from a religious point of view that one could only be a real Jew if one followed strictly the religious principles of the faith. Some would say from a nationalist point of view that one could only be a real Jew if one lived in Israel or at least genuinely wished to live in Israel. This sort of confusion brings out the difficulty of laying down rules for who is authentic and who is not. We might take the analogy of following a sports team here, since it has many resemblances with being a Jew. Some people are passionate in their following of a team, they go to all the games, they listen to news about their team, they have many things in their house with the symbol of the team on them; in short, their lives are dominated by their passion for the team. Other people do few of these things, yet they still regard themselves as supporters. Fans sometimes say when their team wins an important match that it is the happiest day of their life, while another fan might wish their team to win but put the game into a less weighty category. We might be tempted to say that the passionate supporter is the authentic fan, but we should be careful about this, for who is to say that someone who is less demonstrative is consequently less of a fan? It is like saying that someone who makes a huge fuss at a funeral is more sad than someone who is reserved in the expression of her feelings.

How different should the Jews be? This issue arises often especially in modern times in relation to the State of Israel. Should Israel be just another state, or should it be better than other states? When Israel is criticized for what it does the reply is often that this is what countries do when trying to survive and prosper. Some argue that Israel should not behave like other states but better, since a Jewish state should embody a high standard of ethics, in just the same way that Judaism embodies a high standard of ethics. As we can see when examining ethnic groups who have suffered at the hands of others in the past, when they are in power they do not necessarily behave any better than their previous oppressors. This is also true in the case of individuals. But should they? One of the unpleasant labels pinned to Israel is to connect them with the Nazis, and there is indeed a connection. For a period the German army was successful in beating its enemies, and Israel is also. The Nazis did occupy territories, and so has Israel; the Nazis did build walls around their subject peoples, and so has Israel. Whatever one thinks of Israel, though, here the comparison surely ends, since the systematic murder, robbery, and dehumanization that went on under the Third Reich is very far from anything that Israel has done. Yet, this comparison is supposed to work rhetorically to weaken the idea that the Holocaust provides a justification for the State of Israel since the Jews turned out to be "just as bad as the Nazis." If we pursue this argument a little we can see that it can be taken in a different direction, since some argue that the oppression that the Jews suffered under the Nazis should make them more sensitive to the sufferings of others and so avoid the sort of *Realpolitik* that implies the use of oppressive strategies. This argument is often provided by Jews who are themselves opposed to the Israeli government and its treatment of the Arabs both within Israel and the occupied territories. It rests on a notion, usually not a religious notion, that the Jews ought to be better than everyone else in their behavior, and the fact that in the past people have been so bad to them means that a higher standard of morality must be employed.

This argument has a converse, and that is that since people have in the past been so bad to the Jews, the Jews now are justified in being worse behaved to others than would have been the case otherwise. It is not clear how either argument is supposed to work. There are moral standards which are incumbent on us as human beings and surely these should be followed whatever our experiences in the past or those of our ancestors. Many psychologists would suggest that previous negative experiences shape our present behavior, in the sense of causally explaining it, so that if we were treated poorly in the past we might find our future behavior is affected by that. We might for instance be desensitized to the sufferings of others or indeed more sensitive to the sufferings of others. The Bible itself refers to this when it tells the Jews to care for the stranger, "for you were strangers in Egypt" (Ex 22:20, a phrase in one variant or another repeated over thirty times in the Bible). However, past events cannot justify what we do, although it might excuse it to a degree, and should play no part in whether an action is right or otherwise. They can help us work out how to behave, though, and play a role in transforming us into better people. From a moral point of view it would be difficult to argue that the experience of the Jews in history provides them with any different system of morality than anyone else, and so the notion that the Jews should be better than anyone else morally is vacuous. Of course, so is the antisemitic idea that they are worse than anyone else, but then we knew that already.

The boundaries of Zionism

One of the interesting aspects of Zionism is that it reproduces all the uncertainties of this debate. Even the boundaries of Israel are undefined by Zionism. There is a reference (Gen 15:18) to "from the river of Egypt to the mighty Euphrates." Yet, this was far from the case in the past. In the First Temple period, for example, Gaza, Ashkelon, and Ashdod belonged to the Philistines, while the northern coastal strip was controlled by the Phoenicians. In fact, Solomon gave twenty cities in Galilee to King Hiram of Tyre (I Kings 9:11–13). There is also a reference to the Negev belonging to the people of Edom, the descendants of Esau (Deut 2:5), which if it is taken seriously suggests that the south of present-day Israel was not in Israel at all. It is worth reminding ourselves of these passages when religious people insist that the boundaries of Israel were established once and for all by God.

Not only are the boundaries not defined by halakhah (Jewish law) but whether the Jews should return to Israel at all is a lively legal issue. Maimonides does not even seem to count living in the Land of Israel as a commandment or mitzvah at all. He does not mention it in his list of 613 biblical commandments in his *Sefer ha-Mitzvot*. This is something for which he was criticized by Ramban (Nahmanides), who refers to the passage from Numbers 33:53–4 where God says "And you shall dispossess the inhabitants of the land and dwell in it, for I have given you the land to possess it, and you shall divide the land for an inheritance." As we have seen earlier when looking at the notion of justifying war, Ramban calls the war to conquer the land an obligatory war, not something to be done when we feel like doing it, but an obligation on us at all times and in all places. Now, other texts such as the *Megillat Esther* take the line that this positive obligation is only really obligatory when the Jews lived in the land and not later when they were exiled. Of course, once the Messiah comes then they will all return to the land, but until then there is no obligation, positive or otherwise, to capture it and settle there.

So this would see the commandment as being limited by time and human circumstance, as something that we could not reasonably be expected to do when the conditions are inappropriate. On the other hand, Maimonides could be interpreted as valuing the commandment much more directly by arguing that it is implied by the commandment "and you shall surely smite them" (Deut 7:2), since the violence was designed to help establish Jewish occupation of the land. An even stronger argument can be established, since we could refer to the fourth principle of the *Sefer ha-Mitzvot* which urges us not to count as mitzvot those that include the entire Torah. It might be thought that the obligation to live in Israel was just such a commandment, since it enables a much smoother application of all the commandments and so need not be specifically mentioned. Yet, the sorts of principles that

Maimonides had in mind here were very general ones which do not point to specific actions, and the obligation to settle the land is rather specific. On the other hand, there is some strength in the idea that some of the *mitzvot* are only relevant to living in Israel, so this does imply the necessity of living in the land.

Even if we accept that there is an obligation to live in the land, does this mean that there should be a Jewish state? On the face of it, there is no reason why Jews should not feel obligated to live in the land, but not as its rulers. Jews did live in Israel for many years as a minority, or even as a persecuted majority. This could be used as the basis of an argument that Jews have to control the land, since otherwise they will not be able to practice their religion or indeed live freely. Just living in a particular place where perhaps one's religion is persecuted is not going to be a pleasant experience, and it is unlikely then to be commanded. This would suggest there are two *mitzvot*, one is living in the land and the other controlling the land. These only become practical at particular times, but the fact that there are periods when they do not seem plausible restricts their role as options for us, but not necessarily their continuing to be commandments.

Chapter 13

The future of Judaism versus Jewish futures

If we look to the future of Jewish thought, it is difficult to doubt that the things that were done in the past and are being done now will continue to be done in the future, since the sources of debate and argument in Judaism do not change much. There are the basic texts, the Bible and the commentaries on it, and their legal offshoots, that will continue to be dealt with and commented on yet more. Changing circumstances will no doubt call for changing perspectives and the vitality of the commentary tradition will respond yet again to new challenges and issues. New thinkers and theories will be employed to analyze traditional issues in the Jewish tradition, as has always happened in the past. So for much Jewish culture it will be business as usual, as it has been for the last few thousand years. The surprising question arises, though, whether Jewish thought will be pursued by Jews and whether there will be Jews to participate in future intellectual debates of any kind.

Judaism without Jews/Jews without Judaism

One of the intriguing features of contemporary Europe is that there are places in which there is Jewish culture without Jews. This is because Jews are largely absent in significant parts of the world, and even where they exist they are in such small numbers that their effect on cultural life is minor. Not that numbers are the crucial factor, of course, Jews have often managed to punch above their weight in the sense that they have had a disproportionate presence in cultural life with respect to their nominal slice of the population, a presence that often in the past led to resentment and ultimately murder. Antisemitism has often managed to survive after the Jews themselves were long gone, murdered or driven out. Yet, in places like Poland, Lithuania, and Slovakia, for instance, there is something of a revival of Jewish culture in the sense of music and food often through the efforts of gentiles. The few remaining Jews have experienced the strange phenomenon of it being cool to be a Jew, as opposed to a death sentence.

Since the Jewish population all over the world is rapidly shrinking, the experience of those living in these remote outposts of Jewish life might be an indication of the future. Will Jewish culture and religion in the future be experienced largely as a nostalgic mixture of anecdotes, snacks, and tunes?

Let us look at some of the possible reasons for low numbers of Jews in the world in the future. First of all the birthrate for the Jewish population is lower than it is for most other ethnic groups, and this means that more Jews are currently dying than are being born. Birth rates tend to go up and down but there are good reasons to think that the Jewish birthrate will remain dire. One reason is that Jews tend to be disproportionately involved in education and training of one sort and another, and this leads to putting off and restricting the size of families. Then there is the undoubted fact that many Jews are entirely assimilated into their local culture and only regard themselves as Jews in limited ways. They often marry non-Jews and do not bring their children up as Jews. The inevitable result of all these factors is that the Jewish population, however it is defined, is shrinking rather than growing. To a degree this is mitigated by high rates of birth among Orthodox Jews, but this takes place in a small proportion of the Jewish population and does not do much to alleviate the general decline in the absolute Jewish population. In any case, plenty of members of the Orthodox community leave and are lost to the Jewish world entirely. As numbers of Jews decline, it becomes progressively unlikely that Jews will meet other Jews and so the scope for marrying Jews becomes progressively limited in a society where arranged marriages are not the norm.

There are parts of the world from which Jews are today almost totally absent. Many countries in Eastern Europe saw their Jewish populations destroyed in the Holocaust, often with the enthusiastic participation of the locals, and the remnant persecuted once again by the succeeding communist governments. The Arab world has become largely free of Jews, and the wider Islamic world has not on the whole been a friendly place for anyone who could be linked however tangentially to Israel. Jews are widely suspected of a vast range of international crimes, and conspiracy theories thrive in the Islamic world. It is still believed by large numbers of people that the September 11, 2001 attack in New York and Washington were carried out by Israel and Jews in order to hurt the reputation of the Islamic world. In fact, while theories and doctrines like communism have obviously now gone very much out of fashion, antisemitism is the most persistent and successful political doctrine in the world, since it has never been out of fashion and indeed is much stronger now than it ever was.

In the same way that we are beginning to see Judaism without Jews, we can also observe antisemitism without Jews. In fact, antisemitism flourishes much better without Jews since then one need discount any contrary evidence. This might be called a very postmodern form of prejudice, and people who think that the *Protocols of the Elders of Zion* are genuine reports of a meeting that took place often reject any evidence that it is a forgery, by insisting that they have a right to their opinion of its veracity. Another aspect of postmodernism is the determination of some people to assert that they are Jews when they are not, according to any even vaguely halakhic (legal) definition of Jew. Whether the current situation will result in a happier state of affairs where people are more tolerant of religious and cultural differences remains to be seen, but as a tiny minority in a world where sizable populations hate or at best suspect Jews, the future will likely be quite precarious.

Being hated can strengthen communal dynamics, of course, but it can also lead to a flight to countries which are friendlier, and this has resulted in the emptying of large parts of the world of Jews, a phenomenon that is not sufficiently noted. In fact, the Middle East is also experiencing a rapid decline in Christians, and they are also fleeing to more tolerant climes, as are other minorities, a sad state of affairs in that a large part of the world that in the past supported a good deal of religious and cultural variety is rapidly becoming uniform and inevitably less interesting as a result. It is often remarked how intellectually limited much of the Middle East is today with low rates of literacy, scientific research, and academic freedom, and one wonders what effect the ever-increasing homogenization of culture is having. After all, during the heyday of Islamic scientific and intellectual superiority it was precisely the blending of cultures and religions that helped bring about such an outpouring of talent and progress, a blend in which the Jews played a large part.

In a world without Jews the role of the Other has to be played by other groups, but no one plays it as well as the Jews. The absence of obvious Jews leads to theories about the Jews who are behind everything, perhaps from far away, or even the Jews who get gentiles to do their dirty work for them. As antisemites often remark, with some accuracy, the idea that Jews control the world is not far-fetched. Jews are very few in number yet in many places very successful and able to exercise influence. Israel has annoyed huge numbers of people and yet remains in existence, stronger than it ever was, and despite its many problems is able to draw on the support of more powerful players in world politics, such as the United States. So it perversely seems to many that while the *Protocols of the Elders of Zion* is not factually accurate, the idea behind it is valid, that a small bunch of Jews can manipulate gentiles to doing their bidding.

This is something that we must acknowledge about racism, that it is apparently based on facts. Critics often write as though racism is an irrational or inaccurate view of reality, but this is far from the case. The antisemite has evidence for his views, masses of evidence, and the more evidence he acquires the more grounded his views become. In any case, in a world where there are many places without Jews they become the perfect postmodern source of hatred, since they can be seen nowhere and yet blamed for everything. From an intellectual point of view the ways in which political attitudes are often seen as quite arbitrary fits in nicely with antisemitism, since a theory about the Jews does not then need to be backed by evidence, if one is disinclined to look for evidence. And if one is interested in evidence it can always be found somewhere or other. The fewer Jews around, the more Other and exotic they appear, and the more can be ascribed to them.

One aspect of a diminishing Jewish population is that the remainder becomes fascinated by its rapid reduction, a bit like the way a man who is losing his hair spends a lot of time looking at and touching what is left. This can result in a declining interest in what concerns the culture as whole, as gradual introspection sets in. The great explosion of Jewish participation in secular culture in the last 200 years may have had something to do with the increasing confidence of Jews as members of society at a time when they were more and more accepted, and their numbers were relatively large, especially in particular areas and cities. This is clearly not the likely situation in the future, and declining self-confidence may lead the Jews to participate less in general cultural life.

Jewish populations

An aspect of this growing defensiveness may reflect the general opprobrium under which the State of Israel has come really since the 1967 war. This is not the place to speculate why this has happened or whether it is a result of antisemitism. What is relevant is that Jews have to expend considerable effort in defending Israel, if they are sympathetic to Israel as most Jews are, which again draws them away from general social issues. This constant defensiveness is not conducive to the isomorphic relationship which in the past linked the Jews and Western societies, and it should be expected to play a restrictive role in the future of Jewish involvement in those communities and cultures.

Does size matter? How significant are declining Jewish population figures? As far as we can tell, the small size of the Jewish population is very much the norm. In the middle ages and the early modern period, there were probably only a million Jews in the world. Although they lived all over the world, often they were heavily restricted in the space they could occupy and subject to unstable living conditions. Forced conversions, expulsions, poverty, and poor health may not have helped natural growth. On the other hand, there are plenty of examples of communities flourishing in terms of numbers despite difficult living conditions, so this is not a likely explanation for relatively low population expansion.

We may find some useful information about a period of undoubted rapid expansion. Poland saw a population explosion, from around half a million in 1650 to one-and-a-half million in 1800, and then 5 million in 1900.

Fortunately for the Jews this surplus was going on at the same time as emigration to the United States became a possibility, and huge numbers took that path, leaving the difficult economic and political conditions of Eastern Europe for the new democracy over the Atlantic. Unfortunately, by the second decade of the twentieth century restrictions were increasingly used to restrain what came to be seen as a flood. America, South Africa, Australia, and Britain started to enact legislation establishing quotas. Even Palestine, which by 1932 had received many Jews, was shut off after the 1939 White Paper. So to the delight of the Nazis the world seemed to turn its back on the Jews just when their need for rescue was greatest. The Germans could then point to the hypocrisy of those countries who criticized German racism. Although many now criticize the democracies for not taking in more Jews, it is worth considering how plausible such a criticism is. We do know that there was a good deal of antisemitism in high places and as a result a disinclination to import more Jews into the country. On the other hand, the rescue of enormous numbers of Jews would not have gone down well with the local population either, so one has to bear in mind the pragmatic political considerations that governments had in mind at the time. Immigration then as now was a lively political issue, and in the 1930s, the chief problem was unemployment.

The shrinking synagogue population

There have in recent years been some interesting changes in religious affiliation in Jewish life. More and more Jews opt out of synagogue membership and for a variety of reasons. Intermarriage of course may be a potent factor here, since non-Jewish spouses may not want to go to the synagogue or temple, nor may he or she be welcomed there. Then there is often a reaction against the sorts of ritual and display that go on in synagogues in more prosperous parts of the world such as the United States and Europe, where synagogues and temples may be seen as more to do with fashion parades and social meeting places than religious centers that mean anything to many people. It may also be the case that individuals are less likely in the twenty-first century to wish to celebrate tradition en masse and seek a more individual and relevant form of religious expression. This often results in Jews leaving Judaism entirely, in their seeing it as only a secular aspect of their lives, or in trying to adapt it to more personal forms of spiritual expression. A sort of "Judaism lite" then may emerge, where it becomes identified with liking smoked salmon sandwiches, learning a bit of kabbalah for Dummies, and developing one's own ritual.

It is worth pointing out also the diversity of the Jewish communities throughout the world, which seem to become more diverse as they shrink in size and age in profile. For example, in the United States about 10 percent upward of the Jewish population are African-American, Asian-American,

Latino, Sefardi, Middle Eastern, or mixed race. Some of the Latinos see themselves as returned Jews who were forced in earlier centuries to hide their religion due to the Spanish Inquisition. There are also communities in the major urban centers of black Americans who regard themselves as Jews and form their own congregations in much the way that black churches exist. And then there are around 1 million people who are closely linked with Jews as spouses, children, parents, siblings, and those who identify with the Jewish community to some degree, although only in varying ways if at all with the religion.

Another development which seems to be going in a different direction is that the more radical institutions such as the Reform movement have become more orthodox in tone, while the traditional groups have often become more accessible to a wider Jewish public. The Reform movement in its early decades was skeptical of Zionism and abandoned long-standing institutions such as the bar mitzvah and prayer in Hebrew. But as time has gone on these practices and beliefs have changed. Israel is a fact and the Reform movement can hardly turn its back on the millions of Jews who live there. The revival of some aspects of traditional ritual is interesting also, and reveals perhaps a visceral desire to relate more closely to the past, a past in which many Jews take renewed pride.

Jewish futures

As we have suggested, most Jews today are not members of a religious congregation such as a synagogue, and live quite happily outside such a social context. One might assume that this would only increase, but this would be a dangerous prediction. After all, who could have predicted that the Reform movement would have become a bit more traditional in the twentieth century or that Israel would have survived for so long in the midst of such overwhelming hostility from well-financed and stocked enemies? This unaffiliated majority is likely to continue to express itself in eccentric ways, and without paying much attention to the traditional ways of defining Judaism. A sort of secular Judaism, or Jewish humanism is emerging in accordance with which religion or culture is seen as an interesting aspect of the individual's background, but does not define him or her in any way. It is more of an aesthetic feature than anything else. The implications for the future of Jewish thought are intriguing and unpredictable, but there can be little doubt about the increasing influence on it of the secular world and its interests and enthusiasms. But then it was ever thus.

A popular saying in Hebrew may be translated into English as: "All the world is a very narrow bridge and the important thing is not to have any fear." The idea here is that we travel through life and we do not know exactly where we are going or what dangers lurk along the way, rather like walking across a narrow bridge. It is always possible to fall off, or for the bridge to collapse while we are on it. Fear should be avoided since we can be confident that as far as possible we have some idea of our route and what may interfere with our making progress along it. Jews should be able to equip themselves with something from their intellectual armory that leads them to step out along the way with some confidence. That is not to say that the past, even the recent past, gives much scope for optimism, but unless Jews try to foster a positive attitude they will turn their thoughts and prayers into nothing more than a martyrology. Now, how each individual avoids fear will depend on his or her particular background and religious commitments, if any, and perhaps the influence that literature such as the Bible has had on them. It is in this continuing dialogue with the sources and avoidance of fear that Jewish thought may be said to have its heart, and those who value the diversity of human intellectual life will hope that that heart continues to beat well into the future.

Bibliography

Abrams, D. (1994) *The Book Bahir*. Los Angeles, CA: Cherub Press.

Abrams, J. (1995a) *Learn Talmud: How to Use the Talmud*. Northvale, NJ: Jason Aronson.

—— (1995b) *The Women of the Talmud*. Northvale, NJ: Jason Aronson.

Adler, R. (1998) *Engendering Judaism: An Inclusive Theology and Ethics*. Philadelphia, PA: Jewish Publication Society.

Alpert, R. (1998) *Like Bread on the Seder Plate*. New York: Columbia University Press.

Alter, R. (1983) *The Art of Biblical Narrative*. New York: Basic Books.

—— (ed.) (2005) *The Five Books of Moses: A Translation with a Commentary*. New York: W.W. Norton.

Altmann, A. (1973) *Moses Mendelssohn: A Biographical Study*. Philadelphia, PA: Jewish Publication Society.

Antonelli, J. (1997) *In the Image of God: A Feminist Commentary on the Torah*. Northvale, NJ: Jason Aronson.

Armstrong, K. (1996) *In the Beginning: A New Interpretation of Genesis*. New York: Alfred A. Knopf.

Astren, F. Karaite (2004) *Judaism and Historical Understanding*. Columbia, SC: University of South Carolina Press.

Baskin, Judith R. (ed.) (1999) *Jewish Women in Historical Perspective*. Detroit, MI: Wayne State University Press.

Benz, W. (2004) *Was ist Antisemitismus?* Munich: C.H. Beck.

Berger, D. (ed) (1979) *The Jewish-Christian Debate in the High Middle Ages*. Philadelphia, PA: Jewish Publication Society.

Berkovits, E. (1973) *Faith after the Holocaust*. New York: Ktav Publishing House.

Biale, R. (1995) *Women and Jewish law: The Essential Texts, Their History, and Their Relevance for Today*. New York: Schocken Books.

Blidstein, G. (1997) *In the Rabbis' Garden: Adam and Eve in the Midrash*. Northvale, NJ: Jason Aronson.

Börne, L. (1999) "On Shylock," in *The German-Jewish Dialogue: An Anthology of Literary Texts 1749–1993* (ed.) R. Robertson. Oxford: Oxford University Press, 69–81.

Boyarin, D. (1997) *Unheroic Conduct: The Rise of Heterosexuality and the Invention of the Jewish Man*. Berkeley, CA: University of California Press.

Brody, R. (1998) *The Geonim of Babylonia and the Shaping of Medieval Jewish Culture*. New Haven, CT: Yale University Press.

Buber, M. (1955a) *Tales of the Hasidim: The Early Masters*. London: Thames & Hudson.
—— (1955b) *Tales of the Hasidim: The Later Masters*. London: Thames & Hudson.
—— (1970) *I and Thou*. (trans.) Kaufman, W. New York: Scribner's.
Cohen, M. (1986) "Islam and the Jews: Myth, Counter-Myth, History." *Jerusalem Quarterly*, 38: 125–37.
—— (1995) *Under Crescent and Cross*. Princeton, NJ: Princeton University.
Cohen, R. (ed.) (1986) *Face to Face with Levinas*. Albany, NY: State University of New York Press.
Cohn-Sherbok, D. (1997) *The Jewish Messiah*. Edinburgh: T.&T. Clark.
—— (2003) *Judaism: History, Belief and Practice*. London: Routledge.
Cragg, K. (1994) *The Event of the Qur'an*. Oxford: Oneworld.
—— (1999) *Jesus and the Muslim: An Exploration*. Oxford: Oneworld.
Davidman, Lynn and Tenenbaum, Shelly (eds) (1995) *Feminist Perspectives on Jewish Studies*. New Haven, CT: Yale University Press.
De Lange, N. and Freud-Kandel, M. (eds) (2005) *Modern Judaism: An Oxford Guide*, Oxford: Oxford University Press.
Derrida, J. (2002) *Acts of Religion*. New York: Routledge.
Dershowitz, A. (1997) *The Vanishing American Jew: In Search of Jewish Identity for the Next Century*. Boston, MA: Little, Brown.
Dorff, E. and Newman, L. (eds) (1998) *Contemporary Jewish Theology: A Reader*. Oxford: Oxford University Press.
Dorfman, R. and Dorfman, B. (2000) *Synagogues without Jews: And the Communities that Built and Used Them*. Philadelphia, PA: Jewish Publication Society.
Ellis, M. (2002) *Practicing Exile: The Religious Odyssey of an America Jew*. Waco, TX: Baylor University Press.
Fenton, P. (1996) "Judaism and Sufism," in *History of Islamic Philosophy* (eds) Nasr, S. and Leaman, O. London: Routledge, 755–68.
—— (2003) "Judaism and Sufism," in *Cambridge Companion to Medieval Jewish Philosophy* (eds) Frank, D. and Leaman, O. Cambridge: Cambridge University Press.
Firestone, T. (1998) *With Roots in Heaven: One Woman's Passionate Journey into the Heart of her Faith*. New York: Dutton Books.
Fishbane, M. (1998) *The Exegetical Imagination: On Jewish Thought and Theology*. Cambridge, MA: Harvard University Press.
Fox, E. (ed.) (1997) *The Five Books of Moses: Genesis, Exodus, Leviticus, Numbers, Deuteronomy: A New Translation with Introductions, Commentary, and Notes*. New York: Schocken Books.
Frank, D. (1989) "Humility as a Virtue: A Maimonidean Critique of Aristotle's Ethics," in Ormsby, E. (ed.) *Moses Maimonideas and His Time*. Washington, DC: The Catholic University of America Press, 89–99.
Frank, D. and Leaman, O. (eds) (2003) *Cambridge Companion to Medieval Jewish Philosophy*. Cambridge: Cambridge University Press.
Frank, D., Leaman, O., and Manekin, C. (eds) (2001) *The Jewish Philosophy Reader*, London: Routledge.
Frankel, Ellen (1996) *The Five Books of Miriam; A Woman's Commentary on the Torah*. New York: Putnam.

Gibbs, R. (1992) "A Jewish Context for the Social Ethics of Marx and Levinas," *Autonomy and Judaism: The Individual and the Community in Jewish Philosophical Thought* (ed.) Frank, D. Albany, NY: State University of New York Press, 161–92.

—— (1992) *Correlations in Rosenzweig and Levinas*. Princeton, NJ: Princeton University Press.

Gilman, S. (2005) *Kafka*. London: Reaktion Books.

Glick, L. (1999) *Abraham's Heirs: Jews and Christians in Medieval Europe.* Syracuse, NY: Syracuse University Press.

Goitein, S. (1966) *Studies in Islamic History and Institutions*. Leiden: Brill.

—— (1974) *Jews and Arabs: Their Contacts Through the Ages*. New York: Schocken Books.

Goldberg, M. (2004) *The Mehitzah in the Synagogue* (trans.) Villa, D. Jerusalem: Shechter Instiute of Jewish Studies.

Goodman, L. (1992) *On Justice*. New Haven, CT: Yale University Press.

Gottlieb, L. (1995) *She Who Dwells Within: A Feminist Vision of a Renewed Judaism*. San Francisco, CA: Harper.

Grabar, I. (1996) *The Shape of the Holy: Early Islamic Jerusalem*. Princeton, NJ: Princeton University Press.

Green, A. (1992) *Seek My Face, Speak My Name: A Contemporary Jewish Theology*. Northvale, NJ: Jason Aronson.

Greenberg, B. (1994) *On Women and Judaism: A View from tradition*. Philadelphia, PA: Jewish Publication Society.

Gruen, E. (1998) *Heritage and Hellenism: The Reinvention of Jewish Tradition*. Los Angeles, CA: University of California Press.

Hand, S. (1989) *The Levinas Reader*. Oxford: Blackwell.

—— (ed.) (1996) *Facing the Other: The Ethics of Emmanuel Levinas*. Richmond: Curzon.

Handelman, S. (1991) *Fragments of Redemption: Jewish Thought and Literary Theory in Benjamin, Scholem and Levinas*. Bloomington, IN: Indiana University Press.

Harper Jacobs, L. (1995) *The Jewish Religion: A Companion*. Oxford: Oxford University Press.

Harshav, B. (2004) *Marc Chagal and His Times: A Documentary Narrative*. Stanford, CA: Stanford University Press.

Hartman, D. (1985) *A Living Covenant: The Innovative Spirit in Traditional Judaism*. New York: Free Press.

Hasson, I. (1996) "The Muslim View of Jerusalem, the Qur'an and Hadith," in *The History of Jerusalem: The Early Muslim Period* (eds) Prawer, J. and Ben-Shammai, H. Yad Izhak Ben-Zvi: Jerusalem: 349–85.

Hegel, G. (1970) *Phenomenology of Spirit* (trans.) Miller, A.V. Oxford: Clarendon Press.

—— (1977) *Faith and Knowledge* (trans. and ed.) Cerf, W. and Harris, H.S. Albany, NY: State University of New York Press.

—— (1984–87) *Lectures on the Philosophy of Religion* (trans.) Hodgson, C.P. and Brown, R.F. Los Angeles, CA: University of California Press.

Herder, J. (1997) *On World History: An Anthology* (ed.) Adler, H. and Menze, E. (trans.) Menze, E. with Palmer, M. Armonk: M.E. Sharpe.

Hertzberg, A. (ed.) (1991) *Judaism: The Key Spiritual Writings of the Jewish Tradition*. New York: Simon & Schuster.

Heschel, A. (1996) *God in Search of Man: A Philosophy of Judaism*. San Francisco: Harper.

Hirsch, S. (1959) *Judaism Eternal* (trans.) Grunfeld, I. London: Soncino.

Homolka, W., Jacob. W., and Seidel, E. (eds) (1997) *Not by Birth Alone: Conversion to Judaism*. London: Cassell.

Hughes, A. (2005) *Jewish Philosophy A–Z*. Edinburgh: Edinburgh University Press.

Jacobs, L. (1995) *We Have Reason to Believe*. London: Valentine Mitchell.

Jewish Study Bible (2004) (eds) Berlin, A. and Brettler, M. New York: Oxford University Press.

Josephus (1981) *The Jewish War*. Harmondsworth: Penguin.

Katz, J. (1983) *Exclusiveness and Tolerance: Studies in Jewish-Gentile Relations in Medieval and Modern Times* (Scripta Judaica, 3) New York: Behrman House.

Leaman, O. (1988) "Maimonides, Imagination and the Objectivity of Prophecy," *Religion*, 18, 69–80.

—— (1992) "Philosophy vs. Mysticism: An Islamic Controversy," in *Philosophy, Religion and the Spiritual Life* (ed.) McGhee, M. Cambridge: Cambridge University Press, 177–88.

—— (1995a) *Evil and Suffering in Jewish Philosophy*. Cambridge: Cambridge University Press.

—— (1995b) "Is a Jewish Practical Philosophy Possible?" in *Commandment and Community: New Essays in Jewish Legal and Political Philosophy* (ed.) Frank, D. Albany, NY: State University of New York Press, 55–68.

——(1997a) "The Future of Jewish Philosophy," in *The History of Jewish Philosophy* (eds) Frank, D. and Leaman, O. London: Routledge, 895–907.

—— (1997b) "Jewish Existentialism," in *History of Jewish Philosophy* (eds) Frank, D. and Leaman, O. London: Routledge, pp. 799–819.

—— (1997c) *Moses Maimonides*, London: RoutledgeCurzon.

—— (1998) "The Philosophy of Religion," in *The Future of Philosophy* (ed.) Leaman, O. London: Routledge, 120–33.

—— (2002) "Ideals, Simplicity, and Ethics: The Maimonidean Approach," *American Catholic Philosophical Quarterly*, 76: 107–24.

—— (2004) *Islamic Aesthetics: An Introduction*. Edinburgh: Edinburgh University Press.

—— (ed.) (2006) *The Qur'an: An Encyclopedia*. New York: Routledge.

Levinas, E. (1969) *Totality and Infinity* (trans.) Lingis, A. Pittsburgh, PA: Duquesne University Press.

—— (1974) *Autrement que d'être*, The Hague: Nijhoff. [Translated as *Otherwise than Being or Beyond Essence* by Lingis, A. (1981) The Hague: Nijhoff].

—— (1990a) *Difficult Freedom* (trans.) Hand, S. London: Athlone.

—— (1990b) *Nine Talmudic Readings* (trans.) Aronowicz, A. Bloomington, IN: Indiana University Press.

—— (1994a) *Beyond the Verse: Talmudic Readings and Lectures* (trans.) Mole, G. London: Athlone.

—— (1994b) *In the Time of the Nations* (trans.) Smith, M. Bloomington: Indiana University Press.

Lewin, R. (1911) *Luthers Stellung zu den Juden: Ein Beitrag zur Geschichte der Juden in Deutschland während des Reformationszeitalters*. Berlin: Trowitzch und Sohn.

Lewis, B. (1995) *Cultures in Conflict: Christians, Muslim, and Jews in the Age of Discovery*. New York: Oxford University Press.

Maimonides, M. (1963) *The Guide of the Perplexed* (trans.) Pines, S. Chicago, IL: University of Chicago Press.

——— (1982–) *Mishneh Torah*, Yale Judaic Series. New Haven, CT: Yale University Press.

Mendes-Flohr, P. and Reinharz, J. (eds) (1995) *The Jew in the Modern World: A Documentary History.* Oxford: Oxford University Press.

Mishnah (1933) (trans.) Danby, H. Oxford: Oxford University Press.

Momigliano, A. (1990) *Alien Wisdom: The Limits of Hellenization.* Cambridge: Cambridge University Press.

Most, A. (2004) *Making Americans: Jews and the Broadway Musical.* Cambridge, MA: Harvard University Press.

Nemoy, L. (1952) *Karaite Anthology.* New Haven, CT: Yale University Press.

Neusner, J. (1991) *The Mishnah: A New Translation.* New Haven, CT: Yale University Press.

——— (1994) *The Midrash: An Introduction.* Northvale, NJ: Jason Aronson.

Numbers Rabbah (1939) (trans.) Slotki, J. London: Soncino.

Ochs, V. (1999) *Words on Fire: One Woman's Journey into the Sacred.* Boulder, CO: Westview.

Patterson, D. (2005) *Hebrew Language and Jewish Thought.* London: RoutledgeCurzon.

Peli, P. (ed.) (1996) *Soloveitchik on Repentance: The Thought and Oral Discourses of Rabbi Joseph B. Soloveitchik.* Northvale, NJ: Jason Aronson.

Peperzak, A (ed.) (1995) *Ethics as First Philosophy: The Significance of Emmanuel Levinas for Philosophy, Literature and Religion.* London: Routledge.

Peretz, I. (1987) "Bontshe the Silent," in *Man's Search for Values* (eds) Martin, T., Chamberlin, D., and Wieler, I. Scarborough, ON: Gage Educational Publishing.

——— (1998) "If Not Higher," *Oxford Book of Jewish Stories* Stavans, I. (ed.) Oxford: Oxford University Press.

Pirke Avot: A Modern Commentary on Jewish Ethics (1998) (ed. and trans.) Kravitz, L. and Olitzky, K. New York: Union of American Hebrew Congregations.

Plaskow, J. (1997) "Jewish Feminist Thought," in *History of Jewish Philosophy* (eds) Frank, D. and Leaman, O. London: Routledge, 885–94.

Polliack, M. (2003) *Karaite Judaism: A Guide to Its History and Literary Sources.* Leiden: Brill Press.

Quinn, P. (2005) *Philosophy of Religion A–Z.* Edinburgh: Edinburgh University Press.

Raphael, M. (2003) *Judaism in America.* New York: Columbia University Press.

Rapoport-Albert, A. (ed.) (1997) *Hasidism Reappraised.* Oxford: Littman Library.

Ravitsky, A. (1991) "Hatzivi lakh tziyunim:gilgulo shel ra'ayon," in *Eretz Yisrael bahagut hayehudit biyemei habeinayim* (eds) Halamish, M. and Ravitzky, A. Jerusalem: Yad Yitzkhak Ben Tzvi, 1–39.

Sarana, N. (1995) *On the Book of Psalms: Exploring the Prayers of Ancient Israel.* New York: Schocken Books.

——— (1996) *Exploring Exodus: The Origins of Biblical Israel.* New York: Schocken Books.

Scholem, G. (1970) *On the Kabbalah and Its Symbolism* (trans.) Mannheim, R. New York: Schocken.

Scult, Mel (ed.) (1991) *Dynamic Judaism: The Essential Writings of Mordecai M. Kaplan.* New York: Fordham University Press.

Seeskin, K. (2000) *Searching for a Distant God: The Legacy of Maimonides*. New York: Oxford University Press.

Sfar, J. (2005) *The Rabbi's Cat* (trans.) Siegel, A. and Singh, A. New York: Pantheon.

Shatzmiller, J. (1994) *La deuxième controverse de Paris*. Leuven: Peeters.

Soloveitchik, J. (1983) *Halakhic Man* (trans.) Kaplan, L. Philadelphia, PA: Jewish Publication Society.

Steinsaltz, A. and Eisenberg, J. (2000) *The Seven Lights: On the Major Jewish Festivals*. Northvale, NJ: Jason Aronson.

Stern, D. (1991) *Parables in Midrash: Narrative and Exegesis in Rabbinic Literature*. Cambridge, MA: Harvard University Press.

Sternberger, G. (1995) *Pharisees, Saducees, Essenes*. Minneapolis, MN: Fortress Press.

Talmud Bavli (1998) The Schottenstein Edition, Artscroll Series. Brooklyn, NY: Mesorah.

Wasserstrom, W.M. (1995) *Between Muslim and Jew: The Problem of Symbiosis under Early Islam*. Princeton, NJ: Princeton University Press.

Wieseltier, L. (2000) *Kaddish*, New York: Vintage.

Wittgenstein, L. (1994) *Vermischte Bemerkungen* (eds) von Wright, G.H. and Nyman, H. Werkausgabe, Frankfurt: Suhrkamp, 498.

Wolfson, E. (1994) *The Speculum that Shines: Vision and Imagination in Medieval Jewish Mysticsm*. Princeton, NJ: Princeton University Press.

—— (2000) *Abraham Abulafia—Kabbalist and Prophet: Hermenutics, Theosophy, Theurgy*. Los Angeles, CA: Cherub Press.

Wright, T. (1997) "Translating the Bible into Greek: The Jewish Thought of Emmanuel Levinas," *Le'Eyla*, October, 41–5.

Zornberg, A. (1996) *The Beginning of Desire: Reflections on Genesis*. New York: Image Books.

Index

Due to their ubiquity in the text, there are no separate entries for Bible, commentary, interpretation, or Torah.

eBooks – at www.eBookstore.tandf.co.uk

A library at your fingertips!

eBooks are electronic versions of printed books. You can store them on your PC/laptop or browse them online.

They have advantages for anyone needing rapid access to a wide variety of published, copyright information.

eBooks can help your research by enabling you to bookmark chapters, annotate text and use instant searches to find specific words or phrases. Several eBook files would fit on even a small laptop or PDA.

NEW: Save money by eSubscribing: cheap, online access to any eBook for as long as you need it.

Annual subscription packages

We now offer special low-cost bulk subscriptions to packages of eBooks in certain subject areas. These are available to libraries or to individuals.

For more information please contact webmaster.ebooks@tandf.co.uk

We're continually developing the eBook concept, so keep up to date by visiting the website.

www.eBookstore.tandf.co.uk